Discourse and the translator

LANGUAGE IN SOCIAL LIFE SERIES

Series Editor: Professor Christopher N. Candlin

Discourse
and the translator

B. Hatim
I. Mason

An imprint of **Pearson Education**

Harlow, England · London · New York · Reading, Massachusetts · San Francisco
Toronto · Don Mills, Ontario · Sydney · Tokyo · Singapore · Hong Kong · Seoul
Taipei · Cape Town · Madrid · Mexico City · Amsterdam · Munich · Paris · Milan

Pearson Education Limited,
Edinburgh Gate, Harlow,
Essex CM20 2JE, England
and Associated Companies throughout the world.

Visit us on the World Wide Web at:
www.pearsoned.co.uk

First published 1990

British Library Cataloguing in Publication Data
Hatim, B. (Basil)
  Discourse and the translator. – (Language in social
  life series)
  1. Languages. Translation. Semantic aspects
  I. Title II. Mason, Ian, 1994–
  418′.02

ISBN 0-582-05925-9 CSD
ISBN 0-582-02190-1 PPR

Library of Congress Cataloging in Publication Data
Hatim, B. (Basil), 1947–
  Discourse and the translator / B. Hatim, I. Mason.
    p.   cm. — (Language in social life series)
  Bibliography: p.
  Includes index.
  ISBN 0-582-02190-1 (PPR) 0-582-05925-9 (CSD)
  1. Translating and interpreting.   2. Discourse analysis.
  I. Mason, I. (Ian), 1994–   II. Title.   III. Series
  P306.2.H38   1989   89–2619
  418′.02–dc20   CIP

Set in 10/12pt Palatino Linotron 202

Printed in Malaysia, PPSB

16 15 14 13 12
08 07 06 05 04

Contents

General Editor's Preface

If the existence of metaphor constitutes one of the key problems that face translators, seeking like metaphor itself, to express one world in terms of another, it is equally true that understanding the metaphors that have been employed to capture the nature and purpose of translating itself poses a difficulty for the non-specialist reader. Scientific study or artistic endeavour, researchable theory or technical craft, a branch of linguistics or of literature, all have their advocates among translators and those who have sought to characterise its theory and its practice.

In approaching this latest contribution from Basil Hatim and Ian Mason to the new *Language in Social Life Series*, let me suggest that readers take a more investigative and less pigeonholing approach, beginning from George Steiner's telling comment that when we read or hear any language from the past, or when we receive as human beings any message from any other human being, we perform an act of translation. What does such an act involve? At least, an understanding of the cultural and experimental worlds that lie behind the original act of speaking or of writing, ways into their schemata, if you like. Secondly, an understanding of the potential of the two semiotic systems in terms of their image-making. Third, and most obviously, a making intelligible of the linguistic choices expressed in the message. Fourthly an opportunity to explore the social psychological intentions of the originator of the message matched against one's own. Lastly, a challenge to match all of these with our appropriate response in our semiotic and linguistic system, and our culture.

Seen from this perspective, translation not only parallels human communication itself, it rises above those disciplinary memberships and those general labels with which I began. It allows us to put language into perspective by asserting the need to extend beyond the apposite selection of phrases to an investigative exploration of the signs of a culture, and to the social and individual motivations for particular choices. It offers the possibility of unravelling the complex of human and conceptual relations which go to make up the contexts in which we communicate. As such, it is as much social as linguistic. Insofar as unpacking the metaphors of communication involves all of us in cognitive work, it suggests a way in which we can characterise the psychological processes that human beings bring to bear on exchanging meanings. Furthermore, it gives us a motivation and a means to uncover the structure and textuality of the texts of a society, the communicative products which are both the starting point and the conclusion of our everyday translating activity.

What translation does, then, is to make strange and denaturalise those powers and outcomes of communication which we commonly take for granted. It sets us a problem. It asks us to explore our ideologically and culturally-based assumptions about all those matters on which we utter, in speech or in writing, or in signs. It tests our communicative competence, both linguistic and cognitive, to the utmost, and, most intimately, it requires us to cooperate with our fellow communicators in coming to our understandings. More than just problem-posing, however, translation (or better, translating) suggests how we might go about problem-solving. Here the somewhat sterile debates about translation as process or translation as product give way to fresh opportunities to cohere the semiotic, the linguistic, the social, the cultural and the psychological perspectives on communicating. In short, it offers a broader conception of what it means to understand.

Such a speculative sweep needs however to be kept in its place. Translating after Babel is a costly business, after all, and keeps large numbers of professionals in communicative work. It requires understanding if their efficacy is to be evaluated. Internationalism in commerce and in migration make it necessary, as does the creativity of artists and writers, and for those reasons alone, it ought not to remain a mystery; it needs translating. We have a right to know how translators do what they do, as specialist professionals in conveying and in part recreating, other people's messages.

We might think this a tall order for a library, let alone a book. That depends on the stance to translating you take and how well you can weave the contributing disciplines into the theme from the start (out of their own self-interest to understand their own practices, if for no other reason) and how authentic you can make your links to the profession. I have no doubt that Basil Hatim and Ian Mason achieve both goals. Their professional (and intercultural) biographies give them that credibility , and that breadth of view. More to the point in terms of the ethos of the *Language in Social Life Series*, they have a particular argument to advance, that of the translator as mediator, the topic of their final Chapter in this book. This is where the process of exploring and understanding translation began for me, as General Editor, though for other readers their motivations will lie elsewhere. How can we make use of the experiences of translating to understand the differences and the parallels between alternative social and cultural frames of reference? How can we as particular communicators, develop that double understanding, so difficult for many, which is a translator's normal activity? From that experience of exploring the metaphor of translating can we derive general benefits for language and cultural education?

Christopher N Candlin
General Editor
Macquarie University, Sydney

Foreword

The title of this book might lead some to believe that our intention is, somehow, to teach translators how to translate. Nothing could be further from the truth. Quite apart from the presumptuousness of such an aim, there is a real sense in which it is translators who are providing us with the evidence for what we know about translating. As translators ourselves, how often have we felt that, at a particular point in our work, something interesting was taking place, some procedure or solution which deserved to be recorded, some regularity of the process of translating which could be systematised and tested against other data, if only we had the time to pause in our work, forget about deadlines and be reflective for a while. But that is a luxury which translators can rarely afford – except, of course, when they can take time off from translating.

Meanwhile, interesting developments are taking place in the world of theoretical studies. The gap between theory and practice in translation studies has existed for too long. Now, thanks to work being done in several different but related areas, there is an opportunity to narrow that gap. Recent trends in sociolinguistics, discourse studies, pragmatics and semiotics, together with insights from the fields of artificial intelligence and conversation analysis, have advanced our understanding of the way communication works. The relevance to translation studies of all of this is obvious as soon as translation is regarded not as a sterile linguistic exercise but as an act of communication. This, then, is our aim: to relate an integrated account of discourse processes to the practical concerns of the translator. In so doing, we hope also to be able to provide pointers to areas for further research. For there is much that remains to be done. Studies in cross-cultural communication and in contrastive discourse linguistics are, relatively speaking, still in their infancy. But it is this very fact which provides a note of optimism for the future. The way is now open for fruitful analysis of translation processes. It is our hope that, in some small measure, we have been able to make a contribution to this important area of applied linguistics research.

Many people – friends, colleagues, former students – have helped us in our work on this book. In particular, we owe a debt of gratitude to those who have read and commented on earlier drafts of individual chapters: Ruqaiya Hasan, Diarmuid Bradley, James Dickens, Hugh Keith, Margaret Lang, Jerry Payne, Miranda Stewart, Anthony Stanforth, Bob Vanderplank and Malcolm Williams; and for help with examples to: Rainer Kölmel, Isabelle Lenoir, Mike Parry, Mireille Poots, Bjarne Thomsen, Gavin Watterson, Shona Whyte and many others. We are also indebted, above all, to the Series Editor of the Language in Social Life Series, Chris Candlin, whose guidance and suggestions have pointed us in new directions and helped us avoid many a pitfall. It goes without saying that we alone are responsible for any shortcomings which remain.

BH/IM

Acknowledgements

We are grateful to the following for permission to reproduce the following textual copyright material:

Carcanet Press Ltd and New Directions Publishing Corporation, Inc for the poem 'This Is Just To Say' by William Carlos Williams in *The Collected Poems 1909–1939* edited by A Walton Litz and Christopher MacGowan and *Collected Poems Vol I 1909–1939*, US Copyright 1938 by New Directions Publishing Corporation; Editorial Gredos, S A for the poem 'Serenata Sintectica' by Cassiano Ricardo in *En torno a la traduccion* by Garcia Yebra (1983).

We are grateful to the following for permission to reproduce the following illustrative copyright material:

(Text 1C$_1$) Claire Bretécher for the cartoon excerpt from 'Les Pionniers', published in *Les Frustrés* (1978 p.66); (Text 1C$_2$) Methuen for the English translation of the above, published in *More Frustration* (1983 p.23); (Text 1D$_1$) Les Éditions Albert René for a cartoon from *Les Lauriers De César* by Goscinny and Uderzo (1972 p.7); (Text 1D$_2$) Les Éditions Albert René and Hodder & Stoughton for the English translation of the above, published in *Asterix and the Laurel Wreath* by Goscinny and Uderzo and translated by Anthea Bell and Derek Hockridge (1974 p.7); (Text 8J) Honda (UK) Ltd for excerpts from their advertisement and the original artwork; (Figure 3.4) Routledge and Kegan Paul for a diagram from *Language and Situation: Language Varieties and the Social Contexts* by Michael Gregory and Susanne Carroll (1978 p.47).

Standard Abbreviations

FSP   Functional Sentence Perspective
MT   Machine Translation
R   Rheme
T   Theme
SL   Source Language
TL   Target Language
ST   Source Language Text
TT   Target Language Text

ONE

Issues and debates in translation studies

Translation is a useful test case for examining the whole issue of the role of language in social life. In creating a new act of communication out of a previously existing one, translators are inevitably acting under the pressure of their own social conditioning while at the same time trying to assist in the negotiation of meaning between the producer of the source-language text (ST) and the reader of the target-language text (TT), both of whom exist within their own, different social frameworks. In studying this complex process at work, we are in effect seeking insights which take us beyond translation itself towards the whole relationship between language activity and the social context in which it takes place. Thus, much of what we shall have to say in this book about translating is equally applicable to other forms of language use, considered not in isolation but as part of social life.

As soon as we begin to consider the work of the translator, we are aware of the multifarious nature of the activity. The social conditions in which translations are produced vary considerably as between the work of literary, religious, scientific and technical translators, between staff and freelance translators, and so on. Social and institutional divisions, functional differences: none of these can be denied. Translating activity is undoubtedly highly diverse. But dwelling on these demarcations would mask the important similarities that exist between all types of translating. It is the task of the theorist to discern regularities and patterns of behaviour where these exist, to incorporate diversity of function within an overall model of the translating process. Kelly (1979: 226) suggests a functional approach:

> It is only by recognizing a typology of function that a theory of translation will do justice to both Bible and bilingual cereal packet.

It is clear that in this case, variation of function is being referred to in the sense of contextually determined variation in language use. The predominant function of creative literature is not the same as that of an administrative memorandum or religious exegesis. But it will be important for us to operate with other, more subtle distinctions than these broad categories. On the one hand, different language functions, such as 'conceding', 'deducing', 'suggesting', may be discerned within literature, just as within other kinds of discourse. On the other hand, as Fowler (1986) convincingly argues, the boundary between 'literature' and 'non-literature' is an artificial one and, if 'creative use of language' is taken to be one of the criteria for recognition of the former, it can be shown that many non-literary texts display the same creative devices, used to the same ends, as in what is recognised as belonging to the category 'literature'. In fact, it proves very difficult to devise criteria for distinguishing, in any systematic way, between what constitutes literary and non-literary discourse; whatever is said to characterise the one will also be present, to some degree at least, in the other. But once all texts are seen as evidence of a **communicative transaction taking place within a social framework**, the way is open to a view of translating which is not restricted to a particular field – religious, literary, scientific – but which can include such diverse activities as film subtitling and dubbing, simultaneous interpreting, cartoon translating, abstracting and summarising, etc. This is the view we adopt in this book. Our ability to recognise texts as instances of a type – exposition, argumentation, instruction – depends on our experience of previous instances of the same type, in other words, on our ability to recognise texts as signs. The way we recognise and respond to these signs is, as we shall see in Chapter 6, a regularity of language use which transcends boundaries of genre.

To introduce our topic of discourse and the translator, we propose to review some of the traditional issues in translation studies, as they emerge from commentaries on translation. The text definitively commits the translator, whose only outlet for commentary is then either the footnote or the translator's introduction. Whereas the former is limited in scope and has the accompanying disadvantage of drawing attention to the inadequacy of translation, the translator's commentary has always provided an outlet for rationalisation about the approach adopted or judgements made and an opportunity to reflect on the nature of the process of translating.

In this chapter, then, we shall be selective, relating our review to the central concern of this book: **translating as a communicative process which takes place within a social context**. In selecting a limited number of themes, we hope to make some tentative links between theoretical points to be made in later chapters and some of the views and stances adopted by commentators in the past. Each theme has to do with the position of the translator, either as a problem-solver or as the occupier of a social role. By relating these familiar themes to the notion of translation as communicative discourse, we hope to be able to move beyond the rather inconclusive nature of traditional debates on such issues.

PROCESS AND PRODUCT

It is in the nature of things that the target text displays only the translator's final decisions. Readers perceive an end-product, a result of a decision-making process; they do not have access to pathways leading to decisions, to the dilemmas to be resolved by the translator. What is available for scrutiny is the end-product, the result of translation practice rather than the practice itself. In other words, we are looking at translation as **product** instead of translating as **process**. The distinction is an important one, as Widdowson (1979: 71) points out. Bell (1987) suggests that the tendency to ignore the process involved in the act of translating lies behind the relative stagnation of translation studies in recent years. If we treat text merely as a self-contained and self-generating entity, instead of as a decision-making procedure and an instance of communication between language users, our understanding of the nature of translating will be impaired. It is a problem which besets all attempts to evaluate translations by analytic comparison of ST to TT, a product-to-product comparison which overlooks the communication process. Critiques of individual translations abound. But from the perspective of translation studies, what is needed is systematic study of problems and solutions by close comparison of ST and TT **procedures**. Which techniques produce which effects? What are the regularities of the translation process in particular genres, in particular cultures and in particular historical periods?

The view that underlies this book then, is of translation as a process, involving the negotiation of meaning between producers and receivers of texts. In other words, the resulting translated text is to be seen as evidence of a transaction, a means of retracing the pathways of the translator's decision-making procedures. In the same way, the ST itself is an end-product and again should be treated as evidence of a writer's intended meaning rather than as the embodiment of the meaning itself. In translating metaphor, for example, there is little point in seeking to match target-language words with those in the ST in isolation from a consideration of the writer's whole world-view. Occurrences of metaphor have a cumulative effect which suggests a particular perception of reality and it is this which the translator seeks to capture.

In this sense, texts can be seen as the result of **motivated choice**: producers of texts have their own communicative aims and select lexical items and grammatical arrangement to serve those aims. Naturally, in translating, there are potentially two sets of motivations: those of the producer of the source text and those of the translator. Consequently, in the first half of this chapter we shall consider how translators respond to what they perceive as the motivations behind ST procedures; subsequently, we give consideration to the translator's own motivations.

OBJECTIVITY/SUBJECTIVITY

Inevitably, both translating and discussing translations involve making judgements. But can judgements about translations be made objectively? Recently, serious attempts have been made to establish translation criticism on a proper footing (e.g. Reiss 1971, Simpson 1975, House 1976, Wilss 1982). To replace the impressionism and unsubstantiated opinion which often characterises judgements about the merits and demerits of particular translations, these authors propose methodical and systematic criteria for evaluation, based on ST analysis and consideration of available translation procedures. But does this mean that subjectivity can at last be eliminated from translation assessment and that objective evaluations can be made by literary critic and translation teacher alike? There seems to be little prospect of this, given the nature of human language processing itself. Every reading of a text is a unique, unrepeatable act and a text is bound to evoke differing responses in different receivers. On this point, we agree with Reiss (1971: 107):

. . . any analysis, however concerned it may be to achieve total objectivity, ultimately amounts to interpretation.

(*Our translation*)

and with House (1976:64):

> It seems to be unlikely that translation quality assessment can ever be completely objectified in the manner of the results of natural science subjects.

What can be done, however, is to elaborate a set of parameters for analysis which aim to promote consistency and precision in the discussion of translating and translations. A common set of categories is needed and a set of terms for referring to them, a metalanguage for translation studies. It is one of our aims in this book to suggest a model of the translation process based on just such a set of categories.

'LITERAL' VERSUS 'FREE'

In the light of all this, let us re-examine some basic notions. The primary time-honoured debate concerns the degree of latitude the translator is permitted in representing the source text in translation. The 'literal' versus 'free' controversy has been more or less a constant in translation studies, no matter how far back one goes. The extreme case is that referred to by the fourteenth-century translator Salah al-Din al-Safadi who, writing about earlier generations of Arab translators, complains that they

> look at each Greek word and what it means. They seek an equivalent term in Arabic and write it down. Then they take the next word and do the same, and so on until the end of what they have to translate.
>
> (Quoted in Badawi 1968: 33 – *our translation*)

Al-Safadi faults this method of translating on two counts:

1. It is erroneous to assume that one-for-one equivalents exist for all lexical items in Greek and Arabic.
2. The sentence structure of one language does not match that of another.

One could continue the list: word order, sentence length, ways of presenting information, and so on; all are language-specific. More fundamentally still, it is erroneous to assume that the meaning of a sentence or text is composed of the sum of the meanings of the individual lexical items, so that any attempt to translate at this level is bound to miss important elements of meaning. The arguments are, no doubt, familiar ones. Yet the debate continues even today and literal translation has its defenders. Newmark (1988: 68–69), who is careful to distinguish literal translation from word-for-word translation, maintains that

> literal translation is correct and must not be avoided, if it secures referential and pragmatic equivalence to the original.

Pragmatic equivalence, however, as we shall see later, is frequently at variance with referential equivalence. Text 1A is taken from a multilingual advertisement for a well-known brand of after-shave.

Text 1A

DRAKKAR
Audacieux, franc et tenace
Bold, vigorous and tenacious
Kühn, freimütig und haftfest

Here, equivalence is sought not at referential level (e.g. *franc* does not have the same referential meaning as *vigorous*) but at the connotative level of the virile qualities of adventurers (the brand name in French denotes a Viking longboat). At this level *franc*, *vigorous* and *freimütig* (i.e. 'free-spirited') are indeed equivalent. Conversely, the German term *haftfest*, while relaying most of the referential meaning of *tenace/tenacious* – i.e. that the substance 'clings' – is less successful in conveying the desired connotations.

Of course, in this case we are looking at a particular kind of translating activity and our judgements are made in terms of what the text is trying to achieve. It is this fact which may lead us to a reassessment of the traditional 'literal' versus 'free' debate. The problem is that the issue is all too often discussed without reference to the context in which translating takes place; the social circumstances of translation are lost from sight. In fact, the beginnings of a solution to the problem will depend, to borrow a well-known sociolinguistic formula, on: who is translating what, for whom, when, where, why and in what circumstances?

FORMAL AND DYNAMIC EQUIVALENCE

In this respect, Eugene Nida's (1964) reformulation of the problem in terms of types of equivalence appropriate to particular circumstances is a positive move. By distinguishing **formal equivalence** (closest possible match of form and content between ST and TT) and **dynamic equivalence** (principle of equivalence of effect on reader of TT) as basic orientations rather than as a binary choice, Nida shifts attention away from the sterile debate of free versus literal towards the effects of different translation strategies. Formal equivalence is, of course, appropriate in certain circumstances. At crucial points in diplomatic negotiations, interpreters may need to translate exactly what is said rather than assume responsibility for reinterpreting the sense and formulating it in such a way as to achieve what they judge to be equivalence of effect. Similarly, a frequently-employed technique in this book will be to give formal English versions of text samples from languages such as Arabic, to which relatively few readers have access. Formal equivalence is, in other words, a means of providing some degree of insight into the lexical, grammatical or structural form of a source text.

Orientation towards dynamic equivalence, on the other hand, is assumed to be the normal strategy. Although most translations may fall somewhere on the scale in between the two types, Nida (1964: 160) claims that 'the present direction is toward increasing emphasis on dynamic equivalences'. Newmark (1981: 39) prefers the terms **semantic** and **communicative** translation. The advantage of this formulation is that the categories, as defined, cover more of the 'middle ground' of translation practice. Semantic translation – attempting 'to render, as closely as the semantic and syntactic structures of the second language allow, the exact contextual meaning of the original' – is less extreme than formal equivalence and therefore conforms more closely to a common translation strategy. Useful as these concepts are, however, they are beset with problems. On the one hand, all translation is, in a sense, communicative. Similarly, a translator who aims at formal equivalence usually has good reasons for doing so and the formally equivalent version may well, in fact, achieve equivalence of reader response.

Naturally, actual effects on receivers of texts are difficult to gauge. Consequently, it seems preferable to handle the issue in terms of equivalence of **intended effects**, thus linking judgements about what the translator seeks to achieve to judgements about the intended meaning of the ST speaker/writer. In other words, we need to consider the issue in terms of the degree of motivation of particular strategies in both ST and TT. We are here in the domain of pragmatics, a discipline which over the last twenty years has brought considerable insights into the nature of intended meaning, the relation of meaning to communicative environment and the principles of cooperation and communication between producers and receivers of texts. These issues will be looked at in detail in Chapter 5.

There is also a problem concerning the use of the term 'equivalence' in connection with translations. It implies that complete equivalence is an achievable goal, as if there were such a thing as a formally or dynamically equivalent target-language (TL) version of a source-language (SL) text. The term is, of course, usually intended in a relative sense – that of closest possible approximation to ST meaning – and this is the sense in which we use it here. But the concept of 'adequacy' in translation is perhaps a more useful one. Adequacy of a given translation procedure can then be judged in terms of the specifications of the particular translation task to be performed and in terms of users' needs.

FORM VERSUS CONTENT: THE TRANSLATION OF STYLE

Closely related to the literal versus free issue is the debate on the primacy of content over form or vice versa. Should content be faithfully rendered at all costs, and form only if the translation of content allows? As with other issues, the translator is here faced with what amounts to a conflict of interests. The ideal would of course be to translate both form and content, without the one in any way impinging on the other. But many would claim that this is frequently not possible. The form of a source text may be characteristic of SL conventions but so much at variance with TL norms that rendering the form would inevitably obscure the 'message' or 'sense' of the text. So how, when and to what extent is the translator justified in departing from the style or manner?

For some modern theorists (e.g. Nida), the overriding criteria are type of discourse and reader response. Thus, adherence to the style of the source text may, in certain circumstances, be unnecessary or even counterproductive since:

> the standards of stylistic acceptability for various types of discourse differ radically from language to language. What is entirely appropriate in Spanish, for example, may turn out to be quite unacceptable 'purple prose' in English, and the English prose we admire as dignified and effective often seems in Spanish to be colourless, insipid and flat. Many Spanish literary artists take delight in the flowery elegance of their language, while most English writers prefer bold realism, precision, and movement.
>
> (Nida 1964: 169)

To modify style on these grounds, however, is to deny the reader access to the world of the SL text. More importantly, it is a step on the road to adaptation, the logical outcome to which is to turn the producer of the SL text into someone else: to give him the expression – and therefore the outlook – of a member of the TL community. One has only to think, for example, of the peculiar Englishness of the dialogue in many of Harold Pinter's plays to realise that any attempt to modify it in translation, for the sake of TL stylistic conventions, would inevitably transform the characters into different people and, no doubt, affect the unstated undercurrents of meaning on which much in the plays depends. In such cases, the 'style' is the 'meaning'. Henri Meschonnic (1973: 349) is critical of Nida's willingness to detach style from meaning:

> . . . meaning and form: there are not two dissociable, heterogeneous entities. A text is a whole entity, to be translated as a whole. (*Our translation*)

The style, in other words, is an indissociable part of the message to be conveyed. This much is undeniable. But it seems to us that there is a more fundamental problem, namely, the term 'style' itself. Rather than try to resolve the style and content debate, we shall, in this book, re-examine the terms in which the conflict has been traditionally stated. For the indiscriminate use of relatively ill-defined terms such as 'style' and 'message' has not, in general, helped to clarify the debate.

REDEFINITION OF 'STYLE'

The term 'style' seems to have become a kind of umbrella heading, under which are lumped together all kinds of textual/contextual variables. Analysis is needed of the separate components of 'style', in this sense of the term, and the development of register analysis by Halliday, McIntosh and Strevens (1964) and others has gone a long way towards improving our understanding of what is involved. In Chapter 3, we look at how individual contextual variables affecting both language users and the use to which language is put are relevant to the translation/translatability of texts. 'Style' may be seen as the result of motivated choices made by text producers; thus, we shall distinguish style from (1) idiolect, the unconscious linguistic habits of an individual language user; and (2) the conventional patterns of expression which characterise particular languages. Stylistic effects are, in this sense, traceable to the intentions of the text producer and these are what the translator seeks to recover. But there is a further development which adds a social dimension to stylistic effects. Through intertextuality – the tendency of text producers to be influenced by other texts they have experienced (see Chapter 7) – stylistic options come to be characteristic not of the entire language system but of particular **social roles** and particular **kinds of language activity**. Style can thus be either individual or social.

Style, then, in the sense we are retaining, is not a property of the language system as a whole but of particular language users in particular (kinds of) settings. The translator, as a language user in a setting which is generally not that of the ST producer, has to be able to judge the **semiotic** value which is conveyed when particular stylistic options are selected. This and related matters will form the basis of our discussion in Chapter 6.

MEANING POTENTIAL

Let us now consider the selection of options in a text from the reader's point of view. As G. Steiner (1975) points out, and as much research into the reading process has shown, each act of reading a text is in itself an act of translation, i.e. an interpretation. We seek to recover what is 'meant' in a text from the whole range of possible meanings, in other words, from the **meaning potential** which Halliday (1978: 109) defines as:

> the paradigmatic range of semantic choice that is present in the
> system, and to which the members of a culture have access in their
> language.

Inevitably, we feed our own beliefs, knowledge, attitudes and so on into our processing of texts, so that any translation will, to some extent, reflect the translator's own mental and cultural outlook, despite the best of impartial intentions. No doubt, the risks are reduced to a minimum in most scientific and technical, legal and administrative translating; but cultural predispositions can creep in where least expected. In the field of translating for international organisations, for example, there have to be strict in-house rules for such matters as the names of sovereign states, variants of which inevitably reflect ideological attitudes. Such rules, however, and any norms enshrined in official glossaries cannot cover all cases; the subtle emphases of SL and TL texts are bound to differ wherever subjective discourse is involved.

In literary translating, the process of constant reinterpretation is most apparent. The translator's reading of the source text is but one among infinitely many possible readings, yet it is the one which tends to be imposed upon the readership of the TL version. Beaugrande (1978) suggests that a common failing in translators of poetry is the urge to resolve polyvalence, a crucial feature of poetic discourse, and to impose a particular reading of the text. Yet since an important feature of poetic discourse is to allow a multiplicity of responses among SL readers, it follows that the translator's task should be to **preserve, as far as possible, the range of possible responses; in other words, not to reduce the dynamic role of the reader.**

'EMPATHY' AND INTENT

It is a fact recognised by all translators that familiarity with the ideas and underlying meaning of the writer of a SL text is a vital aid to translating, whereas unfamiliarity breeds lack of confidence, or at least the inability to anticipate meaning when a text is in some way defective, obscure or just elliptical. The best translators of works of literature are often said to be those who are most 'in tune' with the original author. The translator must 'possess' the spirit of the original, 'make his own' the intent of the SL writer: such are the frequently used terms. The imagery is akin to that used by G. Steiner (1975: 298): 'The translator invades, extracts, and brings home.'

It is perhaps the very elusiveness of intentionality which

encourages the use of metaphor to refer to the notion. The view that intention should be relayed in translation is no longer controversial; but appeal to it still tends to be couched in vague and impressionistic terms. How can we pin down that part of meaning which we refer to as intention? We believe that for translation theory, the most fruitful approach is that developed within pragmatics, which attempts to account for the ways in which we perceive underlying meaning on the basis of what we already know or assume to be the case. These ideas are explored in Chapters 4 and 5, where examples of intended meaning are discussed.

Clearly, there is a link between intentionality and such matters as the structure and wording (or texture; see Chapter 10) of TL texts. Translation is a matter of choice, but choice is always motivated: omissions, additions and alterations may indeed be justified but only in relation to intended meaning. Even within the eighteenth-century canon of translation-as-imitation, departures from the original text were not indiscriminate. According to T. R. Steiner (1975: 42), ideal mimesis involved fidelity to the 'design' of the source text, in the light of which certain elements may be judged superfluous; and 'it is to mimetic theory that we can attribute many eighteenth-century licenses to omit, simplify, and beautify'. The relevance of these ideas to present-day translating is to be found in the close link between the translator's choices and the intentionality of the producer of the ST. Our discussion of texture in Chapter 10 is based upon this assumption.

THE TRANSLATOR'S MOTIVATION

In discussing intention and other matters, we have focused mainly on the producer of the source text. The intentions of the translator add a second dimension to the process and it is to this that we now turn.

The translator's motivations are inextricably bound up with the **socio-cultural context** in which the act of translating takes place. Consequently, it is important to judge translating activity only within a social context. Before there is translation, for example, there has to be a need for translation. The need may be client-driven, as when someone commissions, asks for or otherwise requires a translation; it is often market-driven, when publishers perceive demand for a work of foreign literature; it may even be translator-driven, as when a work of ancient literature is translated or re-translated because someone feels that, by doing so, he or she can communicate something new. Moreover, the status of the source text as a social product, its intended readership, the socio-economic circumstances of its production, translation and reception by TL readers are all relevant factors in the study of the translation process. From the eighth-century Caliph of Baghdad who had philosophers brought from Egypt to translate from Greek and Coptic and established the *bayt al-hikma* (or House of Wisdom) to the present-day work of staff translators for international organisations, from the translations of the classics by gentlemen-scholars to the evangelising work of Bible translators, the activity of translators has always been a function of, and an influence upon, the social life of their times. To study translations in isolation from the factors affecting their production is consequently to miss out an important dimension of the phenomenon. In fact, the social context of translating is probably a more important variable than the textual genre, which has imposed such rigid distinctions on types of translating in the past ('literary translation', 'scientific and technical translation', 'religious translation', etc.). Divisions of this kind tend to mask certain fundamental similarities between texts from different fields: there are regularities of discourse procedures which transcend the boundaries between genres and which it is our aim to describe.

POETIC DISCOURSE: A TEST CASE FOR TRANSLATABILITY

The view of translating as a part of the communication process between SL writer and TL reader may help to shed some light on an age-old debate within translation studies. It concerns the nature of poetic discourse and whether or not it is translatable from one language into another. The terms of the debate are familiar ones and do not seem to have changed very much over the centuries.

In recent times, Roman Jakobson (1959: 238) is one of those who, from a linguistic perspective, adopt a pessimistic view. In poetry, 'phonemic similarity is sensed as semantic relationship'; formal aspects of the linguistic code became part of the meaning so that translation proper is impossible; 'only creative transposition is possible'. In fact, the point is applicable, well beyond poetry, to all discourse in which properties of the form of the language code are brought to the fore and made to bear particular significance. Advertising and political slogans rely on alliteration and rhyme ('Let the train take the strain': British Rail; 'the workers not the shirkers': Margaret Thatcher, *circa* 1980). Puns also rely on coincidental similarities of form which are rarely replicated in other languages.

A striking example from poetic discourse is provided by García Yebra (1983: 145), who cites a Portuguese poem by Cassiano Ricardo entitled *Serenata sintética*:

> rua
>> torta
>
>>>> lua
>>>>> morta
>
>>>>>>> tua
>>>>>>>> porta.

In this short poem, phonemic form is everything. The words themselves are evocative: a small town with 'winding streets' (*rua torta*), a 'fading moon' (*lua morta*) and the hint of an amorous affair: 'your door' (*tua porta*). But their impact is achieved almost solely through the close rhyme and rhythm; the meaning is raised from the level of the banal by dint of exploiting features which are indissociable from the Portuguese language as a code. García Yebra relates that he gave up the attempt to translate the poem even into Spanish, a language which shares certain phonological features with Portuguese.

In the face of such seemingly insurmountable difficulties as these, translators' reactions have generally been of two kinds. On the one hand are those referred to earlier who adapt or imitate the SL poem, without any attempt to translate in the normal sense of the word. On the other hand, are literalists such as Vladimir Nabokov, who points to the 'charlatanism' of those whose loose versions of an original poem masquerade under the name of translation; only a literal rendering can render the essence of the poem and thus lay claim to the term 'translation':

> Literal: rendering, as closely as the associative and syntactical capacities of another language allow, the exact contextual meaning of the original. Only this is true translation . . . It is when the translator sets out to

render the 'spirit', and not the mere sense of the text, that he begins to traduce his author. (Nabokov 1964: viii–ix)

This view, of course, brings us back into the literal versus free debate, to which, as we have seen, there is no satisfactory resolution. Rather than advancing opinions about what is best in translating discourse of this kind, we would suggest that progress lies in analysing the facts of the matter. Lefevere (1975) provides a useful framework by listing seven different strategies in verse translation:

1. phonemic translation (imitation of ST sounds);
2. literal translation (cf. Nabokov);
3. metrical translation (imitation of metre of ST);
4. prose translation (rendering as much of sense as possible);
5. rhymed translation (added constraints of rhyme and metre);
6. blank verse translation (no constraint of rhyme but still one of structure);
7. interpretation (complete change of form and/or imitation).

Against such categories as these, translations can be judged according to what the translator set out to achieve, instead of some notional criterion of what qualifies as good translation of poetry. Once again, we must place the act of translating within a social context. Since total re-creation of any language transaction is impossible, translators will always be subject to a conflict of interests as to what are their communicative priorities, a conflict which they resolve as best they can. It follows from this that, in assessing translations, the first thing to consider is the translator's own purpose, so that performance can be judged against objectives. In sum, it should be possible to arrive at some statement, along the lines of Jakobson's, of what can and what cannot be achieved and then to discuss results in terms of what the translator is aiming at, and for what kind of reader: do the results match up to the stated aims?

'LAWS' OF TRANSLATION

In contrast to this procedural approach is the long-standing tradition in translation studies of formulating sets of rules to which the translator should theoretically adhere. A. F. Tytler, whose *Essay on the Principles of Translation*, first published in 1791, was the first whole book in English devoted to translation studies, propounds three 'laws of translation':

> I. That the Translation should give a complete transcript of the ideas of the original work.
> II. That the style and manner of writing should be of the same character with that of the original.
> III. That the Translation should have all the ease of original composition.
>
> (Tytler 1907: 9)

The trouble with 'laws' such as these is that they imply that the three objectives are entirely compatible and achievable; whereas, if matter and manner are indeed separable entities, then I, II and III are, at least in part, mutually exclusive.

A more recent formulation of the 'basic requirements' of a translation are to be found in Nida (1964: 164). The similarities are striking:

1. making sense;
2. conveying the spirit and manner of the original;
3. having a natural and easy form of expression;
4. producing a similar response.

The fourth requirement is an addition to Tytler's list, reflecting modern concern with reader response. In other respects, however, the points are essentially the same, although 'making sense' seems to be far less constraining than conveying the 'ideas' of the source text. Recognising that the requirements are in conflict, Nida suggests that correspondence of meaning should, in the last resort, have priority over correspondence of style – an issue we reviewed earlier. Let us now consider these conflicts in terms of the divided loyalties of the translator.

AUTHOR-CENTRED AND READER-CENTRED TRANSLATING

Instead of prescribing abstract rules for translator behaviour, it seems preferable to begin by taking into consideration differences in the basic orientation of the translator. Thus it is that some commentators speak of author-centred translating, text-centred translating and reader-centred translating. The distinction between author-centred and text-centred has to do with the status of the source text: translators of modern literature are often acquainted or in contact with the author of the source text and interpret in the light of what they know about the intended meaning. For translators of, say, EEC directives or legal contracts, on the other hand, authorship is far less important than the nature of the text itself and its range of possible meanings. Where translating is reader-centred, these preoccupations are still present but priority is accorded to aiming at particular kinds of reader response. Given that, in any case, translating involves a conflict of interests, it is all a question of where one's priorities lie. There are parallels here to the reading process itself, in the sense that, as shown in Alderson and Urquhart (1985: xviii), 'the product of reading will vary according to the reader's purpose and motivation'.

For many translators of religious texts, first loyalty is at all times with the source text. For others in the same field of translating, concern for the reader is paramount. A simple example will serve to illustrate the point. Texts $1B_1$, $1B_2$ and $1B_3$ are taken from three major translations of the Parable of the Labourers in the Vineyard (Matthew 20, 1–16).

Text $1B_1$

> For the kingdom of heaven is like unto a man that is an householder, which went out early in the morning to hire labourers into his vineyard. And when he had agreed with the labourers for a penny a day, he sent them into his vineyard. And he went out about the third hour, and saw others. . .

Text $1B_2$

> For the kingdom of heaven is like a householder who went out early in the morning to hire labourers for his vineyard. After agreeing with the labourers for a denarius* a day, he sent them into his vineyard. And going out about the third hour he saw others. . .
>
> *The *denarius* was worth about seventeen pence.

Text $1B_3$

> The kingdom of Heaven is like this. There was once a landowner who went out early one morning to hire labourers for his vineyard; and after agreeing to pay them the usual day's wage he sent them off to work. Going out three hours later he saw some more men. . .

Evidence of the translators' different orientations is to be found in the mention of a sum of money. Whereas the producer of Text $1B_1$ (the Authorised Version of 1611) offers a simple functional equivalent, token for token (i.e. basic unit of currency in TL culture for basic unit in SL culture), Text $1B_2$ (the Revised Standard Version 1881 and 1954) is scrupulous in relating the precise denomination referred to in the source; it is a text-centred version. A footnote is then offered as a concession to communicative requirements. For the translator of Text $1B_3$ (New English Bible, 1961), however, both of these solutions are inadequate; neither 'a penny' nor 'a denarius' communicates anything (and any attempt to translate the actual sum into modern prices has built-in obsolescence). In opting for *the usual day's wage*, the translator is departing from the letter of the source text in order to ensure an adequate communicative response in readers of the translation: it is a clear case of reader-centred translating. As is frequently the case, the differences are traceable to the translators' brief. Whereas the Revisers of 1881 had been instructed 'to render the same Greek word everywhere by the same English word', the New English Bible translators were asked to produce 'a genuinely new translation' for English readers in 'the current speech of our own time' (NEB 1961: vii–viii).

In case it should be thought that all this is of merely historical interest, Texts $1C_1$ and $1C_2$ are offered as a contemporary example of similar procedures at work. They are fragments of, respectively, a cartoon by Claire Bretécher and the corresponding English translation. Here, references to French political institutions are exchanged for equivalent British ones. The result is, of course, that the cartoon characters themselves become, in translation, British. It is worth noting that, whereas the translator of Bretécher systematically adapts from a French to a British setting, the translators of the famous *Astérix* cartoon series do not, since the humour in this case is dependent on national identities: Astérix has to remain a Frenchman and Parisian driving habits must remain Parisian, as Texts $1D_1$ and $1D_2$ illustrate. The stereotype is strong enough to be recognisable to the foreign reader, whereas Bretécher's left-wing intellectuals need to be transposed to another setting. In each case, the translator is guided by a different overall purpose.

It hardly seems useful to debate whether or not **adaptation** is still translation. It is a procedure appropriate to particular circumstances (e.g. translating for the stage), which aims to achieve a particular kind of equivalence. Once again, judgements need to be made in terms of the adequacy of given procedures for achieving particular ends.

Text 1C₁

Text 1C₂

Text 1D₁

Text 1D₂

CONDITIONS OF PRODUCTION

From a social point of view, the position of translators in each of the various fields of translating is naturally very different. Few can earn a living from literary translating, which is often done for the sake of the intellectual or aesthetic pleasure it procures. Many freelance technical or administrative translators rely on regular work from agencies or direct from clients in order to make a living. Staff translators for large firms or international organisations form yet another category; their work may be repetitive and often involves performance under pressure of time. Such basic matters as these are bound to influence attitudes and to ensure that translators in each category have more in common with each other than with those working in other fields of translating. As Kelly (1979: 126) observes, Meschonnic's (1973) criticism of Nida derives largely from the fact that, for the former, literary expression is the predominant function of language whereas for Nida, as a Bible translator, the passing of information is paramount. In other words, it is often the difference in function of translation which produces differences of outlook.

Yet there are many issues of common concern. Similar problems are faced in widely differing fields of translating, as Texts $1B_{1,2,3}$ and $1C_{1,2}$ show. Our aim in this chapter has been to review certain common themes in translation studies and to show that, in all cases, translators are involved in communicative activity which takes place within a social context. The translator's purpose and priorities are to be seen within this context: such traditional issues as the 'literal' versus 'free' debate, the problems of interpretation of any source text, the adequacy of particular translations for particular purposes are all relatable to the social conditions in which translating activity occurs. How then can the whole process be studied? To what extent has the twentieth-century discipline of linguistics contributed to translation studies and helped to promote a systematic approach to evaluating the translation process? This is the subject of our next chapter.

TWO

Linguistics and translators: theory and practice

THE TRANSLATOR AT WORK

Our purpose in this chapter is to consider the impact of linguistics on the work of the translator and to look for areas where the theoretical study of language can continue to bring insights to the translator's task. We begin our analysis at the workplace: the contemporary professional translator, faced with a lengthy, semi-technical document to translate into his or her language of habitual use. Let us take the case of the freelance translator, working from home but equipped with the tools for the job, including some of the aids made available by modern technology. In addition to a range of dictionaries (monolingual and bilingual), one-volume encyclopaedias and, perhaps, documentation in specialised subject areas, the translator frequently works either with a word processor or, in the case of work for agencies, with a dictaphone. On-line access to information retrieval at the workstation is also a realistic possibility in the near future: not just multilingual glossaries but also databases providing access to technical fields of writing and to encyclopaedic information. In broad terms, the translator needs access to specific information in the fastest possible search time: information which will facilitate comprehension of the source text or information which will serve as a guide to TL terminology and text conventions.

Aids to translators are improving all the time, but the basic problems faced by translators in their work remain the same. In broad and general terms, these can be listed as follows:

1. Comprehension of source text:
   (a) parsing of text (grammar and lexis)
   (b) access to specialised knowledge
   (c) access to intended meaning.

2. Transfer of meaning:
   (a) relaying lexical meaning
   (b) relaying grammatical meaning
   (c) relaying rhetorical meaning, including implied or inferrable meaning, for potential readers.

3. Assessment of target text:
   (a) readability
   (b) conforming to generic and discoursal TL conventions
   (c) judging adequacy of translation for specified purpose.

As a specification of the cognitive and linguistic tasks carried out by the translator, this list is simplified and incomplete. The full range of processing activities deployed in translating will, we hope, become clear as our study proceeds in later chapters. But for the moment, our checklist will serve as a guide to the points on which linguistic theory might be expected to be of relevance to translation practice.

The emergence of linguistics as a new discipline in the twentieth century brought a spirit of optimism to the pursuit of language study, a feeling that the groundwork was at last being laid for a systematic and scientific approach to the description of language. Insights into the way language functions as a system might be expected to shed light on – and perhaps provide solutions to – the kinds of language problems experienced in social life. Many areas of social life called for investigation from a linguistic standpoint: the teaching of modern languages, the treatment of language disorders, the role of language in education, the status and treatment of minority languages, language planning policy in emergent nations and, of course, translation.

HUMAN AND MACHINE TRANSLATION: ACTUAL AND VIRTUAL PROBLEMS

One obvious application of linguistics is the attempt to develop a device for carrying out automatic translation. The search for 'fully automatic high-quality translation' might be expected to provide a point of contact between linguists and the translating profession; in reality, it has largely been a case of separate development. Instead of initiating a thorough investigation into the actual process as carried out by human translators, early research into machine translation

(MT) chose to concentrate on problems of syntactic parsing and resolving lexical polysemy in sample sentences. An unstated underlying assumption was that translation involved overcoming the contrasts between language systems. Source-language syntactic structures had to be exchanged for TL structures; lexical items from each language had to be matched and the nearest equivalents selected. While a huge investment was made (in terms of both effort and funding) in research into how to resolve such problems, the whole notion of context was deemed to be intractable and, consequently, beyond the bounds of machine processing.

Early models of MT were more a reflection of current pre-occupations in linguistics than an attempt to simulate the work of the translator or to model the cognitive processes involved. A small sample of unedited MT output from this period will serve to illustrate the point. Text 2A is an example of output from an IBM Mark I French–English system of the late 1950s, quoted in Hutchins (1986: 69).

Text 2A

> The algebraic logic which is the subject of this course/s is conceived here as the part the most elementary (of) the mathematical logic. Later we/us will specify what we/us hear/mean signify by the word 'algebraic'. But one needs indicate immediately in what consists the mathematical logic whose algebraic logic constitutes the first part.

It must firstly be said that, despite its shortcomings, Text 2A is a comprehensible stretch of English and provides evidence of definite successes at this relatively early stage of MT research. One instance is the selection of *which*, rather than *who*, in line 1, referring back to an inanimate subject noun. But the problems are obvious. Leaving aside the inability of the system at this stage to distinguish subject and object pronouns, problems to be resolved obviously include noun/adjective inversion (*the part the most elementary*), use of the definite article (*the mathematical logic*), polysemy of the French verb *entendre* (*hear/mean*) and certain categories of pronouns (*in what consists; whose* – the latter should no doubt read 'of which'). All of these, of course, constitute problems of linguistic analysis but they are definitely not translation problems, in the sense that no competent translator would regard them as anything other than automatic transfer procedures which do not on the whole involve any choice: *la partie la plus élémentaire* becomes 'the most elementary part', and so on. Human translators, on the other hand, may well feel inclined to relay the rhetorical drift of the argument which underlies Text 2A, for example:

> We shall specify later. . . For the moment, however, we must indicate. . .

The rhetorical development of a text, beyond the limits of the individual sentence, lay beyond the scope of MT research, at least for the time being. Consequently, problems in early MT and problems of human translating simply did not coincide: what was of concern to the one was of scarcely any concern to the other.

After early success on a modest scale, results of the application of MT to naturally occurring texts proved to be disappointing. By 1964, V. H. Yngve of MIT was forced to admit that:

> We have come face to face with the realisation that we will only have adequate mechanical translations when the machine can 'understand' what it is translating and this will be a very difficult task indeed.

(Yngve 1964, quoted in Hutchins 1986: 164)

In 1966, the Automatic Language Processing Advisory Committee (ALPAC), set up by the US National Academy of Sciences to enquire into the state of MT, reported – perhaps over-pessimistically – that there was 'no immediate or predictable prospect of useful machine translation'. Funding for MT in the United States was drastically reduced and, for a while, interest in MT began to wane. Research has, however, continued and we shall refer to more promising approaches to MT later in this chapter. Many systems are now operational and users report relative satisfaction with the results. It would nonetheless be fair to say that much of the output of MT systems in use still requires extensive post-editing of a fairly basic kind.

Naturally, the integration of MT into the work of large-scale translation services has not been without attendant problems. Translators whose training had led them always to produce high-quality work now found themselves spending a considerable proportion of their time on tedious correction of poor-quality machine output. In these circumstances, job satisfaction tends to suffer as tasks become repetitive and frustrating (see, e.g., discussions reported in Melby 1982 and Picken 1985: 85–91). In response to this, **interactive systems** have been developed, thus putting translators back in control of the translation process and allowing them to intervene at every stage. In these systems, the machine initiates requests for help by offering alternative translations of certain words or phrases. The human editor selects one of these options or types in a better version. The editor can also decide at this stage whether or not to update the system's dictionary by keying in new entries. Only when these stages are completed does the system generate the target text. (For further discussion, see Melby 1987).

STRUCTURE VERSUS MEANING

Before looking at promising developments over the last two decades, we shall now suggest some of the reasons why earlier developments in linguistic theory were of relatively little interest to translators. Structural linguistics sought to describe language as a system of interdependent elements and to characterise the behaviour of individual items and categories on the basis of their distribution (i.e. the complete range of linguistic contexts in which they could occur). Morphology and syntax constituted the main areas of analysis, largely to the exclusion of the intractable problem of meaning, which was either ignored or else dealt with purely in terms of the distribution of lexical items. Bloomfield's (1933: 140) famous statement is symptomatic:

> The statement of meanings is therefore the weak point in language study, and will remain so until human knowledge advances very far beyond its present state.

Since meaning is at the very heart of the translator's work, it follows that the postponement of semantic investigation in American linguistics was bound to create a gap between linguistics and translation studies. Quite simply, linguists and translators were not talking about the same thing. Moreover, linguistic description was in general limited to single language systems. The complexities involved in analysing distributions and systemic contrasts of sounds, word forms and sentence constituents within a language system were taxing enough in themselves, without clouding the issue by introducing contrasts and comparisons between languages. For the translator, meanwhile, every problem involved two language systems; a statement of the distribution of an item in one language is of no particular value. In Text 2A above, for example, an analysis of the complete set of distributions of the

French verb *entendre* might have helped in the formulation of a rule for MT selection of a correct English equivalent. It would not, on the other hand, help the human translator who knows that what is required in this context is 'what we mean by. . .' and whose real preoccupations lie elsewhere, namely, in maximising readability of a technical text.

CONTRASTS BETWEEN LANGUAGE SYSTEMS

Structuralist theories of language were, nevertheless, influential in translation theory and there were some serious attempts to apply structuralist notions to translation problems. Catford (1965), for example, attempts to build a theory of translation on the current state of 'linguistic science'. The work is, in fact, firmly based on the British linguistic tradition of J. R. Firth and M. A. K. Halliday, which differs from American structural linguistics in its emphasis on contextual meaning and the social context of situation in which language activity takes place. Moreover, the work draws on more than a single language system and examples are drawn from a commendable variety of closely related and unrelated tongues, ranging from Gaelic to Indonesian. Yet much of the discussion is about structural contrasts between language systems rather than about communication across cultural barriers and about individual, de-contextualised sentences instead of real texts. Thus, translation theory becomes a branch of contrastive linguistics, and translation problems become a matter of the non-correspondence of certain formal categories in different languages. For Catford (1965: 32):

> A formal correspondent is any TL category which may be said to occupy, as nearly as possible, the 'same' place in the economy of the TL as the given SL category occupies in the SL.

The assumption that 'formal correspondence' thus defined is of relevance to translation studies leads naturally to an investigation of 'equivalence probability' – an attempt to arrive at a statistical calculation of the degree of probability that a given SL category will, in any given text, be rendered by an equivalent TL category. Thus, the probability that French *dans* will be rendered by English *in* is calculated, in the case of a particular pair of texts, at 73 per cent. It is then hoped that statistical analysis of a large sample of texts might lead to the formulation of 'translation rules'. Manifestly, however, any such extrapolation can lead only to statements about language systems, not about the communicative factors surrounding the production and reception of texts. The notion of equivalence probabilities between such categories as prepositions may be relevant to certain elementary errors in raw MT output, as in Text 2A. But it is of no concern to the human translator, for whom translation of *en quoi consiste la logique mathématique* as *what mathematical logic consists of* is not a problem.

A similar concern with contrasts between the mechanics of different languages underlies Jakobson's (1959: 236) assertion that 'languages differ essentially in what they *must* convey and not in what they *can* convey'. In other words, all natural languages have the capacity to express all of the range of experience of the cultural communities of which they are part; and the resources of particular languages expand to cater for new experience (via borrowings, metaphor, neologism, etc.); but grammatical and lexical structures and categories force language users to convey certain items of meaning and it is here, according to the contrastive/structuralist view, that real translation problems lie. Typically, such non-correspondences are to be found in the categories of **deixis**, that is, those categories which relate an utterance to the personal, spatial and temporal characteristics of the speech situation. In the personal pronoun system of English, for example, gender and number are expressed in the third person (*he/she/it/they*); number but not gender in the first person (*I/we*); and neither number nor gender in the second person (*you*). The same asymmetrical pattern is not, of course, found in all languages. Chinese has no gender distinction in the third person; Bahasa Malaysia has two first-person plural pronouns according to whether or not the addressee is included in the reference; and many languages make a singular/plural distinction in the second person, overlaid with the polite/familiar pronouns of address. In Romanian, there is a three-way polite/familiar distinction (*tu/lei/dumneavoastra*). According to Levinson (1983: 69–70), village Tamil has as many as six second-person pronouns, reflecting various gradations of addresser/addressee relationship.

Pronouns of address: a problem of structural contrast

It is beyond dispute that this lack of a one-to-one relation-ship between grammatical categories, including tense systems, demonstratives and adverbs of time and place, creates problems for the translator. For illustration, let us consider in more detail the distinction made in many languages between so-called 'polite' and 'familiar' forms of address, as manifested in pronouns and verb endings, e.g. *tu* and *vous* in French. Following the convention in linguistics, we shall use T and V to refer to these forms, irrespective of the language involved. Problems arise, typically, in literary translating and in film subtitling, where dialogues often involve a significant shift from the V- to the T-form of address. The significance of the shift cannot be rendered in English by pronominal means; there has to be some kind of lexical compensation for the inevitable loss. Text 2B is a fragment of dialogue taken from H-G Clouzot's film *Le salaire de la peur* (in English, *The Wages of Fear*). The French screenplay (including some Spanish, on account of the action being situated in Latin America) is printed on the left, the corresponding English subtitles on the right.

Text 2B

A:	Allez, viens-là mon petit gars.	Come here kid.
	Otra copita para mi compadre	Another glass for my buddy
	Assieds-toi	
B:	Merci, vous êtes bien aimable	You're very kind
A:	Non, tu me tutoyais tout à l'heure	No, we're friends.
	Je m'appelle Jo . . . pour toi	To you, my name's Jo

To a SL audience, speaker B's use of the V-form in *Vous êtes bien aimable* is significant in that it marks an attempt to maintain a certain distance in interpersonal relations. The subsequent reference by speaker A to the use of T-forms via the delocutive verb *tutoyer* is cohesively linked to this use of the V-form, with *Non* used to comment anaphorically on speaker B's utterance. In the subtitles, cohesion is established with difficulty. The use of *We're friends* to compensate for information loss is, in itself, successful enough (and is a device which is often used in solving this subtitling problem) but, especially in conjunction with *No*, the utterance appears unmotivated and coherence is more difficult to perceive than in the source text; it involves perceiving *No* as a reaction to the relative formality of the previous utterance:

'You're very kind' – 'No, we're friends'

On the other hand, satisfactory alternative solutions to the problem are not easy to find (given the particular constraints of subtitling) and some communicative loss seems inevitable. Text 2C offers a possible alternative sequence, with greater internal coherence.

Text 2C

   A: Another glass for my buddy
   B: Thank you, Mr . . .?
   A: Come off it! We're friends.
      To you, my name's Jo.

Lyons (1979) investigates the use of T- and V-forms in Tolstoy's *Anna Karenina*, where characters who are aristocratic social equals use both T- and V-forms in Russian according to the current state of their relationship, reflecting changes of mood or emotion; but they also occasionally switch to French, in which, in their social group, only *vous* is allowable, thus avoiding the awkward choice between the Russian V-form (seen as 'cold') and the T-form (seen as too intimate and therefore 'dangerous'). Noting that English translations of *Anna Karenina* fail to render the significance of these switches between T and V, Lyons concludes (1979: 249)

> that there may be semantic distinctions drawn by one language-system that either cannot be translated at all or can only be roughly and inadequately translated in terms of some other language-system.

From this point of view, it is but a short step to conclude, in the words of Lyons's title, upon 'the impossibility of translation'.

IS TRANSLATION IMPOSSIBLE?

Recognition of the non-correspondence of categories within languages is also at the root of a view which, for a while, was highly influential in linguistics. The view, which has developed out of statements made by Edward Sapir (1921) and research among the Hopi Indians by B. L. Whorf (e.g. 1956), holds that language is the mould of thought, so that our ways of thinking and conceptualising are determined by the language we speak. In its strongest form, this linguistic determinism would suggest that we are, in fact, prisoners of the language we speak and incapable of conceptualising in categories other than those of our native tongue. It is now widely recognised that such a view is untenable. The very fact that people are capable of learning a second language to a high degree of competence and fluency considerably weakens the hypothesis. And translators who are not bilinguals are, in fact, successful in relaying meaning from one language into another. In doing so, they are able to conceptualise meaning independently of a particular language system. Full accounts of the Sapir/Whorf hypothesis and of various counter-arguments are provided in many linguistics textbooks (e.g. Sampson 1980, Lyons 1981) and we do not propose to repeat them here. We can note, however, that preoccupation with formal categories (Whorf saw Hopi as a 'timeless' language because, e.g. there is no tense system) leads to pessimistic assumptions about untranslatability which do not entirely correspond to the experience of the practising translator.

These assumptions about insuperable problems in translating are similar to the views of Nida (1959) in his contention that non-correspondence of grammatical and lexical categories is the main source of information loss and gain in translation. The latter occurs when an SL category lacks information which is obligatorily expressed in the corresponding TL category; for example, in a dialect of Zapotec, 'it is obligatory to distinguish between actions which occur for the first time with particular participants and those which are repetitious'. The addition to the TL text of information not expressed in the SL text seems inevitable – but only as long as translation itself is regarded as an activity in which each meaningful SL text item has to be represented by an equivalent TL text item and vice versa.

In all these discussions, the communicative value in particular contexts of the items under scrutiny is not considered. It is as if translating involved reflecting the idiosyncracies of SL structure at every stage of the way. In theory, translating from Chinese, a language which does not have verbal tenses, into English, in which verbs are obligatorily marked for tense, would inevitably result in addition of information. Yet in practice, Chinese-to-English translators will confirm that the English tense to be selected is normally apparent from context and does not necessarily add meaning to what is expressed in the source text. Thus, wholly different conclusions are reached by those who start from the point of view of the translator at work from those who begin with comparison of language structures. Theory and practice do not seem to match.

At the same time, the influence of contrastive structural linguistics has made itself felt in translation teaching methodology. The assumption that translation problems are best examined at the level of contrasts between grammatical and lexical categories underlies a number of published manuals of translating which devote separate sections to the translation of verbs (tense, mood, voice, aspect), adjectives, pronouns, prepositions, etc. (see, for example, García Yebra 1982, Astington 1983). As Chau (1984) has noted, there appears to be a time-lag between the currency of ideas in general linguistic theory, their subsequent passage into works on translation theory and their eventual pedagogical application in manuals of translating, so that more recent trends within linguistics are not yet reflected in manuals of translating while the structuralist approach is still influential here and there. Conversely, there has been an influence on linguistics of work done in the area of translation studies. The use of translating as a tool in language teaching has been of interest to many in applied linguistics (e.g. Widdowson 1979, Dagut 1986) while psycholinguistics and the study of bilingualism are concerned with the evidence provided by 'natural' or spontaneous translation. Finally, the field of contrastive linguistics inevitably involves consideration of correspondences and non-correspondences between languages and, therefore, of translation.

THE LANGUAGE-AND-MIND APPROACH

Among the insights brought by Chomsky and others to language analysis was the distinction between 'surface structure' and 'deep structure' – that is, the notion that the arrangement of elements on the surface of discourse, 'the words on the page', so to speak, mask an underlying structural arrangement, reflecting the actual relations between the concepts and entities involved. This secondary level of representation seemed appealing to some theorists of translation and Nida (1964: 68) went as far as to suggest that the activity of translating involved:

1. Breaking down the SL text into its underlying representation or semantic 'kernels'.
2. Transfer of meaning from SL to TL 'on a structurally simple level'.

3. Generation of 'stylistically and semantically equivalent expression' in the TL.

The psychological exactness of this hypothesis would be difficult to validate; scientific investigation of the sequences of processes in translators' mental activity is problematic and has not yielded conclusive results. As Aitchison (1976: 175) observes,

> the hypothesis that we recover a Chomsky-like deep structure when we comprehend a sentence has not been disproved, but is on the whole unlikely.

Moreover, the deep structure in question was conceived of as a syntactic entity; transformational generative grammar was not primarily interested in the representation of lexical and other forms of meaning. Like structural linguistics, it continued to work exclusively on descriptions of grammatical systems in single languages (usually English). Once again, no unit larger than the single sentence was analysed and the data were nearly always idealised and de-contextualised. Utterances such as

John is eager to please

or

These men are more clever than Mary

cannot, in the absence of a plausible context, form the basis for a useful discussion of translation.

Finally, in its insistence on according priority to the investigation of 'competence' (the ideal speaker/hearer's language faculty) over the investigation of 'performance' (the implementation of competence in production and reception of particular texts), transformational grammar drew attention away from language as communication, the very substance of the translator's work.

THE SOCIO-CULTURAL CONTEXT

It was Dell Hymes who questioned the limitations of the notion of grammatical 'competence', as narrowly conceived within Chomskyan linguistics. Like much of the data used in its investigation, linguistic competence is an abstraction which ignores the relevance of socio-cultural features to language acquisition:

> The controlling image is of an abstract, isolated individual, almost an

unmotivated cognitive mechanism, not, except incidentally, a person in a social world.

(Hymes 1972: 272)

In place of this, Hymes recommends that linguistics address itself to accounting for the fact that children acquire the ability to produce utterances which are not only grammatical but also appropriate. In other words, they acquire **communicative competence** or 'competency for use'.

The concept is, of course, directly relevant to translation studies; the translator's communicative competence is attuned to what is communicatively appropriate in both SL and TL communities and individual acts of translation may be evaluated in terms of their appropriateness to the context of their use. Widdowson (1979: 8) makes a useful distinction between **usage** and **use**. Usage, as codified in dictionaries and grammars, is a 'projection of the language system or code'. The artificial data we have referred to in this chapter may be seen as exemplification of usage; it should never be mistaken for the actual use of language in communication. It now becomes clear that the preoccupation in translation studies with non-correspondence of grammatical categories in individual languages was an exercise in usage rather than in use, in language-as-system rather than in language-as-communication.

CURRENT TRENDS: INTENTIONS AND UNDERSTANDING

In recent years, the scope of linguistics has widened beyond the confines of the individual sentence. Text linguistics (see, for example, Beaugrande and Dressler 1981) attempts to account for the form of texts in terms of their users. If we accept that meaning is something that is negotiated between producers and receivers of texts, it follows that the translator, as a special kind of text user, intervenes in this process of negotiation, to relay it across linguistic and cultural boundaries. In doing so, the translator is necessarily handling such matters as intended meaning, implied meaning, presupposed meaning, all on the basis of the evidence which the text supplies. The various domains of sociolinguistics, pragmatics and discourse linguistics are all areas of study which are germane to this process.

Returning once more to Text 2A, our sample of MT output, we

can see how some of these notions apply to any human translation of the source text from which Text 2A is derived. Beyond the elementary task of decoding grammatical and lexical relations, the human translator would require not just to be generally aware of the mathematical principles to which the text alludes but also to be able to perceive the text producer's intentions more or less as being:

1. to situate *algebraic logic* and *mathematical logic* with respect to one another;
2. to postpone definition of *algebraic*, in order to focus the reader's attention on the nature of *mathematical logic*.

As suggested in the initial list of the translator's tasks with which we began this chapter, the objective is then to facilitate retrieval of these intentions by the reader of the target text, in conformity with TL norms. Text 2D is an attempt to post-edit Text 2A on the basis of these requirements.

Text 2D

> Algebraic logic, which is the subject of this course, is considered here to be the most elementary component of mathematical logic. We shall define later on what we mean by the term 'algebraic'. But for the moment, our most important task is to state what mathematical logic consists of since algebraic logic is but the first part of it.

Research in machine translation has also gone far beyond the limitations of the early models referred to previously. Ambitious projects are once again under way. For example, the EUROTRA project aims to construct a 'pre-industrial prototype MT system', capable of handling the official EEC languages, and to

> provide reasonable-to-good quality translations without significant human involvement, for texts from limited subject domain (information technology) and text type (official community documents such as EEC Council decisions).

> (Arnold and des Tombe 1987: 115).

In the United States, research based on artificial intelligence (AI) now seeks to fill the gaps left by the excessive concentration of earlier systems on syntax to the exclusion of semantics. On the assumption that translating involves 'understanding' – in the sense of forming a representation of intended meaning in a text – the AI approach not only brings semantic analysis to the fore but also incorporates 'knowledge bases' which simulate the necessary amount of world knowledge to which human translators resort during the translation process. A pioneering study in this area is that of Schank and Abelson (1977), who assert that 'understanding is knowledge-based' and attempt to formalise this knowledge in terms of **scripts** (standard sequences of events), **plans** (general information about the connectivity of events) and **goals** (recognisable aims of a person's behaviour). The state of the art is at present far from achieving fully automatic high-quality translation but the approach seems a promising one, based as it is on the factors that are actually involved in the process of human communication by language. At Colgate University, the TRANSLATOR MT system incorporates a knowledge base which aims to 'represent the expert knowledge of a human translator' (Tucker 1987: 38). Conversely, the representation of knowledge in terms of **frames** (patterns of common-sense knowledge about a topic), plans and scripts is also relevant to the process of human translating and is discussed in detail by Neubert (1985: 36–48).

Taken together, all of these developments (context-sensitive linguistics, sociolinguistics, discourse studies and artificial intelligence) have provided a new direction for translation studies. It is one which restores to the translator the central role in a process of cross-cultural communication and ceases to regard equivalence merely as a matter of entities within texts. Beaugrande (1978: 13) heralds this new orientation:

> The focus of translation studies would be shifted away from the incidental incompatibilities among languages toward the systematic communicative factors shared by languages. Only in light of this new focus can such issues as equivalence and translation evaluation be satisfactorily clarified.

In Chapters 3 to 8, we propose to examine these communicative factors, beginning with the analysis of **register** which, although limited in scope, is a promising approach to the investigation of context.

THREE

Context in translating: register analysis

Against the background described in Chapter 2, a new approach developed by Michael Halliday and his colleagues in Britain in the 1960s and 1970s provided translation studies with an alternative view which approached language as text. Halliday (1971: 331) explains what this approach involves:

> By a functional theory of language I mean one which attempts to explain linguistic structure, and linguistic phenomena, by reference to the notion that language plays a certain part in our lives; that it is required to serve certain universal types of demand.

This social theory of language, known as the **systemic-functional** model, owes its existence to a variety of sources. Basically, however, two sets of insights from anthropology and linguistics were particularly influential. The first of these comes from the work of Malinowski (1923, 1935) and the second from that of Firth (e.g. 1935).

MALINOWSKI: CONTEXTS OF SITUATION AND CULTURE

From our point of view, it is perhaps a striking coincidence that Malinowski's theory of context was originally developed with the translator in mind. Working with people who belonged to a remote culture (Melanesian peoples in the Trobriand Islands of the Western Pacific), Malinowski had to face the problem of how to interpret it for the English-speaking reader. The problem became one of translation since the cultures concerned were studied through their emergence in texts (oral tradition, narration of fishing expeditions, etc.). What was the best method for portraying these texts in English: free translation, literal translation or translation with commentary? Free translation would be intelligible but convey no cultural insights. Literal translation, on the other hand, superficially preserves the original but would be unintelligible to the English reader. In consequence, Malinowski opted for translation with commentary.

What the extended commentary did was to 'situationalise' the text by relating it to its environment, both verbal and non-verbal. Malinowski referred to this as the **context of situation**, including the totality of the culture surrounding the act of text production and reception. He believed the cultural context to be crucial in the interpretation of the message, taking in a variety of factors ranging from the ritualistic (which assumes great importance in traditional societies), to the most practical aspects of day-to-day existence.

FIRTH: MEANING AND LANGUAGE VARIATION

A colleague of Malinowski at London University, J. R. Firth, maintained that the study of meaning was the *raison d'être* of linguistics and that it should be viewed in terms of 'function' in 'context'. In other words, the meaning of an utterance has to do with what the utterance is intended to achieve, rather than merely the sense of the individual words. This view of language built on some of the notions expounded by Malinowski, such as those of situation and culture. Context of situation could now include participants in speech events, the action taking place, other relevant features of the situation and the effects of the verbal action. These variables are amenable to linguistic analysis and are therefore useful in making statements about meaning.

Firth (1951) proposes a number of levels of meaning, each of which has its own contribution to make and confronts the translator with particular problems: phonological, grammatical, collocational and situational. It is in terms of these levels of meaning that, for Firth, the limits of translatability are to be found. For example, in translating certain types of verse (Firth takes the example of Swinburne), the lower modes of phonetics and phonology present insurmountable problems, leading to commonly heard statements that poetry is untranslatable. But, as Gregory (1980) suggests, Firth is merely indicating the limits of translatability in the strict sense of the word, as opposed to recommending that no attempt should be made to translate a text where one mode of meaning proves to be problematical.

SITUATIONAL DESCRIPTION

Under the influence of Firth and Malinowski, description of **communicative events** is now fairly widely recognised as a proper goal of linguistic analysis. These events are as amenable to sociologically conscious linguistic description as any other kind of data. In fact, as Gregory (1967: 178) points out,

> The difference between situational and other kinds of linguistic description has been greatly exaggerated. Much of the absence. . . of development of contextual and situational statement has been due to what might be termed a remarkable failure of nerve, a fear as to what is a describable relevant situational feature, a situational 'fact'.

But what can be said to constitute a relevant set of situational features? Naturally, criteria of relevance vary. As we have seen in Chapter 2, linguists, applied linguists and translation theorists have different interpretations of what has to be described. In translation studies, for example, a systematic description of the translating process is a priority. Translators, for their part, have long been aware of the role of situational factors (source, status, client, use to be made of translation, etc.); it was only in linguistics that the realisation was slow to come about.

THE NOTION OF REGISTER

Catford (1965: 83) neatly expresses the point of view of translation theorists who have addressed themselves to the question of text context:

> The concept of a 'whole language' is so vast and heterogeneous that it is not operationally useful for many linguistic purposes, descriptive, comparative, and pedagogical. It is therefore desirable to have a framework of categories for the classification of 'sub-languages' or varieties within a total language.

So what determines variation in language use? We can approach this problem in terms of several different dimensions: the medium by which language is transmitted (phonic, graphic), formal patterning (lexico-grammatical arrangement), and situational significance (relevant extra-linguistic features).

Halliday, McIntosh and Strevens (1964) recommend a framework for the description of language variation. Two dimensions are recognised. One has to do with the user in a particular language event: who (or what) the speaker/writer is. User-related varieties (Corder 1973) are called **dialects** which, while capable of displaying differences at all levels, differ from person to person primarily in the phonic medium. The second dimension relates to the use to which a user puts language. Use-related varieties are known as **registers** and, unlike dialects, differ from each other primarily in language form (e.g. grammar and lexis). For example, the distinction between

> (1) I hereby declare the meeting open

and

> (2) Shall we make a start now?

is use-related. On the other hand, the difference in voice quality or the way a particular vowel is pronounced when (1) and (2) are uttered by an Australian, an American or an Englishman is one of phonic medium and is, therefore, user-related.

USER-RELATED VARIATION

Depending on the user, language varies in several respects. We shall here distinguish idiolectal, geographical, temporal, social and standard/non-standard variation. These are represented in Fig. 3.1.

LANGUAGE VARIATION

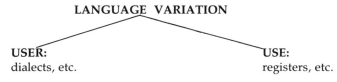

USER:
dialects, etc.

1. geographical
2. temporal
3. social
4. (non-) standard
5. idiolectal

USE:
registers, etc.

Figure 3.1   The use–user distinction

Geographical dialects

Language varieties correspond to geographical variation, giving rise to different geographical dialects. It should be noted that demarcation lines between regional varieties are drawn not always on linguistic grounds but often in the light of political or cultural considerations (e.g. the situation of Dutch *vis-à-vis* German, where a geographical boundary based on linguistic considerations alone would be difficult to determine). Another misconception surrounding geographical variation is that a given variety has the same status throughout the area where it is spoken (e.g. the notion that only one variety of English is used in, say, southern England). The dynamics of geographical variation are too complex to pigeonhole neatly; the notion of a 'continuum' with inevitable overlaps may be necessary for a better understanding not only of geographical variation but of other types of dialect as well.

An awareness of geographical variation, and of the ideological and political implications that it may have, is therefore essential for translators and interpreters. Accent, for example, is one of the more recognisable features of geographical variation and is often a source of problems. We recall the controversy in Scotland a few years ago over the use of Scottish accents in representing the speech of Russian peasants in TV dramatisation of a foreign play. The inference was allowed that a Scottish accent might somehow be associated with low status, something which, no doubt, was not intended. Like producers and directors, translators have to be constantly alert to the social implications of their decisions. The representation in a ST of a particular dialect creates an inescapable problem: which TL dialect to use? In Molière's *Dom Juan*, the speech of Pierrot is made to resemble that of the *patois* of the Ile-de-France, as in Text 3A$_1$.

Text 3A$_1$

> Aga, quien, Charlotte, je m'en vas te conter tout fin drait comme
> cela est venu; car, comme dit l'autre, je les ai le premier avisés, avisés
> le premier je les ai. . .

One English translator offers 'a synthetic west country alternative. . . with suitable diffidence' (Molière 1953: xxvii), as in Text 3A$_2$.

Text 3A$_2$

> Lookee, Lottie, I can tell 'ee just 'ow it did come about. 'Twas me as
> clapped eyes on 'em first in a manner o' speak'n'; first to clap eyes on
> 'em, I be. . .

One can understand the translator's reluctance: why West Country?
How synthetic? The extent of these problems may be appreciated
by comparison to another translation (Molière 1929: 14), given in
Text 3A$_3$.

Text 3A$_3$

> Eye, marry, Charlotta, I'se tell thee autright haw it fell aut; for,
> as the zaying iz, I spied 'um aut ferst, ferst I spied 'um aut. . .

The difficulty of achieving dialectal equivalence in translation
will be apparent to anyone who has translated for the stage.
Rendering ST dialect by TL standard has the disadvantage of
losing the special effect intended in the ST, while rendering
dialect by dialect runs the risk of creating unintended effects
(cf. the discussion of Text 3C below). At a more general level,
sensitivity to the various accents and lexico-grammatical features
of different geographical dialects is the hallmark of the competent
interpreter at international conferences. Whereas training for
non-native speakers often focuses on the Received Pronunciation
(RP) variety of English, speeches in international conferences may
display features of Australian English, Nigerian English, Indian
English, etc.; interpreter training programmes need to reflect this
dialectal diversity of English.

Temporal dialect

Temporal dialects reflect language change through time. Each
generation has its own linguistic fashions, and, whereas change
is generally imperceptible, one has only to read a pre-war
advertising text to measure the extent of this diversity. Terms
such as 'ghetto-blaster' and 'video nasties' define a text as a
product of the 1980s. Such recent coinages may constitute a
translation problem particularly if dictionaries (monolingual and
bilingual) are not keeping pace with current usage. Translators
of texts from earlier times encounter considerable problems to do
with the use of either archaic language or the modern idiom in their
target text. In literary translation, there is the added consideration

of aesthetic effect. In Text 3B, taken from *Macbeth*, the lexical item *petty* is potentially a problem.

Text 3B

> Tomorrow, and tomorrow, and tomorrow,
> Creeps in this petty pace from day to day,
> To the last syllable of recorded time;

> (*Macbeth*, Act V, Scene V)

The problem can be one of comprehension because *petty* is intended in the sense of 'slow' and not 'trivial' as in current temporal dialect. However, one Arabic translator, despite recognising the intended sense and preserving the referential meaning of 'slow', ran into another problem. He selected *batii'* which is restricted to the Modern Standard and therefore jars with the aesthetic effect achieved by the rest of the text. The item *wa'iid* ('unhurried', 'slow'), on the other hand, would have successfully preserved both the reference and the aesthetic values of Classical Arabic.

Social dialect

In addition to the geographical and the temporal dimensions, social differentiation is also reflected in language. Social dialects emerge in response to social stratification within a speech community. As translators and interpreters, we are here up against problems of comprehensibility with ideological, political and social implications. Principles of equivalence demand that we attempt to relay the full impact of social dialect, including whatever discoursal force it may carry. Yet liaison interpreters working with interlocutors of vastly differing social status (e.g. barrister and accused person) find themselves tempted to neutralise social dialect in translation for the sake of improved mutual comprehension, and to avoid appearing patronising. But how far can the interpreter legitimately go in attenuating the ideological significance of social dialect? The implications of issues such as these will occupy us in Chapters 5 and 6.

Standard dialect

Range of intelligibility is defined in terms of the distinction between 'standard' and 'non-standard' dialect. Although the notion of 'standard/non-standard' is a function of prestige, like social dialect, it should not be understood as implying any linguistic value judgement. Nor is the prevalence of standards simply a question of statistics (minority, majority, etc.). Rather, the way a standard evolves is a complex process which is enhanced or hindered by factors such as education and the mass media. In understanding and describing standards/non-standards, it is, therefore, important to take into consideration functional variation and the way this finds expression in language. In situations where two or more codes coexist in a speech community, code switching is not random and the translator or interpreter, like all language users, must be able to recognise the question of 'identity' involved. For example, when non-standard forms of language are used in advertising to promote a product, identification with the values of a particular social group or class is being evoked.

Finally, it is of course the case that these user-related varieties overlap considerably. Let us take the case of Arabic, where there is a 'standard' or literary dialect which varies only slightly from one region to another or from one period to another. This 'classical' standard is chosen as the target dialect when the source text happens to be in a standard dialect too. But how does the translator into Arabic cope when the source text is in a non-standard dialect (for example, Cockney in *Pygmalion*)? Catford (1965: 87–8) offers one general solution to this kind of problem:

> the criterion here is the 'human' or 'social' geographical one. . . rather than a purely locational criterion.

Thus, the equivalence in the translation of *Pygmalion* into Arabic will be established functionally. The aim will be to bring out the user's social/linguistic 'stigma', not necessarily by opting for a particular regional variety but by modifying the standard itself. The user's status may have to be reflected not primarily through phonological features but through non-standard handling of the grammar or deliberate variation of the lexis in the target language. The same solution could well apply to the Molière example quoted in Texts $3A_{1,2,3}$.

Idiolect

An important aspect of user-related variation, which clearly illustrates the overlap between the different varieties, is the individuality of a text user, or **idiolect**. It has to do with 'idiosyncratic' ways of using language – favourite expressions, different pronunciations of particular words as well as a tendency to over-use specific syntactic structures. Although it is difficult to isolate and describe these idiolectal differences on the basis of, say, one text or a single encounter, the uniqueness of an individual's speech represents an important aspect of language variation in general. In fact, idiolectal variation subsumes features from all the other aspects of variety discussed above: temporal, geographical, social, etc. This conforms to the notion that all types of variation may be viewed in terms of a 'continuum', with features from the several areas of variation in constant interaction.

The question for the translator is: since idiolects are normally on the margin of situationally relevant variation, is it necessary or possible to translate them? But if variation within any given domain of linguistic activity is systematic (and we believe it is), much more than the actual descriptive label for a given instance of variation is involved. One's idiolectal use of language is not unrelated to one's choice of which standard, geographical, social or temporal dialects to use. It is also linked to the purpose of the utterance and will ultimately be found to carry socio-cultural significance. Thus, in the French original of Samuel Beckett's *Waiting for Godot*, Vladimir's idiolect is marked by a predilection for the subjunctive mood and for the occasional use of third-person forms of address (*Peut-on savoir où Monsieur a passé la nuit? Monsieur a des exigences à faire valoir?*). The exaggerated formality of these devices contrasts strongly with the tramp's physical condition and is a significant feature of his character.

The important status accorded to idiolects is recognised by O'Donnell and Todd (1980: 62), who posit the notion of idiolect as the basis of a distinction between dialect and style:

'dialect', as the kind of variety which is found between idiolects, and 'style' as the kind of variety found within idiolects.

Thus, the ways in which various individuals pronounce 'round the twist', for example, are dialectal variations, whereas an individual's use of 'round the twist' as opposed to 'peculiar' or 'eccentric' is to be accounted for in terms of 'style'. This notion of style identifies the kind of variation occurring within a given idiolect and not between idiolects. Politicians make subtle and conscious use of colloquialisms for particular effects. Thus, when Neil Kinnock, leader of the British Labour Party, uses in a speech the expression 'off his trolley', it would be important for an interpreter to identify this not as a feature of Kinnock's idiolect but rather as a conscious stylistic choice aimed at producing a particular effect.

We can now summarise the relevance of user-related varieties to translating by means of a real example. Text 3C contains utterances of the game-keeper, Mellors, in D. H. Lawrence (1960).

Text 3C

> 'Tha mun come ter th' cottage one time', he said. . . 'Ah mun ta'e th' lantern', he said. 'The'll be nob'dy'.

In terms of 'user', we can analyse Text 3C as in Fig. 3.2.

Geographical dialect:	Midlands of England	cannot be relayed
Temporal dialect:	contemporary with publication; now dated	
Social dialect:	working class	could be relayed
Standard:	non-standard	
Idiolect:	[unmarked]	

Figure 3.2   Characterisation of user in Text 3C

It is interesting that, in translations of this passage into other European languages (French, German and Danish versions were consulted), no attempt is made to render the dialectal speech, e.g.:

> 'Du mußt mal zu meinem Haus kommen,' sagt er. . . . 'Ich muß die laterne nehmen', sagt er, 'es wind schon niemand unterwegs sein'.

> (Lawrence 1960)

These translators are unanimous in rejecting the artificiality of some TL dialectal equivalent. Yet it is also true that the alienating effect of the use of non-standard speech in the source text is inescapably lost.

USE-RELATED VARIATION

The distinction between dialect and style in the account of language variation sheds light on the conscious stylistic choices made by language users. But what are the factors which affect this choice? Within the user-use framework (developed by Halliday *et al.* 1964, Gregory and Carroll 1978, and others), a relationship exists between a given situation and the language used in it. **Register** is the term employed for the kind of variety which is distinguished in this way, i.e. according to use. In the words of Halliday *et al.* (1964:87),

> The category of register is postulated to account for what people do with their language. When we observe language activity in the various contexts in which it takes place, we find differences in the type of language selected as appropriate to different types of situation.

That is to say, registers are defined in terms of differences in grammar, vocabulary, etc., between two samples of language activity such as a sports commentary and a church service. We distinguish three main types of register variation, as in Fig. 3.3.

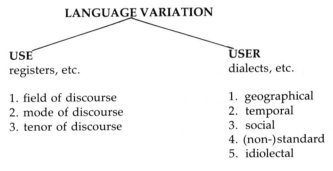

Figure 3.3   Use-related variation

In isolating registers, Halliday *et al.* (1964) make a number of pertinent remarks about how the notion is to be understood. Firstly, the category 'situation' is not to be restrictively interpreted as the event or state of affairs being talked about. These by themselves do not determine the linguistic choices made. What is of more importance in establishing the situation–use relationship is the 'convention' that a given linguistic utterance is appropriate to a certain use. This insight is particularly relevant to translators and revisers who have to cope with the inappropriateness of texts such as the news report reproduced in Text $3D_1$, which appeared in an English-medium magazine.

Text 3D$_1$

> The newly formed Babylon Company for the Production of Cinema
> and TV films decided to produce three TV serials in the coming months
> including 'The Last Days' and 'An Evening Party.'
> It is noteworthy that Babylon Company was formed on February
> 7, 1980 with a capital of over 6 million Dinars.
>
> (IRAQ 8.2.1980)

The text is undoubtedly a translation from Arabic, but it is
problematic because of the nebulous nature of the relation
between the language of the text (particularly that of the second
paragraph) and the situational conventions surrounding it (those
of news reporting). News reports in English do not normally
contain expressions such as *it is noteworthy* to signal background
information. If the text is to achieve its goal, significant modifications are called for. At the stage of revising the translation, in
all probability a reviser would opt for deleting those parts of the
text which violate situational appropriateness and modifying the
order of presentation, perhaps along the lines of Text 3D$_2$. (See
also Chapter 9 on text structure.)

Text 3D$_2$

> The Babylon Company for Production of Cinema and TV films,
> established yesterday with a capital of over ID 6 million, has decided
> to produce three television serials over the coming months, including
> *The Last Days* and *The Evening Party*.

A second observation in the early formulation of register theory
by Halliday and his colleagues is that it is often the collocation of
two or more lexical items and not the occurrence of isolated items
that determines the identity of a given register. By the same token,
although grammatical and lexical features can separately point to a
given register, it is common to find that the combination of features
from both these levels is significant. Sentences (1) and (2) below are
equivalent in terms of propositional content:

(1) I am sending you. . .
(2) Please find enclosed. . .

However, the collocational format of (2) violates the conventions
of personal notes and would therefore be inappropriate as an
informal note to a friend.

Thirdly, the category 'situation type' includes any number of similar situations (tokens) of the general type. Thus, making your next appointment with the dentist's receptionist is a particular token of a recognised type of situation. It is suggested that users' awareness of conventional situation types facilitates effective communication. A common core of grammatical and lexical features appropriate to many situation tokens can be identified. There are here the seeds of a theory of text types, which we shall develop in Chapter 8. For the moment, let us note that this insight is of immediate relevance to the translator. Translator-training programmes are often based on situational syllabuses, e.g. legal translating, technical, administrative, etc. Within this framework the benefit of concentrated work on terminology is obvious and aspects of language use such as those reviewed below should not be underestimated.

Field of discourse

Three basic aspects of register can be distinguished: **field of discourse, mode of discourse** and **tenor of discourse**. Field, or the reference to 'what is going on' (i.e. the field of activity), is the kind of language use which reflects what Gregory and Carroll (1978) call 'the purposive role', or the social function of the text (e.g. personal interchange, exposition, etc). This is similar to Crystal and Davy's (1969) 'province', which additionally emphasises the occupational, professional and specialised character of fields (e.g. a religious sermon). Whichever account of register one chooses, there is general agreement that field is not the same as subject matter. Firstly, it is often the case that we encounter fields that are characterised by a variety of subject matters (e.g. political discourse as a field may be about law and order, taxation or foreign policy). Secondly, in certain fields (e.g. a swimming lesson), use of language is ancillary. Put differently, it is only when subject matter is highly predictable in a given situation (a physics lecture) or when it is constitutive of a given social activity (courtroom interaction) that we can legitimately recognise a close link between field and subject matter.

In translating and interpreting, field can become a problem when working from a source language such as English which has developed a scientific and technical culture and, consequently, a wide variety of what Gregory (1980) calls 'marked fields of discourse' to reflect this 'world experience'. Translators working into target languages in the developing world face the challenge of forging new expression in these fields – an activity which transcends issues of bilingual terminologies and broaches wider questions of identity, ideology, etc. By the same token, English and French as target languages would also have problems with 'the myriad praise names of the Yoruba Oba' (Gregory 1980: 464).

Mode of discourse

Mode refers to the medium of the language activity. It is the manifestation of the nature of the language code being used. The basic distinction here is that between speech and writing and the various permutations on such a distinction (e.g. written to be spoken, etc.). Gregory and Carroll (1978: 47) illustrate the extent of mode variation by means of a diagram, reproduced here as Fig. 3.4.

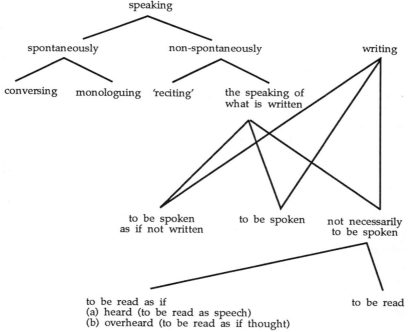

Figure 3.4   Mode of discourse

Channel, as the vehicle through which communication takes place, is an important aspect of mode. It transcends speech vs writing to include other communicative occurrences such as the telephone conversation, the essay, the business letter, etc. Also included here are differences in language use between dialogues and monologues. In Halliday's later writings (e.g. 1978: 144–5), mode even includes rhetorical concepts such as expository, didactic, persuasive, descriptive and the like.

It is quite common, however, for fluctuations in mode to be inappropriately reflected in translated material. This is true not only of some translations of literary classics, but even of instances of journalistic translation: an off-the-cuff remark often reads as ponderously as the journalist's considered opinion. Likewise, when films are subtitled, certain phonological features of mode have to be represented in writing. This mode shift can create problems, such as how to represent in writing the slurred speech of a drunkard. The area is worthy of greater investigation than it has so far received.

Tenor of discourse

Tenor relays the relationship between the addresser and the addressee. This may be analysed in terms of basic distinctions such as polite–colloquial–intimate, on a scale of categories which range from formal to informal. On such a cline, various categories have been suggested ('casual', 'intimate', 'deferential', etc.) but it is important that these should be seen as a continuum and not as discrete categories.

This kind of variation is relevant in translating between languages which are culturally distinct from one another. Namy (1979) relates how interpreting between American and French trade union officials involves a constant shift of tenor. Whereas the French make deliberate use of an educated formal tenor, their American counterparts conventionally do the opposite, displaying their working-class allegiance with liberal use of colloquialisms, etc.

In addition to personal tenor, which covers degrees of formality, Gregory and Carroll (1978: 53) suggest that there is a further kind of tenor, namely **functional tenor**. It can be defined in the following terms:

> Functional tenor is the category used to describe what language is being used for in the situation. Is the speaker trying to persuade? to exhort? to discipline?

In fact, there is overlap between all three variables, field, mode and tenor. The values accruing from the three dimensions of language use help us define and identify registers. The three variables are interdependent: a given level of formality (tenor) influences and is influenced by a particular level of technicality (field) in an appropriate channel of communication (mode). Translators who are required to produce abstracts in a target language from SL conference papers, for example, will be attentive to the subtle changes in field, mode and tenor that are involved. Abstracts are written to be read and normally display a neutral functional tenor. Yet the conference papers from which they are derived may be 'written to be spoken' and are often highly persuasive.

THE INHERENT FUZZINESS OF REGISTERS

In the absence of any stringent formal criteria for distinguishing one register from another, it has always proved difficult to discern the precise boundaries of any given register. The danger always exists that a given register is simply equated with a given situation, giving rise to so-called 'special languages' such as 'the language of politics', 'the language of advertising', 'the language of journalism', etc. These overgeneralisations can be misleading, and it is important to perceive the multifunctional nature of texts, an issue which we look at in detail in following chapters.

It should be noted that this point echoes sentiments expressed in the early days of register analysis. As far back as the early 1960s, Halliday and his colleagues (e.g. 1964: 94) asserted that '[a speaker] speaks . . . in many registers', thus allowing for shifts of register within texts. From the translator's point of view, this kind of fluctuation in one and the same text is of crucial importance. In Text 3E, for example, at least four domains of use are in evidence. These are numbered in Roman numerals and are discussed below.

Text 3E

A back door to war

I { Claudia Wright reveals Israel's involvement in President Reagan's military plans in Central America

Washington

III { 'Americans do not support vacillation,' Colonel Robert McFarlane, currently Deputy National Security Adviser to President Reagan, wrote in a 1978 study of presidential policy in military crises. Americans 'expect their leaders to lead, to be clear, forthright and firm. Particularly when American lives or property have been lost, the American impulse is toward firmness. It must not be reflexive—a knee jerk—but rather thought out and appropriate in strength to the task.'

IV { Since 1981, when McFarlane joined the administration, he has been testing out his theory as principal planner of US military tactics in Central America. As the President's newly appointed Middle East negotiator, he will now have his chance to try out the same methods in another combustible area.

(*New Statesman* 1983)

I (*Claudia Wright reveals . . . Central America*)

Here, we have the editorial 'attention-getting' device. In terms of register analysis, this may be described as follows:

Field: arousing interest in the topic
Tenor: slick, in-the-know salesmanship
Mode: headline-like abstract, written to read as if heard (i.e. it is reminiscent of a TV or radio announcer's introduction)

II (*Americans do not . . . to the task*)

Field: American domestic policy and international current affairs
Tenor: emotive, operative, manipulative use of rhetoric
Mode: political speech, written to be spoken

III (*Colonel Robert McFarlane . . . military crises*)

Field: news reporting
Tenor: detached, factual
Mode: written to be read

IV (*Since 1981 . . . combustible area*)

Field: assessing current affairs (investigative journalism)
Tenor: authoritative, evaluative commentary
Mode: editorialising through seemingly detached reporting;
    written to be read reflectively.

A successful translation will seek to reflect these different
'harmonies' through the appropriate use of language variation.

RESTRICTED REGISTERS

It goes without saying that it is futile even to attempt to
list the total range of language uses. The category of situation
type is only a helpful classificatory device. But in actual analysis
correspondence between situation and language remains vague
and different criteria for grouping texts will have to be investigated
(see Chapter 8). Nevertheless, in attempting to classify language
in terms of the intersection of user–use, we need to start with a
fairly well-defined type of linguistic variation. In this respect, a
promising area of investigation is **restricted registers**.

The restriction in question refers to the purpose of the communication. One basic feature of such registers is the predictable
and limited number of formal (phonological, lexical, grammatical)
items and patterns in use within a fairly well-defined domain of
language activity. An example of restricted registers is the language
of international telecommunications. It is hardly surprising in this
respect that the area in which machine translation has so far found
most success is that of restricted registers: the Canadian system
METEO for translating weather forecasts runs on a restricted

dictionary of some 1500 entries and is said to have an 80 per cent success rate without any need for post-editing.

The degree of register restriction may be viewed as a continuum. At one end we have maximally-restricted registers such as 'diplomatic protocol'. At the other end, we have open-ended registers such as the 'language of journalism'. In between, we may locate registers such as those of weather bulletins, insurance contracts, etc. The continuum establishes the relationship of a given register to its situation, a relationship which is expressed by Gregory and Carroll (1978: 68) in the following terms:

> The more typical or stereotyped the situation, the more restricted will be the range of options from which choices in the field, mode and tenor can be made. . .

It is interesting to note that some organisations which have adopted machine translation systems now encourage their staff to draft texts in restricted registers in order to render them machine-usable.

On the other hand, we need to beware of positing such unrestricted registers as 'commerce' and 'journalism'. To attempt to quantify the frequency of items of vocabulary and grammar in such wide domains cannot lead to any meaningful characterisation of a register. Thus, whereas our concept of register is a fairly adequate device for predicting language use in restricted domains, it becomes less powerful in unrestricted areas. Here, other factors are at work which translators need to respond to. These will be the subject of Chapter 4.

FOUR

Translating and language as discourse

BEYOND REGISTER

In this chapter, we shall suggest an alternative view of the ways in which language users (and therefore translators) react to texts. But we shall continue to assume that identifying the register membership of a text is an essential part of discourse processing; it involves the reader in a reconstruction of context through an analysis of what has taken place (field), who has participated (tenor), and what medium has been selected for relaying the message (mode). Together, the three variables set up a communicative **transaction** in the sense that they provide the basic conditions for communication to take place.

Let us now apply our model of communication to an actual text sample. Text 4A is typical translation material. The journal from which it is reproduced – *World Health Forum* – is one of many published by international organisations, often in several different language versions.

Text 4A

DENTAL PUBLIC HEALTH AND DISEASE PREVENTION

Oral health care does not have the makings of a dramatic issue. Very few people die of oral disease, and its effect on the economies of nations is insignificant. Yet very few people manage to avoid oral disease, and the two major variants – dental caries and periodontal disease – can and do cause irreversible damage. In the process, dental caries can cause some of the most severe pain that the average person is likely to experience in his lifetime. In 1978 a national survey in the United Kingdom, where 4% of the national health budget is spent on dental care, showed that 30% of the adult population was edentulous. . .

Early formulations of register theory (e.g. Halliday *et al.* 1964, Gregory and Carroll 1978) would describe Text 4A as an article in which dental health is assessed from a socio-medical viewpoint (field); as written by a medical academic for semi-specialist readers (tenor); and as written to be read within the conventions of academic writing (mode). Analyses such as these, carried out on a large sample of texts, would then form the basis for establishing a special language known as 'medical English', constituting a recognised area of expertise within translator training and testing.

Studies in register analysis are thus of relevance to translators of all kinds. According to Gregory (1980: 466),

> The establishment of register equivalence can be seen then as the major factor in the process of translation; the problems of establishing such equivalence, a crucial test of the limits of translatability.

Problems involved in translating Text 4A into another language include locating equivalent terminology in the appropriate field (*oral health care, dental caries, periodontal disease, edentulous. . .*) and achieving TL expression in the appropriate tenor and mode (formal, written).

A lot more than this, however, is resorted to by language users in handling context and in tracing the ways it is reflected in actual textual material. For translators, the relevant questions are:

1. Does translating activity consist solely of matching SL and TL registers in accordance with intuitively perceived or externally defined 'stylistic' conventions?

2. Can texts be reduced to compilations of situational variables, recognition of which is sufficient to establish equivalence?

Anything beyond a wholly superficial reading of texts will tell us that this is not so. When an article entitled 'Dental public health and disease prevention' begins with the sentence:

Oral health care does not have the makings of a dramatic issue

the reader automatically infers an underlying intention on the part of the writer to show that oral health care is in fact important. The text-processing mechanisms whereby the competent reader, even before assimilating later portions of text, is able to perceive a communicative intention roughly equivalent to: 'it may not be dramatic but. . .' cannot be accounted for by register analysis alone. A dimension is lacking which would describe the sentence as an entity which, in addition to referring to a topic, performs some kind of action.

From the point of view of translators, this is important not so much because they might be unable to perceive intended meaning (competence in this area being a *sine qua non* of professional translating) but rather because in certain cases expression of intended meaning is subject to subtle variation between SL and TL text norms and equivalence may therefore be more difficult to achieve. A translation may be a faithful rendering in terms of denotative meaning yet fail to carry the conviction of the source text. As Widdowson (1979: 105) points out, equivalence is not just linguistic and semantic; it is also pragmatic. Moreover, he adds,

> we cannot of course, by definition establish pragmatic equivalence by considering isolated sentences but only by considering what utterances count as in context.

THE THREE DIMENSIONS OF CONTEXT

The problem with register analysis, then, is that the insights which it affords into the **communicative** dimension of context, valuable as they are, are not in themselves sufficient. As we have seen, a further dimension of context can be distinguished. It is the **pragmatic** dimension which builds into the analysis values relating to the ability to 'do things with words'. There is, however, a third dimension which we shall call **semiotic** – treating a communicative item, including its pragmatic value, as a sign within a system of signs.

To illustrate all three dimensions, let us return to Text 4A, which includes a statistical statement:

4% of the national health budget is spent on dental care

Handling statistics, percentages, ratios, etc. (field) is, of course, an important part of the technical education which most people receive at school. And the ability to handle figures, etc., at speed is an important skill to be acquired in the early stages of interpreter training. But the significance of statistical statements such as the above can only be adequately grasped when a pragmatic analysis suggests what 'action' is being performed by a given figure: is 4 per cent to be understood as too little ('a mere 4 per cent'?), too much ('as much as 4 per cent'?) or as a neutral statement of affairs ('about right')? Appreciation of these pragmatic glosses is crucial: in some languages explicit markers are used to make a particular pragmatic reading transparent. In liaison interpreting, it is sometimes important to make explicit the significance of figures being quoted. The extent to which a figure 'speaks for itself' is often a matter for the translator's or interpreter's judgement.

Now, each element in a text displays its own 'local' pragmatic meaning, but it is important to realise that pragmatic values in a sequence of elements interact with each other as signs with 'global' semiotic values. That is to say, the gloss 'a mere 4 per cent' is a token belonging to a general type which also includes other signals such as 'deplorable', 'disgraceful', etc. In Text 4A, this token plays a part in an overall plan ('arguing for dental care'

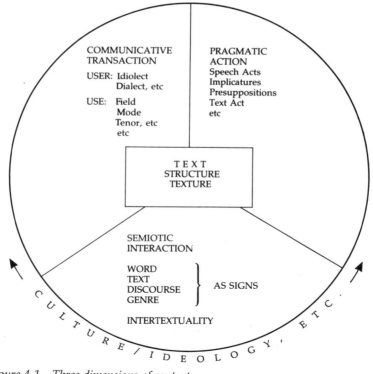

Figure 4.1   Three dimensions of context

by underlining present inadequacies). This interactive dimension of context is semiotic. It takes pragmatic reading a step further and helps the reader to locate a given message within an overall system of values appropriate to a given culture (the ideological stance of the writer as a scientist, arguing for a particular course of action). It is the perception of pragmatic and semiotic values such as these which enables translators to transfer the entirety of the message into their TL version.

Figure 4.1 is a representation of the three dimensions of context which are to be elaborated in what follows.

THE PRAGMATIC DIMENSION

Pragmatics has been defined as the study of the relations between language and its context of utterance. Stalnaker (1972: 380) offers the following, more helpful definition:

> Pragmatics is the study of the purposes for which sentences are used, of the real world conditions under which a sentence may be appropriately used as an utterance.

It was the Oxford philosopher J. Austin (1962) who first investigated the ability of sentences to perform actions, to effect some communicative purpose over and above the sense conveyed by the sum of the individual lexical items which the sentence comprises. Beginning with the so-called performative verbs whose pronouncement (in the first person singular, present tense) actually serves to accomplish the action conveyed (as in 'I name this ship . . .' or 'I do solemnly swear . . .'), Austin noted that in fact all utterances, in addition to meaning something, actually have some communicative force which is the dynamic element in communication, the element which moves communication forward. Accounts of Austin's theory of speech acts and the refinements and advances made by Searle (1969, 1976) abound in linguistics textbooks. It is not our intention here to review these theories in detail but rather to remind ourselves of the main findings and to apply them to the work of the translator as an analyser of texts.

Austin distinguished three different kinds of actions which are performed when a language user produces an utterance:

1. **Locutionary act**: the action performed by uttering a well-formed, meaningful sentence.

2. **Illocutionary act**: the communicative force which accompanies the utterance, e.g. promising, warning, conceding, denying, etc.
3. **Perlocutionary act**: the effect of the utterance on the hearer/reader; i.e. the extent to which the receiver's state of mind/knowledge/attitude is altered by the utterance in question.

In terms of the first sentence in Text 4A, we could say that the locutionary act involves encoding a set of notions into lexical items arranged according to the constraints of English syntax. The illocutionary act involves making a statement in the form of a concession which will later be countermanded. The perlocutionary effect might be to achieve the reader's assent to what is initially to be accepted as a non-controversial point. (It should of course be noted that the actual perlocutionary effect may be quite other than that intended by the writer; readers' reactions are not subject to his control.) Essentially, then, it is the illocutionary act which lends communicative force to an utterance. Together, the locutionary, illocutionary and perlocutionary acts constitute what is referred to as a **speech act**.

SPEECH ACTS

Various attempts have been made to classify speech acts. For our purposes, it will suffice to outline the classification proposed by Traugott and Pratt (1980), following Searle (1976):

1. **Representatives**: acts which seek to represent a state of affairs (such as stating, telling, insisting, etc.).
2. **Expressives**: acts which give expression to the speaker's mental and emotional attitude towards a state of affairs (e.g. deploring, admiring, etc.).
3. **Verdictives**: Acts which evaluate and relay judgement (e.g. assessing, estimating, etc.).
4. **Directives**: Acts which seek to influence text receivers' behaviour (e.g. ordering, requesting, daring, etc.).
5. **Commissives**: Acts which commit the speaker to a course of action (e.g. promising, vowing, pledging, etc.).
6. **Declarations**: Acts whose utterance performs the action involved (e.g. blessing, baptising, dismissing, etc.).

In principle at least, any stretch of utterance could be analysed into a sequence of speech acts such as those listed. Thus, Text 4B consists of a series of speech acts which may be identified as follows.

Text 4B

> Sir—Did Dr Dugdale intend to imply that the superiority of breast-feeding had not been adequately demonstrated? If so, he should look again. It is clearly superior in all settings, not just for babies in the Third World for whom the WHO code was intended. Although the reasons are complex, deaths and a variety of non-fatal illnesses (not just diarrhoea) are much less frequent among breast-fed infants even in industrial nations. I have compiled a bibliography of the accumulating evidence, which I should be happy to send to anyone who requests it.

(*World Health Forum*)

We would classify the question in the first sentence as a verdictive on the grounds that the implied criticism of Dr Dugdale's judgement is a verdict. The second sentence is also a verdictive in that it is a judgement. There follow two expressives, classified as such because of the evaluative elements *clearly* and *much less*, which relay the writer's point of view. The fifth sentence consists of a representative (*I have compiled. . .*) and a commissive (*which I should be . . .*), whereby the writer commits himself to a course of action. Over and above the referential meaning of individual elements, the translator will seek to relay the illocutionary force of each speech act in turn.

Now, in his study of performatives, Austin showed that, in order for sentences to count as commissives, declarations, etc., certain conditions had to be fulfilled. Take, for example, the sentence:

The meeting is adjourned.

Apart from its value in certain contexts as a statement of fact, we are aware that its utterance alone may in certain circumstances serve to perform the action indicated, that is, the adjournment of a meeting. But it is not true that anyone can successfully adjourn a meeting merely by uttering the sentence. In particular, the speaker has to be a participant in a meeting; the speaker has to have the necessary authority as, say, chairperson; the meeting (normally) has to have begun and an acceptable pretext for adjournment to have been adduced, etc. Such conditions for a successful outcome of speech acts are known as **felicity conditions**.

Court interpreters in particular will be aware of the conditions governing appropriate utterances in various judicial contexts. Leaving aside formulaic utterances (taking the oath, sentencing, etc.), participants' roles in courtroom interaction would seem to predetermine the range of speech acts which they can successfully utter. For example, the accused may not order, question, discuss, etc.; a barrister may assert, question, threaten, etc.; while it is the prerogative of a judge to advise, pronounce, adjourn. Whenever there is more than one language of court, interpreters are under pressure to ensure that their performance accomplishes the appropriate speech acts; the consequences of transferring, say, a request into what is perceived as a command may be serious.

THE COOPERATIVE PRINCIPLE AND GRICEAN MAXIMS

Felicity conditions depend on the assumption that, in communication, being sincere is a social obligation (the sincerity condition; Searle 1969). Such notions of cooperation, truthfulness, intention, etc., are central to another development in pragmatics initiated by Grice (1975, 1978). Rather than elaborating rules for successful communication, Grice prefers to speak of maxims which participants conventionally adhere to in communication. Briefly stated, they are as follows:

1. **Cooperation**: make your conversational contribution such as is required by the accepted purpose or direction of the talk exchange in which you are engaged.
2. **Quantity**: make your contribution as informative as (but not more informative than) is required.
3. **Quality**: do not say what you believe to be false, or that for which you lack adequate evidence.
4. **Relation**: be relevant.
5. **Manner**: be perspicuous, avoid obscurity of expression, avoid ambiguity, be brief, be orderly.

Taken together, the maxims could be summed up as: how to be maximally effective and efficient in communication. Underlying them is the assumption that participants normally pursue their goals in communication in accordance with such unwritten conventions as the above; any deviation from them is perceived by other participants as involving **implicature**. For example, consider the exchange:

A: There's going to be trouble when John finds out.
B: Why? What's going on?
A: It's a nice day today, isn't it?
B: Oh, come off it!

Speaker A apparently violates the maxim of relation. But B is not fooled: rather than assume that A is seeking to initiate a conversation about the weather, B infers that the violation is motivated by an attempt by A to indicate that B is prying. Relevance is thus re-established. As Beaugrande and Dressler (1981: 123) put it:

> conversational participants will infer unexpressed content rather than abandon their assumption that discourse is intended to be coherent, informative, relevant, and cooperative.

It is worth noting that there is some evidence to the effect that the maxims may not be universal; Keenan (1976) relates that speakers of Malagasy often disregard the maxim of quantity. Further research into these complex phenomena is needed. But for the translator, the question remains: are TL receivers as able to infer unexpressed content as SL receivers would be? To what extent can the translator compensate for any deficit on the part of the TL receiver? Is the perlocutionary effect of the translator's utterance (TL text) subject to the translator's control? These issues will be discussed in detail in Chapter 5.

It will be apparent from this cursory presentation of speech acts and conversational implicature that the whole issue is being judged primarily from the point of view of the oral mode of discourse, involving a speaker, a hearer and a situation of utterance. The applications to liaison interpreting are obvious; it is perfectly possible for the interpreter to translate competently the locutionary act involved in an utterance (in the sense of finding appropriate equivalents for ST words and relating them correctly and appropriately in TL syntax) while failing to perceive or otherwise misrepresenting the illocutionary force of the utterance in context. Thus, in a negotiating session involving a trainee liaison interpreter, an English speaker reacted to a point made by his interlocutor (French) in the following terms:

Text 4C$_1$

> If we are content merely to condemn the American position, it is perhaps not a very positive attitude to the problem. It might be preferable. . .

The interpreter turned to the French speaker and said:

Text 4C$_2$

> Votre attitude n'est pas positive. . .

At this point, the French speaker shifted his previously cooperative negotiating stance and became reserved and distant. The interpreter had inadvertently transformed an attempt to introduce a new point in the debate (and an indirect indication of dissatisfaction) into a direct accusation, thus falsifying the illocutionary force of the utterance and achieving an unintended perlocutionary act. An error of which the written translator may occasionally remain unaware (because the consequences are not immediately obvious) will always be painfully apparent in the activity of liaison interpreting.

NEGOTIATING MEANING IN TRANSLATION

Despite the orientation of speech act theory towards the oral mode of discourse, the findings are of course equally applicable to written texts. Felicity conditions are easier to perceive in relation to the speech situation because an interlocutor is present and the ways in which utterances are regulated in accordance with speakers' and hearers' intentions can be calculated. In written discourse, on the other hand, the reader's somewhat shadowy presence interacts with the text producer only to the extent that the latter intuits the reactions of the former and shapes his discourse accordingly. But this interaction is still crucial to the view of human language activity (and therefore, translating activity) as a process, not as a product. Seeing the meaning of texts as something which is negotiated between producer and receiver and not as a static entity, independent of human processing activity once it has been encoded, is, we believe, the key to an understanding of translating, teaching translating and judging translations.

In essence, our initial investigation of the pragmatic dimension of context has brought out the ways in which intentions are perceived in communication. The translator, in addition to being a competent processor of intentions in any SL text, must be in a position to make judgements about the likely effect of the translation on TL readers/hearers. But so far, our analysis is not powerful enough to cope with the detailed nature of intentionality in texts. This will be our subject in Chapter 5. But as we suggested earlier, there is a third dimension of context which accounts for the interaction of speech acts as signs. In analysing Texts 4A, 4B and 4C, we have implicitly relied on assumptions which have to do with the role of interaction between the various speech acts involved. This is the semiotic dimension of context.

COMMUNICATIVE, PRAGMATIC AND SEMIOTIC INTERPLAY

We can demonstrate the interdependence of the communicative, pragmatic and semiotic dimensions by considering a particular translation problem. The following text samples illustrate the use of 'honorifics'. They are taken from published translations from Arabic.

Text 4D

> **Sayyid Faisal bin Ali**, the Minister for National Heritage and Culture, left Muscat yesterday for New York.

Text 4E

> **HH the Amir Shaikh Isa Al Khalifa** received **Shaikh Mohammad Al Khalifa**, the Foreign Minister, . . . and **Ghazi Al Gosaibi**, Bahrain's ambassador to the United States.

Text 4F

> And when he had accomplished that, there was such a shouting and singing and hustle and bustle, a veritable babel, that was only restrained when **the sheikh**, their father, got up. . .
>
> (Hussain 1932)

In the SL texts, either *sayyid* or *shaikh* (alternative spelling *sheikh*) is used as an honorific in all cases. But when should honorifics be retained or left out in translation? The translators' solutions in Texts 4D, 4E, and 4F may be displayed as in Fig. 4.2

Arabic		English
(4D)	*sayyid*	retained in transliteration
(4E)	*sayyid*	omitted before *Ghazi*
(4E)	*shaikh*	retained in transliteration
(4F)	*sheikh*	retained in transliteration

Figure 4.2   Honorifics in translation

At the communicative level, variation in the use of *sayyid* and *sheikh* can be said to be a problem of tenor or level of formality. In context, however, the items present the translator with a number of problems, the solution to which requires more than knowing the lexical meanings, even if these are learnt with glosses of tenor ('formal', 'informal', etc.) and other pragmatic values (e.g. deference). In dealing with the intricacies involved, the different translators of Texts 4D, 4E, and 4F will have been aware of subtleties, which we can sum up as follows:

1. In Text 4D, the title *sayyid* is retained in transliteration, as the person involved is 'a descendant of the Prophet Mohammad' (with complex political and religious implications). In other contexts, *sayyid* may still be used in Arabic but, when special status is not involved, it may be replaced by the English 'Mr' or may even be dropped. Omission would be appropriate when the Western connotations of 'Mr' would be culturally too obtrusive, as in Text 4E.

2. In Texts 4E and 4F, the title *Shaikh* is retained in transliteration for reasons that are made clear in the footnote to the translation of Text 4F (E. Paxton in Hussain 1932: 8):

   Shaikh or sheikh. Means literally 'an elderly man'. Hence it is used among Bedouins for the chief of a tribe and among civilized Arabs for the head of an order or sect, like the dervishes. Shaikh has many other uses besides. It may mean a learned doctor of religion (there are no priests in Islam) or a senator. Here it is merely used as a title of respect for the author's father, as being the head of the family or one who memorized the Quran.

Even a catalogue of meanings such as the one contained in this translator's footnote is not a sufficient basis for establishing equivalence. In fact, translators are aware of all of the values that the items in question potentially have within the language system (usage). But these potential values are not always applicable in actual contexts and translators need to deduce their own patterns of use. The complex patterning involved in forms of address or reference may even go beyond notions such as 'pecking order' or 'hierarchy'. It can only be learned in terms of the interactive dimension in which these forms behave as 'signs'.

THE SEMIOTIC DIMENSION

The assumptions, presuppositions and conventions that surround discourse reflect the ways in which a given culture constructs and partitions reality. Any given language is bound to express this partitioning in its own way. By the same token, transfer of meanings from one cultural system to another involves a contextual dimension which manages our understanding of the way cultures work in terms of other communicative and pragmatic features.

Semiotics or **semiology** is the science which studies signs in their natural habitat – society. Envisaged by Saussure as part of social psychology, and identified by Peirce as having a distinctly 'logical' bias, semiotics focuses on what constitutes signs, what regulates their interaction and what governs the ways they come into being or decay. As Jakobson (1971: 698) puts it:

> Every message is made of signs; correspondingly, the science of signs termed *semiotics* deals with those general principles which underlie the structure of all signs whatever, and with the character of their utilization within messages, as well as with the specifics of the various sign systems. . . .

The discourse fragments in Texts 4D, 4E, and 4F are of considerable semiotic significance. The various forms of address or reference are signs in that, through them, we exchange meanings within a culture. In television interviews, British politicians very often address their interviewers on first name terms ('Donald') to express informality, solidarity, etc. However, in certain contexts, a switch to use of the surname ('Mr McCormack') signals far more than mere formality. It may, for example, signify 'I am taking you to task for overstepping the limit.'

The interactive dimension of language use does not just operate on the level of individual lexical items. It may also involve larger units. Translators may achieve semiotic equivalence by retaining, modifying or even omitting whole sequences within a text. The SL version of Text 4E includes a sequence which was deliberately omitted in the English version on semiotic grounds. It would, if translated literally, appear as in text 4G.

Text 4G

> . . . Bahrain's ambassador to the United States, who called in order to greet His Highness and enquire about his health on the occasion of returning from his posting in Washington.
>
> (translated from *Gulf News*, Arabic edition)

For an English-speaking target readership, all of the information in Text 4G is already implied in Text 4E: if Bahrain's ambassador to the USA is in Bahrain calling on the Emir, he must have returned from his posting and it is assumed that he will exchange the usual words of greeting! So why should superfluous material occur in the SL text? The answer, no doubt, has to do with the textual conventions of respect for royalty within news reporting in Arabic. (But this in itself is not without semiotic significance, as will be made clear in the course of the following discussion.)

The translator approached the SL version of Text 4G as a sign, i.e. a semiotic unit. In Saussurean terms, the sign is an indissoluble unity of expression and content (or signifier and signified). For us, the string of words *to greet and enquire about his health* (expression/signifier) has as content/signified a complex speech act which may, at the risk of gross oversimplification, be glossed as 'paying due obeisance'. As part of a system of signification, this act is inextricably embedded in Arab culture. It is understood in terms of an obligatory social convention, handed down from generation to generation. It is unique to the culture in question and can only be transferred across socio-cultural boundaries (i.e. inter-semiotically) when the necessary adjustments are made. In this particular case, the translator has correctly perceived that, given an English-speaking expatriate community as the target readership, no functionally equivalent sign to Text 4G exists. This is consistent with Peirce's definition of the sign, namely 'something which stands to somebody for something in some respect or capacity' (*Collected Papers*, Vol. II, para. 228).

INTER-SEMIOTIC TRANSFER

Translation, then, primarily deals with signs and attempts to preserve semiotic, as well as other pragmatic and communicative, properties which signs display. The process of inter-semiotic transfer is not, however, without constraints. There are restrictions entailed by the interplay between values yielded by, say, a given field of discourse and the pragmatic action intended. Metaphoric use of language, for example, invariably conveys additional intended meaning. It is the semiotic status of the metaphor which will be the crucial factor in deciding how it is to be translated. These decisions will at least in part be determined by semiotic categories such as genre, discourse and text.

Generic constraints

Genres are 'conventionalised forms of texts' which reflect the functions and goals involved in particular social occasions as well as the purposes of the participants in them (Kress 1985: 19). From a socio-semiotic point of view, this particular use of language is best viewed in terms of norms which are internalised as part of the ability to communicate. Genres may be literary or non-literary, linguistic or non-linguistic, including forms as disparate as poems, book reviews, christenings, etc. As an example of how genre membership influences the translator's decisions, consider the following translation into English of a literary text from Arabic; it is a continuation of Text 4F.

Text 4H₁

   . . . when the sheikh, their father, got up from his bed and called
for a jug of water in order to wash himself before praying.

The Arabic ST of which Text 4H₁ is a translation may be literally rendered as follows:

Text 4H₂

   . . . when the sheikh, their father, got up from his bed and called
for a pitcher of water to use for his ablutions.

The approach adopted by the literary translator in this instance may be contrasted with that of the journalist translator who, we recall, opted for leaving out a whole segment (Text 4G). Here, the literary translator's solution is to make explicit a given cultural sign (expansion of *ablutions*). Within the constraints of this literary genre, there is a cultural norm which expects the cultural reference, no matter how esoteric, to be preserved and made clearer (i.e. ablutions as a religious rite). Conventions of news reporting in the TL culture in question, however, would not normally admit renderings such as the 'ritual of paying obeisance' as in Text 4G.

The translators' reactions to such discourse samples as Texts 4D and 4E also had to be governed by considerations of genre. Both source texts reflect the semiotics of the social occasions which gave rise to them, i.e. news reporting of official state functions. The genre of the TL texts, however, will be 'News in brief' for an English-speaking expatriate community. There is here an essential difference which is bound to affect translators' decisions. Given the goals of the participants and the purposes of the communication, a formulaic statement of social greeting – . . . *in order to greet His Highness and enquire about his health. . .* – appropriate in the SL genre becomes totally superfluous within the conventions of the TL genre.

Thus, genre and generic membership play an important role in the process of transfer between semiotic systems. Here again, factors such as rhetorical mode and intentionality are at work. But beyond these factors, as Martin (1985) points out, the conventions of genres are indices of particular cultures which exert a strong influence over the way the genres are to be encoded in text.

Discoursal constraints

The participants in the social events which are reflected in genres are bound to be involved in attitudinally determined expression characteristic of these events. The book review as a genre engages reviewers in a typical expression of attitude towards their subject. In this case, the mode of expression is 'evaluative'. Other examples of attitudinal expression might be the 'committed' discourse of pressure groups, the discourse of 'power' of those who exercise authority, etc. Following Foucault (1972) and Kress (1985), these modes of expression will be referred to as **discourses**. The interrelationships between genre and discourse can be represented as in Fig. 4.3.

The conception of discourse developed here can be compared to the **cultural codes** referred to by Barthes (1970). These are conceptual systems which regulate the process whereby the

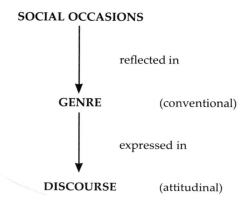

Figure 4.3   Genre and discourse

denotative meaning of an element in a text acquires an extra connotative meaning. This is what happens when culture is seen as imposing itself on the text dynamically. Thus, an ideology, for example, expresses itself through a variety of key terms which take us beyond the text to an established set of precepts. For the expression 'the capitalist press' to become a recognisable feature of the 'committed' discourse of the Left, it has to be perceived within a connotative system of ideological oppositions.

Discourses are then modes of talking and thinking which, like genres, can become ritualised. For example, 'sexist discourse' (or feminist analyses of such discourse) may be taken as a concrete pattern identified within the format of a genre such as rugby songs. The interrelationship between genre and discourse is also culturally determined; there are constraints on which discourses go with which genres and vice versa. For example, 'militant', 'anarchic' discourse is inappropriate for boardroom meetings. By the same token, bureaucratic discourse will be resented at popular mass gatherings.

But different cultures allow different combinations. When Senator Ed Muskie expressed overt emotion, breaking into tears during a televised US presidential campaign, it effectively ended his presidential hopes. Yet, when President Nasser of Egypt addressed the nation after defeat in the Six Day War, his overtly tearful discourse, during which he offered his resignation, led to a popular show of confidence in his leadership and strengthened his political hand.

As an example of how the translator or interpreter copes with such discoursal constraints, consider the discourse sample in Text 4I.

Text 4I

> Fallaci: . . . But you **frighten** people, as I said. And even this **mob** which calls your name is frightening. What do you feel – hearing them **calling out** like this, **day and night**, knowing that they are there, **all of them there sitting for hours, being shoved about, suffering,** just to see you for a moment, and to **sing your praises?**

> Khomeini: I **enjoy** it. I **enjoy** hearing and seeing them. **Because** they are the same ones who **rose up to throw out** the internal and external enemies. Because their applause is the continuation of the **cry** with which the **usurper was thrown out.** It is good that they continue to be **agitated,** because the enemies have not disappeared. Until the country has settled down, the people must remain **fired up,** ready to **march** and attack again. In addition, this is **love,** an intelligent **love.** It is impossible not to **enjoy** it.

> (Johnstone 1987; emphasis added)

Text 4I is taken from an interesting article in which Johnstone (1987) analyses the communication breakdown which occurred when Iran's Ayatollah Khomeini was interviewed for *The New York Times* magazine by a Western journalist in 1979. It is worth noting that this is not an ordinary question-and-answer session; Fallaci is well known for her provocative interviewing style and, on this occasion, she speaks almost as much as Khomeini and with equal commitment.

From the perspective of the two Iranian interpreters who accompanied the Ayatollah, there was an additional set of constraints at work, over and above those of genre (the political interview). The constraints are those associated with emotive, committed discourse. This target text illustrates a different solution to that adopted in Text 4E, the news report concerning the visit of Bahrain's ambassador, where redundant items were omitted. Here, lexical redundancy and syntactic repetition are seen to be motivated and are consequently relayed in their entirety. Thus, the emotiveness of Fallaci's English is matched by the emotiveness of the interpreter's output from Khomeini's Persian. Further investigation of these phenomena would be useful. Johnstone's concern is with culturally determined patterns of reasoning, rather than with translation or interpreting. But the implications of her analysis are of relevance to any enquiry into the impact of discoursal constraints on translation.

Textual constraints

Genre and discourse signals are easily identifiable, but the categories are very broad and diffuse. Within discourse and genre, there are fluctuations which we have to account for. In the book review, for example, differences arise when the discourse of 'objective summarising' gives way to that of 'subjective evaluation'. This shift can be described in terms of a process of problem-solving. Participants perceive differences in situations where the authority of the author being reviewed is challenged. These differences give rise to rhetorical intents such as the need to evaluate through counter-argument, reassertion, etc. Counter-arguments and reassertions constitute what we shall call **texts**. The process of perceiving texts within discourses is summed up by Kress (1985: 12) as follows:

> There are likely to be problems at any time, arising out of unresolved differences in the individual's discursive history, the individual's present discursive location and the context of discourses in interactions. That difference is the motor that produces texts. Every text arises out of a particular problematic. Texts are therefore manifestations of discourses and the meanings of discourses, and the sites of attempts to resolve particular problems.

As concrete entities, therefore, texts are the basic units for semiotic analysis. They concatenate to form discourses which are perceived within given genres. In the process, texts impose their own constraints on the translator. These are indices of rhetorical intents which should be attended to by the translator (see Candlin and Saedi 1983). We shall take such indices to be part of the **textual constraints**. Examples of these in Text 4I are the rhetorical use of the conjunctives (*because, in addition*) as indicators of how the argument is being developed. Together with consideration of genre membership and discourse characterisation, textual indices form the basis of the translator's or interpreter's judgement. Figure 4.4 adds a textual dimension to what was listed in Fig. 4.3 and illustrates the hierarchical relationship between text, discourse and genre.

It is in a process such as that of abstracting that these constraints – genre, discourse, text – come to the fore. An abstract

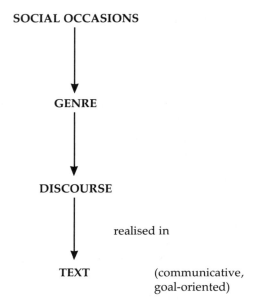

Figure 4.4   Hierarchical relationship between text, discourse and genre

is a genre which has its own conventions. In terms of discourse, abstracts tend towards neutrality. At the textual level, we expect coherence to be maintained. This is hardly the case, however, in Text $4J_1$, which is an English-language abstract of a French article; in addition to violations of genre and discourse, textual development is particularly problematic.

Text $4J_1$

> Is the rise of the Soviet Union to power and domination due
> more to the efficiency of its system and its leaders' know-how
> than to the shortcomings of those who, in the West, hold the
> same responsibilities? No. The present imbalance is the outcome of
> a series of errors in judgement, unfounded speculation, about-faces
> and broken illusions . . .

> (Gallois 1983)

This text needs to be read several times before coherence is established. Yet, the source article of which Text $4J_1$ is an abstract developed a coherent argument that Western leaders have been incompetent and weak in the face of Soviet aggression. In attempting to preserve the committed discourse of the source text (instead of adopting the more usual dispassionate attitude), the translator has adversely affected the cohesive progression of the text. The *series of errors* . . . is not attributed, as it should be, to 'those in the West'. Some phrase such as 'on the part of Western leaders' might at least have maintained cohesion, although in terms of discourse and genre the abstract would still be inadequate. Text 4J$_2$ below is an abstract of the same ST article. This version attempts to respect the generic, discoursal and textual conventions of the English-language abstract.

Text 4J$_2$

> Over the past twenty years, the reasons for the failure of the West to contain Soviet power and domination are to be found in the shortcomings and lack of coordination of Western leaders and their policies . . .

PRAGMATICS AND SEMIOTICS OF REGISTER

The aim of this chapter has been to develop register analysis to a point where it can account for the intricacies of the communicative process. Intentionality lies behind choices made within field, mode and tenor, and affords a new perspective for translators' decisions. At the same time, the semiotic dimension allows us to consider these variables in the way in which they interact. Adding a semiotic dimension to field of discourse (the **experiential** component of context) relates it to genres and their conventions. Similarly, tenor (the **interpersonal** component of context) relates to discourse as an expression of attitude. Finally, genre and discourse find expression in texts through the **textual** component of context. Figure 4.5 represents these interrelationships.

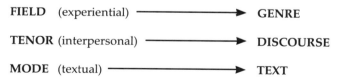

FIELD (experiential) ⟶ **GENRE**

TENOR (interpersonal) ⟶ **DISCOURSE**

MODE (textual) ⟶ **TEXT**

Figure 4.5   Pragmatics and semiotics of context

FIVE

Translating text as action: the pragmatic dimension of context

A brief account was given in Chapter 4 of certain basic notions in pragmatic analysis: speech acts, felicity conditions, and Grice's principles and maxims. The relevance of some of these notions to translating activity was alluded to but not discussed in any detailed way. We now propose to add a socio-cultural element to these basic pragmatic notions and to relate them to the analysis of actual problems of translation.

The value of the notion of the speech act was seen to be that, by adding to utterance meaning the idea of action intended or achieved, we are in fact adjusting our criteria for the judgement of equivalence in translation; equivalence is to be achieved not only of propositional content but also of illocutionary force. At discourse level, communicative failure (relatively speaking) of a translation may be attributed to failure to represent speech acts adequately. In translating official discourse, for example, equivalence of illocutionary force is often subject to difference in cultural norms. Translation of a business letter from a language in which directness is customary may result in offence being given where none was intended, e.g. 'kindly inform us immediately of your intentions. . .' or 'we are sending you instructions. . .' in place of conventional ways of requesting a favour in English such as 'we should be grateful if you would let us know. . .' or 'we should like to suggest. . .'.

ILLOCUTIONARY STRUCTURE

So far, we have assumed that a text consists of a succession of speech acts and that, in order to achieve equivalence in translation, the illocutionary force of each sentence needs to be treated in isolation. Indeed, it is true that much of the literature on speech acts relates to the analysis of individual sentences and that what happens when sentences are concatenated has been relatively neglected. Yet, as Ferrara (1980a,b) has shown, the interpretation of speech acts depends crucially on their position and status within sequences. Put simply, the perceived status of an utterance such as 'There are thirty people in here' varies according to co-text: on the one hand, as the first member of a pair which continues: 'Could you open the window?', it has the status of a subordinate act in a sequence, aiming to achieve the sub-goal of justification for the main goal in the speaker's plan – having a window opened. On the other hand, as a reply to: 'How many people are in here?', its status would be that of compliance with conditions governing what are known as adjacency pairs in conversation (questions tend to be followed by answers, greetings by greetings, offers by acceptances or rejections, etc.). The interrelationship of speech acts within sequences leads to the notion of the **illocutionary structure** of a text, determining its progression and supporting its coherence. In translating, one aims not at matching speech act for speech act but rather at achieving equivalence of illocutionary structure.

A suitable example is provided by the following fragment, taken from a text in which description of the African nightfall is used as a metaphor for the precarious state of the nations of Africa:

Text 5A

> Avant que la nuit s'installe, une parure d'étoiles.
> Trompeuse.
>
> (Pomonti 1979)

Possible translations offered by a group of trainee translators were of three kinds:

(1) As night draws on, the sky is deceptively adorned with stars.
(2) As night draws on, the sky is adorned with stars. It is misleading.
(3) As night draws on, the sky is adorned with stars. But appearances are deceptive.

The inappropriateness of (1) might simply be attributed to the conflation of two ST sentences into one. But little of generalisable value can be derived from such an explanation. Indeed, it could lead one to assume that merging two sentences into one is never justified, or that ST word order must always be respected. Yet, as practising translators will agree, such changes may well be justified in appropriate contexts. But, in the case of Text 5A, it is important to show that the speech act embodied in the single-word ST sentence *Trompeuse* must not only find expression in the target text but must also be translated in a way which is compatible with the illocutionary structure of the source text, where the sub-goal of optimistic description is subordinate and prior to the denial of that optimism; in (1), the optimism is denied before it is even asserted. In (2), on the other hand, each speech act is faithfully rendered in the correct sequence but the implicit relationship of the first to the second sentence in the pair is not made clear. This implicit counter-argument achieved by juxtaposition (a conventional text norm in the source language in this field of discourse) ought to have been made more explicit by some overt signal of contrast. Coherence is achieved here by establishing equivalence of sequentiality rather than equivalence of individual illocutionary acts; hence, the preference for (3) over (2).

TEXT ACTS

Now, the cumulative effect of sequences of speech acts leads to the perception of a **text act** (Horner 1975), the predominant illocutionary force of a series of speech acts. We shall find this notion useful when we come to consider the semiotics of text types in Chapter 8; for the moment, let us retain the idea that equivalence may also be judged at the level of the text act: has the predominant illocutionary force of the source text been preserved in translation? The transfer of such obviously pragmatic notions as irony – which often pervades a whole text – (see below, p. 97) may perhaps best be judged at this level. In other words, what is at issue is whether the pervasive tone of the whole text is being reflected, rather than whether or not the exact degree of irony is achieved in any individual word or phrase.

In liaison interpreting, failure to reflect the predominant illo-cutionary force of one speaker's intervention can lead to the interlocutor not perceiving that a response is required to an offer, a request or an undertaking; the interpreter has not necessarily omitted any formal element; merely, the text act has not emerged from the whole translated utterance with sufficient force. In such situations, we have often observed one interlocutor impatiently waiting for a response which never comes, despite the fact that there has apparently been no hitch in the communication and both the interpreter and the other interlocutor seem content with the current state of the communication. In this case, as elsewhere, a word-by-word comparison of ST and TT would reveal no significant omissions. But, with the aid of text-level criteria such as the text act, judgements on translations can transcend the unsatisfactory level of word-for-word or sentence-for-sentence comparison.

Perceiving a text act depends, of course, on ability to recognise speech acts in a sequence of discourse. But much recent work in pragmatics (e.g. Levinson 1983; Haslett 1987; Van Dijk 1982) is critical of the value of speech-act analysis. Without wishing to reject any of the notions introduced above, we can further refine our pragmatic dimension of context by considering these criticisms and the recent direction which work in pragmatics is following. Broadly speaking, the criticisms are of three main kinds. Firstly, many of the claims made about the role of speech acts in communication lack any empirical substantiation. There is a lack of analysis of actual texts in real interaction. A related point is that the data under consideration usually consist of de-contextualised sentences which, from a communicative point of view, are hardly any advance on the artificiality of the concocted sentences found in some grammar books.

Secondly, the role of the listener in the interaction tends to be neglected. It is as if the illocutionary force and perlocutionary effect are predetermined, with the listener playing an entirely passive role. Yet, listeners (and for that matter readers) are active contributors to the communicative process. Moreover, the boundary between illocutionary and perlocutionary is at best indeterminate, since illocutionary acts themselves have built-in consequences. Finally, the sentences are considered in isolation from any meaningful context, and particularly, from the system of social relations which conditions their utterance. Speech-act analysis fails to account for speakers' motives and beliefs and for such essential matters as background knowledge.

EMPIRICAL ANALYSIS

From the work of Austin onwards, the philosophical tradition in which the discipline of pragmatics has grown up has entailed concentration on the logic of utterance meaning, relying on intuitive judgements about what constitutes a coherent utterance (see Levinson 1983: 286–7). The subtitle of Searle (1969) is *An Essay in the Philosophy of Language* and this is defined (p. 4) as

> . . . the attempt to give philosophically illuminating descriptions of certain general features of language, such as reference, truth, meaning, and necessity. . .

In this framework, language is seen as rule-governed behaviour but, in formulating rules for appropriate linguistic behaviour, there is no attempt to test their value (or rather their descriptive adequacy) on any naturally occurring stretch of utterance; if there were, such speech acts as 'stating', 'describing', 'questioning' would turn out not to be very powerful tools for the analysis of intentionality in discourse. Moreover, identifying a sentence as a 'statement' tells us very little about what strategies might be employed in translating it; yet general speech acts such as 'statements' and 'assertions' are of greater frequency in most texts than are the more closely definable speech acts such as 'threatening' and 'promising'.

Whereas this largely philosophical approach to pragmatics, with its reliance on cognitive criteria, tends to focus on non-occurring sentences, the more recent approach to the analysis of discourse known as **conversation analysis** is wholly empirical in that it looks for 'recurring patterns across many records of naturally occurring conversations' (Levinson 1983: 287). Although such observation of the ways in which participants in conversation interact with each other might seem to be relevant only to informal spoken discourse, the empirical methods and principles involved are in fact equally applicable to the written mode. Once a written text is seen as an act of communication, negotiated between producer and receiver in the same way as conversation is, the way is open to regarding text as process rather than product, and translation as an operation performed on a living organism rather than on an artefact as lifeless as the printed word on the page appears to be.

This is, of course, merely to state in text-linguistic terms what professional translators are ever-conscious of in their day-to-day work. Both ST and TT are produced for a reader ('client', 'consumer') whose needs, expectations, etc., are constantly matched against the communicative intent of the producer of the source text. Thus, where the intention of the producer of ST is to sell a product, any translation of the text as an advertisement must be evaluated in terms of how well it serves that purpose (i.e. the persuasive text act involved), rather than on the basis of a narrow linguistic comparison. On the other hand, a translation of advertising copy may be required purely for information (what are the manufacturers claiming about the product?), in which case the translator's aim will be adjusted accordingly: the communicative purpose of ST is no longer the same as that of TT. Large-scale empirical analysis of 'what is going on' in texts and translated texts, conducted on similar principles to those of conversation analysis, would be a useful contribution to translation studies, and indeed different interpretations of pragmatics could also be evaluated on the basis of their applicability to translating activity.

For the time being, however, the preoccupations of conversation analysis – and therefore its research findings so far – have to do with such issues as turn-taking in conversation, adjacency pairs (question/answer, offer/acceptance, greeting/greeting, etc.), preferred responses (the rank-order of expectedness among possible second parts of adjacency pairs), and so on. As such, they are of more obvious relevance to the process of liaison interpreting than to written translating. How do interpreters cope with the management of turn-taking? Do they intervene in adjacency pairs when, according to Levinson (1983:304), the utterance of such pairs is conditioned by the rule:

> Having produced a first part of some pair, current speaker must stop speaking, and next speaker must produce at that point a second part to the same pair.

Is there always a need for interpreters to intervene? To what extent and how can they intervene successfully? These are the kinds of questions to which empirical research in interpreting studies should address itself. Intuitively, one feels that many of the awkwardnesses and hesitations that occur in liaison interpreting have to do with such problems as these. Yet unfortunately, no substantial empirical work has been carried out into these phenomena, partly due to the relative inaccessibility of recorded data (see, however, Knapp-Potthoff and Knapp 1987). Nevertheless, the scope for research here is tremendous. Many of the issues which conversation analysts are interested in might well be furthered by investigation of what happens in, say, negotiating sessions when the physical channel of communication is altered by the need for interpretation.

ILLOCUTIONARY FORCE IN CONTEXT

The other points on which mainstream speech-act theory is criticised concern the habit of considering the pragmatic meaning of sentences in isolation from any well-defined context. Levinson (1983:18–19) loosely defines an utterance as being 'the pairing of a sentence and a context', yet it is striking that, in the considerable review of the literature of speech acts in that work, the data consist largely of sentences for which no context is posited. Ferrara (1980a:241), on the other hand, states that:

> . . . no evaluation of the appropriateness of an act in a sequence can be carried out without a clear perception of the context, its inherent norms, what is normally believed of it by the members of a society, etc.

From the translator's point of view, it is self-evident that this is true of the evaluation of pragmatic meaning as a whole. And such evaluation is equally crucial to successful translating. A good illustration is provided by Texts 5B and 5C. The background to these texts can be summarised as follows. In July 1985, *Rainbow Warrior*, the flagship of the environmental organisation Greenpeace, was blown up in Auckland harbour, causing the death of one of the crew. Involvement of the French secret services was suspected but those arrested were able to show that they could not have been responsible for planting the bomb, while a second identified team of suspected saboteurs had already left New Zealand before the bomb was planted. By September, an official French government investigator reported that there was no firm evidence to implicate the secret services. Consequently, *Le Monde*'s revelation of the existence of a third team of saboteurs, liaising with the other two and responsible for planting the bomb, was (1) a world exclusive, (2) potentially damaging to the French government, (3) based on reliable evidence, but (4) liable to involve the newspaper in litigation if not framed with extreme care. There can be no doubt that, as in the famous case of the *Washington Post* revelations concerning President Nixon, legal advisers will have meticulously scrutinised the text before it went to press, possibly insisting on changes to reduce the risk of court action. Thus, in a very direct sense, the actual form of the text (lexical selection, attribution of action to agent, selective presentation of information, etc.) is a reflection of the particular circumstances surrounding – and indeed the social conditions governing – its production.

Moreover, the circumstances of the translation are equally important. Produced under the constraints of a short time scale (unless the *Guardian* was able to obtain pre-publication copy from *Le Monde*), it was intended to appear on page one of the following morning's edition of the *Guardian*. This is unusual in that extended direct translations from the foreign press are rarely given such prominence. Similar legal constraints would apply (although the risk of prosecution was no doubt less). But a further – and pragmatically more pressing – constraint is the need for readability which in this case involves adherence to the text-norm conventions of page-one articles in the British press. Naturally, such norms vary from newspaper to newspaper and from cultural community to cultural community. The conventions of *Le Monde* are not those of the *Guardian*, even within the common field of investigative journalism. In short, the translator's task of representing the predominant illocutionary force of the source text ('to allege, with due circumspection') is overlaid by the need to achieve appropriate perlocutionary effect.

Now, in texts of this kind, an interesting instance of contrastive pragmatics arises. It concerns the availability in French of a tense – or as some would say a mood – ('conditional' and 'conditional perfect') for the purposes of allegation. Thus, *seraient* (Text 5B, line 125) and *aurait été coordonnée* (line 156) are conventionally interpreted as allegations for which the text producers have good evidence but which they are not prepared to state as fact. Use of the tense serves virtually as a legal escape clause, an avoidance of liability for the truth of what is alleged. As such, it is a conventional device in journalism. The tense which occupies the same place in the tense system of English ('would be', 'would have been', cf. Text 5C, lines 145–46) does not, however, serve the same, quite specific purpose. The conventional illocutionary force with which it is used is the weaker one of prediction or supposition, as in 'Congress would never agree to that', or 'President Carter would have reacted quite differently', etc. Within the norms of journalism in English, equivalence of intended effect is achieved in other conventional ways, e.g. by passivisation such as 'is said to have. . .', by modals,

Text 5B

Le «Rainbow-Warrior» aurait été coulé par une troisième équipe de militaires français

1 *L'attentat contre le Rainbow-Warrior (un mort, le 10 juillet, à Auckland) aurait été perpétré par*
5 *deux nageurs de combat de l'armée française. Telle est l'information que nous avons recueillie de sources concordantes:*
10 *il y avait en Nouvelle-- Zélande une troisième équipe de militaires français, que les cinq membres de la DGSE*
15 *déjà identifiés, l'équipage du voilier Ouvéa et les faux époux «Turenge» étaient chargés d'épauler.*
20 *Cette révélation contredit formellement la version fournie par la haute hiérarchie militaire à M. Bernard*
25 *Tricot. Dans son rapport, celui-ci assurait que les militaires français n'avaient participé qu'à une mission de sur-*
30 *veillance de Greenpeace et ne mentionnait pas l'existence d'une troisième équipe.*
Dans l'entourage du
35 *ministre de la défense, après avoir qualifié l'attentat de «regrettable, inadmissible et scandaleux», on ajoute: «Ceux*
40 qui ont été arrêtés n'ont pas fait le coup, l'équipage de l'*Ouvéa* pas davantage. Quant à une autre équipe, nous
45 ne connaissons pas

d'autre équipe de la DGSE dans cette affaire et nous ne croyons pas à l'implication d'autres
50 équipes des armées françaises.»
Qui, le 10 juillet au soir, dans le port d'Auckland en Nouvelle--
55 Zélande, a posé deux bombes sur la coque du *Rainbow-Warrior*, le «navire amiral» du mouvement écologiste
60 Greenpeace? Qui, si les auteurs de cet attentat, «*criminel et absurde*» selon M. Mitterrand, sont bien français, leur
65 en a donné l'ordre? Telles sont toujours les deux questions-clés de l'affaire Greenpeace.
La rapport Tricot a
70 confirmé, le 26 août que des agents français se trouvaient alors en Nouvelle-Zélande et que leur mission visait
75 Greenpeace. Mais, il n'a pas été prouvé que les faux époux Turenge, les deux agents français incarcérés en Nouvelle-
80 Zélande, soient les auteurs de l'attentat lui-même; et les autorités militaires, du ministre de la défense à la haute
85 hiérarchie, assurent que la mission confiée aux agents de la DGSE n'était que de surveillance et d'infiltration.
90 Depuis le 10 juillet, du

temps a, cependant, passé et des bouches s'ouvrent.

95 Anciens et proches de la DGSE, «honorables correspondants» de ce service secret, policiers ayant eu connaissance de l'enquête néo-zéland-
100 aise, membres de cabinets ministériels placés à des postes sensibles, militaires du cadre de réserve collaborant avec
105 les partis d'opposition, nombreux sont ceux qui parlent. Et ce qu'ils disent aboutit aux mêmes conclusions. Qui
110 a agi? A les en croire, une troisième équipe, évoquée par *le Canard enchaîné* du 11 septembre, complémentaire
115 de l'équipage du voilier *Ouvéa*, chargé de la logistique, et du faux couple Turenge, lequel aurait servi de «leurre»
120 vis-à-vis des Néo--Zélandais, et aurait réunis le matériel apporté par l'*Ouvéa* aux auteurs de l'attentat. Ces derniers
125 seraient deux nageurs de combat de l'armée française, chacun ayant posé une charge. Nos informateurs ne pré-
130 cisent pas leur base d'affectation, qui ne peut être que le Centre d'instruction des nageurs de combat (CINC) de la
135 base d'Aspretto, en Corse, s'ils relèvent de l'armée de terre, ou Lorient s'ils relèvent de la marine. Mais, tradi-
140 tionnellement, c'est au CINC, lié à la division Action de la DGSE, que le service secret français fait appel pour ce genre
145 d'opérations.
Ces deux militaires

ont la même spécialité qu'Alain Turenge, de son vrai nom Alain
150 Mafart commandant en second de la base d'Aspretto); et que les trois équipiers de l'*Ouvéa* (sous-officiers
155 du CINC).
L'opération aurait été coordonnée par «Philippe Dubast», qui est, en fait, le commandant Louis-
160 Pierre Dillais, «patron» de la base d'Aspretto. A l'exception de Dominique Prieur, alias Sophie Turenge, qui n'était que
165 la couverture maritale d'Alain Mafart, l'opération tout entière semble donc bien avoir été confiée, au plus haut
170 niveau, à des nageurs de combat de l'armée française. Et la DGSE, qui les emploie, a bien, ainsi, participé à l'at-
175 tentat. Les deux auteurs directs de l'attentat, leur mission achevée, ont quitté Auckland par avion, sans être repérés,
180 l'un pour Nouméa, l'autre pour Sydney (Australie).
La réponse à la seconde question (Qui
185 leur a confié cette mission?) est cohérente avec le déroulement de l'opération ...
Il s'agirait des géné-
190 raux Jeannou Lacaze, alors chef d'état-major des armées, et Jean Saulnier, alors chef d'état-major particulier
195 du président de la République, nommé depuis à la tête des armées en remplacement du général Lacaze, mais aussi du
200 ministre de la défense lui-même.
Dans son rapport, M.

Tricot avait insisté sur le rôle de M. Hernu et du
205 général Saulnier dans la prise de décision, mais n'avait pas mentionné le général Lacaze.

Sortir du piège

210 A ce stade, il est impossible de savoir si ces trois personnalités sont directement impliquées, ou simplement
215 concernées en raison de malentendus et de non-dits lors des discussions sur Greenpeace. Le rapport de M. Tricot
220 insistait d'ailleurs sur cette ambiguïté. Le conseiller d'Etat s'est ainsi longuement interrogé sur la signification de la
225 phrase «*anticiper les actions de Greenpeace*» figurant dans une note du 1er mars de l'amiral Fages, au nom de la
230 DIRCEN, et destinée à M. Hernu. ...

BERTRAND
LE GENDRE et
EDWY PLENEL.

(Le Monde 18.9.85)

e.g. 'may have' (cf. Text 5C, line 15) or by vague attribution such as 'according to well-informed sources . . .'. Achieving equivalence of predominant illocutionary force and of illocutionary structure in the target text is of paramount importance.

POWER AND STATUS

In our consideration of the translation of illocutionary force, our scope has now widened to include consideration of the beliefs, perceptions and attitudes of members of SL and TL communities. But we must also widen our horizons to include not only the immediate speech situation but also the social institutions within which linguistic communication takes place. Bourdieu (1982) offers a crucial insight in pointing out that illocutionary force is invested in an utterance not by the words themselves or by any particular combination of them but by the system of social relations which influences the production and reception of utterances in particular situations. The relative power and status of language users within social institutions exercise a determining influence not only on language forms used but also on the intended and perceived illocutionary force of utterances. The translator, who stands between two independent social structures, has to be sensitive

Text 5C

'Third military team involved in sinking'

1 The French newspaper, Le Monde, published a report yesterday on how a "third team," under 5 orders from the French Government may have blown up the Greenpeace boat in Auckland harbour on July 10. We 10 give a partial text of the account by Bertrand Legendre and Edwy Plenel.

The attack on the 15 Rainbow Warrior may have been carried out by two frogmen from the French armed forces.

Information corrobo-20 rated from several sources is that there was a third team from the French armed forces in New Zealand, to which 25 the five members of the DGSE (General Directorate of External Security) already identified—the crew of the 30 yacht Ouvea and the fictitious married couple known as the Turenges—were to give support.

This completely con-35 tradicts the version supplied by the armed forces at a high level to Mr Bernard Tricot, the special investigator. In 40 his report, Mr Tricot said that members of the French armed forces had taken part only in a surveillance mission 45 against Greenpeace.

But who in Auckland harbour, on the evening of July 10, placed two mines on the hull of the 50 Rainbow Warrior, the Greenpeace flagship? If the authors of this attack, which Mr Mitterrand described as 55 "criminal and preposterous!" are indeed French, then who gave them the order?

The Tricot report on 60 August 26 confirmed that French agents were in New Zealand at the time and that Greenpeace was the target of 65 their mission. But it has not been proved that the Turenges, the two French agents imprisoned in New Zealand, 70 were responsible for the attack itself; and the authorities responsible for the armed forces, from the Minister of 75 Defence down to senior officers, declare that the mission entrusted to these DGSE agents was only for surveillance 80 and infiltration.

But former members of the DGSE, those close to it, those who have performed services for 85 it, police officers with knowledge of the investigation in New Zealand, members of ministerial offices in sensitive 90 positions, officers on the armed forces reserve who are working with opposition parties—there are many people 95 who are talking now.

What they say points to the same conclusions: that there was a third team, mentioned by the 100 Canard Enchaîné on

September 11, which was backing up the crew of the Ouvea. It was charged with logistics and to the Turenges, who were to act as a decoy to the New Zealanders and would have handed over the equipment transported by the Ouvea, to the saboteurs.

These would have been two frogmen—one for each explosive device, from the French armed forces, and each would have put one charge in place. Our informants do not specify where they came from, but this can only be the training centre for frogmen (CINC) at the Aspretto base in Corsica, if they were army frogmen, or L'Orient, if they were navy men.

But traditionally the French secret service calls on CINC, which is linked to the action division of the DGSE, for this type of operation.

The two members of the armed forces have the same speciality as Alain Turenge (real identity, Alain Mafart, second-in-command of the Aspretto base) and the three members of the Ouvea crew (NCOs at CINC).

The operation would have been coordinated by "Philippe Dubast", who is, in fact, Louis-Pierre Dillais, head of the Aspretto base. Apart from Dominique Prieur, alias Sophie Turenge, who was only there to provide the cover of a married couple for Mafart, the entire operation seems to have been entrusted at the highest level to French military frogmen. And the DGSE, in making use of them, was therefore involved in the attack. The two men who carried out the attack left Auckland by air, one for Noumea, in the French Pacific territory of New Caledonia, and the other for Sydney.

The reply to the question of who entrusted them with this mission is consistent with the course of the operation. . . .

Those who might have been involved are General Jeannou Lacaze, then head of the army general staff, and General Jean Saulnier, then chief of military staff at the Elysee, who later succeeded General Lacaze, but also the Minister of Defence himself.

At this stage, it is impossible to know if these three were directly implicated or simply involved through misunderstandings and incomplete information during discussions of Greenpeace. Mr Tricot's report, moreover, emphasised this ambiguity. He was persistently questioned about the meaning of the phrase "anticipate the actions of Greenpeace," which appeared in a note dated March 1 from Admiral Fages on behalf of DIRCEN and intended for Mr Hernu.

(The *Guardian* 18.9.85)

to what constitutes the sanctioned norm – or deviation from the norm – in any source text. As Fairclough (1985) has noted, lexical selection tends to be a reflection of social role and status, and alternative lexicalisations may emerge from different ideological positions.

Thus, at a conference on publishing in minority languages held in 1987, one contribution referred to the southern French language, Occitan, not as *une langue minoritaire* ('a minority language') but as *une langue minorisée* (literally 'a language put into a minority position'). To translate this ST item as 'a minority language' on the grounds that the information loss is minimal and the problem of little significance ('what's in a suffix?') would be to ride roughshod over the author's intentions as well as to fail to reflect the power dynamic which provided a primary motivation for the utterance in the first place. The utterance producer's neologism in the source text is not an idle one; it constitutes a strong signal of genre and discourse as defined in Chapter 4, and is a reflection of a whole world-view ('rejection of client status for a language being defended'), born of a particular social situation. The need to reflect this intended meaning leads to an expansion of the ST item into some translation such as 'a language reduced to minority status'. Naturally, problems of this kind are less likely to arise in certain text forms – the scientific laboratory report, say, or a patent. Liaison interpreters, on the other hand, are constantly aware of discourse reflecting ideology and of the sanctioned language forms of particular social institutions. An attested example from the field of court interpreting will serve to illustrate the point.

An English/French interpreter was called in to facilitate a kind of plea-bargaining session between barrister and accused prior to a court appearance. The accused – two Senegalese visitors to Britain – were adamant that they were not guilty, while the barrister was not only convinced that the evidence against them was conclusive, but also that the accused were sufficiently competent in English and had insisted on the services of an interpreter only for the purpose of setting up a smokescreen to hide behind. In this instance, the evident mutual distrust was compounded by the obvious discrepancy between the courtroom discourse of the barrister and the low-status discourse of the accused – which in turn was an inevitable reflection of the balance of power between the participants in the speech situation.

In advancing the view that a plea of not guilty would probably lead to a prison sentence whereas a plea of guilty, although it might involve a fine and/or a short sentence of one or two weeks, would also result in expulsion from the country (the stated aim of the accused), the barrister was employing the language of the court, a discourse of power and authority, and thus establishing in the minds of the accused an identification of the barrister with their accusers. In no way could they perceive him as being their representative. Conversely, the utterances of the accused (in French, which was not their mother tongue) reflected, reproduced and reinforced their position of weakness. In Bourdieu's terms, their own linguistic product was of low value in the particular linguistic market place in which they found themselves. In a situation of this kind, the interpreter is in a precarious position, seen by the barrister as an unnecessary rampart put up by the accused, and by the latter as an agent of the court. Whereas the interpreter is tempted to play a conciliating role (in order to promote real communication), he or she is duty-bound to represent the actual illocutionary force (and hence reproduce the power relationship) of each side of the language exchange.

Such instances are not uncommon. On another occasion, an interpreter mediating between the police and an accused person found that the former felt obliged to justify their actions to the interpreter as if he was taking the side of the accused. In the eyes of authority (police, barristers), the accused appears to acquire some kind of status merely on account of being afforded the voice of an interpreter. To what extent can the liaison interpreter manage a situation such as this? Is there scope for explaining discoursal attitudes as well as reflecting them? Brislin (1980) suggests that there is and that awareness and management of cross-cultural communication difficulties, both verbal and non-verbal, should form part of the interpreter's role. Professionals, certainly, would have decided views on the matter. But it would be an instructive exercise to attempt to set down an adequate code of practice for liaison interpreters.

Significantly, a code of conduct exists for conference interpreting, but the AIIC (Association Internationale des Interprètes de Conférence) which produced it, deems liaison interpreting to be outside its remit. Likewise, the Dubrovnik Translator's Charter covers the work of written translating. It seems that liaison interpreting is the one area where each individual defines her or his own procedures on an *ad hoc* basis.

Both Anderson (1975) and Harris (1981) discuss the interpreter's divided loyalties. The former advances the hypothesis that interpreters are likely to identify more closely with clients who are monolingual speakers of their own mother tongue and notes that, to obviate the problem of conflicting loyalties in the field of international diplomacy, each negotiating team brings its own interpreter:

> This serves the purpose of eliminating many aspects of role strain by making the interpreter responsible to a single client . . . his linguistic ability becomes a part of the negotiating team's arsenal.
>
> (Anderson 1975:217)

The court interpreter, on the other hand, is likely to suffer from 'role conflict'. Harris (1981) notes how even seating position (nearer the defence or nearer the prosecution) can affect clients' trust of the interpreter's neutrality. He also relates that, in the particular case he observed, the interpreter preferred third-person reported speech to first-person speaking in order to mark her own neutrality, thus: 'Le président vous demande. . .' ('the presiding judge is asking you. . .') and 'Die Zeugin antwortet. . .' ('the witness's answer is that. . .'). The need for this distancing device became apparent when one of the witnesses turned on the interpreter and asked: 'Why are you asking me these pointless questions?' (Harris 1981:198), thus obviously identifying the interpreter as an agent of the court.

The impact of a given discourse on a given environment is now seen to involve far more factors than might at first be supposed. We have incorporated into our model of the communication process such notions as the beliefs and perceptions of language users, the social circumstances of the speech/writing event and the effects on language users and their discourse of institutional relations prevailing in society. It follows that the 'meaning' of an utterance cannot be limited to what is expressed on the surface of the text. Pragmatic values are not attached to linguistic forms but accrue from the intentions of the speaker/writer within a given social setting.

The Gricean view is now widely accepted that comprehension of an utterance is not simply a matter of decoding the message which it contains in coded form but rather of seeking to interpret 'speaker meaning'; the hearer infers what the speaker means. Let us now consider the implications of this for the translator. In most cases, the translator, as a receiver of ST but not specifically an addressee (in the sense of the intended receiver of ST), is an observer of the text-world environment of ST. The role of the translator as reader is then one of constructing a model of the intended meaning of ST and of forming judgements about the probable impact of ST on intended receivers. As a text producer, the translator operates in a different socio-cultural environment, seeking to reproduce his or her interpretation of 'speaker meaning' in such a way as to achieve the intended effects on TT readers.

INTERPRETATION AND INFERENCE

There are two important principles underlying such a view. Firstly, instead of limiting our study to consideration of sentence (or text) meaning, we need to consider **speaker meaning** and **hearer meaning** (or writer meaning and reader meaning). Secondly, the notion of comprehension of source text is misleading; it is more accurate to treat reader meaning as being an interpretation of writer meaning. As Green and Morgan (1981: 177) point out,

> To attempt to describe the means by which a hearer 'understood' an utterance might imply a view of discourse in which communication is the simple encoding and decoding of 'thoughts' or 'meanings' in linguistic packages.

Rather, the hearer/reader's task is to construct a model of the speaker/writer's communicative intention, consistent with indications forthcoming from the text being processed and with what he or she knows about the world at large. We are here distinguishing between what Beaugrande and Dressler (1981) call **text-presented knowledge** and **world knowledge.** The factual connotation of the word 'knowledge' is, however, unhelpful and we consequently prefer the term **assumption.** In substituting the notion **assumed familiarity** for what has often been referred to as 'shared knowledge', Prince (1981:232) observes that

> all a speaker has to go on when treating something as given or 'shared' is what s/he assumes the hearer assumes.

We can never 'know' what our interlocutor 'knows'. But we can and do make assumptions about the cognitive environment we both share.

Prince further distinguishes between new discourse entities, textually or situationally evoked entities and inferrable entities. An evoked entity is one which is already active in the discourse model being constructed, whether from co-text or because it is situationally relevant. The important point here, from the point of view of translation studies, is that what is inferrable or situationally evoked for a ST reader may not be so for a TT reader. Operating in different cognitive environments, ST and TT readers are not equally equipped for the task of inferencing. Adjustments in texture arising from these differences will be examined in Chapter 10.

EFFECTIVENESS AND EFFICIENCY IN TRANSLATION

The translator as a text producer is in a similar position to the producer of ST but will often make different assumptions about the separate cognitive environments of source and target text users. Thus, in comparing Texts 5B and 5C, we find:

M. Bernard Tricot (ST lines 24–25)
Mr Bernard Tricot, the special investigator (TT lines 38–39)

The judgements that text producers make about what can be assumed to be shared with text receivers often exert a determining influence on the form an emerging text will take. Any text seeks to achieve a balance between new, evoked and inferrable entities, such that the fusion of the three allows the reader/hearer to infer the producer's communicative intention. The balance is regulated by the principles of effectiveness (achieving maximum transmission of relevant content or fulfilment of a communicative goal) and efficiency (achieving it in the most economical way, involving minimum expenditure of processing effort). Thus, the guiding principle for deciding what to include in a text and what to take for granted may be stated as:

Is the gain in effectiveness sufficient to warrant the extra processing effort involved?

Thus, the translator of Text 5B has decided that inclusion in the target text of the element *the special investigator* meets the requirement as stated. A translation of *M. Bernard Tricot* as merely *Mr Bernard Tricot* is considered not explicit enough on the basis of what the translator assumes about TT receivers' cognitive environment (in this case, awareness of French political affairs). Conversely, a TT version such as:

> *Mr Bernard Tricot, the special investigator appointed by*
> *the French President with the remit of producing a report*
> *on the whole affair and specifically the alleged involvement*
> *of the French secret services. . .*

would indeed convey more 'knowledge'; but a law of diminishing returns operates, whereby the (relatively small) increase in effectiveness is outweighed by the (considerable) extra effort involved in processing the text. It is in this sense that Grice's maxims of quantity are to be understood (see Chapter 4):

> Make your contribution as informative as required.
> Do not make your contribution more informative than
> required

What is 'required' for any given communicative purpose within a TL cultural environment is then a matter for the translator's judgement. It is in these terms that we may define appropriateness. That the translator of Text 5B has fully, yet unobtrusively, exercised this judgement is apparent from the following samples:

> *Les deux auteurs directs de l'attentat. . . ont quitté Auck-*
> *land. . . l'un pour Nouméa, l'autre pour Sydney (Australie).*
> (ST lines 175–182)

> *The two men who carried out the attack left Auckland. . . one*
> *for Noumea, in the French Pacific territory of New Caledonia,*
> *and the other for Sydney.* (TT lines 163–170)

Nida (1964: 130) refers to a process such as this as restoring 'cultural redundancy' to a text. In the light of the Maxim of quantity, the notions ellipsis and redundancy are seen to be pragmatic variables, entirely dependent on assumptions concerning the mutual cognitive environments of ST and TT users. The examples of Noumea and Sydney above are but concrete lexical instances of a process which pervades all texts at a more general level, determining the degree of ellipsis/redundancy present in the text as a function of particular groups of users.

RELEVANCE

Ellipsis and redundancy in texts are also governed by the principle of relevance. Grice's Maxim of Relation is stated as:

> Be relevant.

In elevating the principle of relevance to the status of the central factor governing utterance interpretation, Sperber and Wilson (1986:vii) argue that

> To communicate is to claim an individual's attention; hence, to communicate is to imply that the information communicated is relevant

since in communication we pay attention only to information which seems relevant to us (greatest cognitive effect for minimum processing effort). In developing this view of communication as an ostensive-inferential process (hearers infer meaning from speakers providing evidence of their intentions), Sperber and Wilson suggest (p. 103) that

> the relevance of new information to an individual is to be assessed in terms of the improvements it brings to his representation of the world.

Thus, the interaction of 'new' and 'old' information may give rise to what are called 'contextual effects', of three possible kinds. It may strengthen previously held assumptions (as when 'new' information confirms 'old') or weaken/eliminate unconfirmed/false assumptions (when 'new' contradicts 'old') or the fusion of old and new may serve as premises from which other contextual implications are derived. An assumption is then said to be relevant to a context if it achieves some contextual effect. Returning to Text 5C, we can see how relevance in this sense can be assessed at each level from the individual lexical item (the mention of *frogmen* as an improvement in the reader's model of the *Rainbow Warrior* affair), to the entire discourse event (i.e. elimination of previous assumption of 'government non-involvement'), with the derived implication: 'someone isn't telling the truth'.

Now, if this view of inferential communication is accepted, it will also be appreciated that relevance to a context is a matter of degree and, further, that what is relevant in one (ST) environment may be less or more so in another (TT) environment. Assessing relevance to intended receivers is then another of the translator's tasks. In the case of translations which are selective reductions of STs (on this concept see Sager 1983:122), the process will involve decisions as to which portions of the source text are to be omitted. In comparing the entire articles from which Texts 5B and 5C are taken, it becomes apparent that a reduction has been achieved by eliminating passages where the intentions of the ST writers relate mostly to internal French politics (calculating the political damage to the French President, etc.). Admittedly, in this instance, the selective reduction may have been carried out by an editor rather than by the actual translator; but there are often cases where editor and translator are one and the same person.

Even in full translations, translators can and do take responsibility for omitting information which is deemed to be of insufficient relevance to TT readers. Witness Text $5D_2$, which is a translation of Text $5D_1$. Both are taken from a Spanish airline in-flight magazine.

Text $5D_1$

> Los habitantes no entendían nada, porque aunque la isla es de origen volcánico, desde hacía miles de años, en concreto desde el cuaternario, nunca había habido erupciones.

Text $5D_2$

> The people could not understand what had happened, because the island, although originally volcanic, had never had an eruption.

The translator's decision here is related to what is judged to be relevant in the text-processing environment of the airline passenger seeking entertainment from an in-flight magazine; specification of the 'Quaternary period of pre-history' is not considered to add a contextual effect (as previously defined) in the context of the information that the island is of volcanic origin. It is interesting to note that the discrepancy is also cultural in that whereas 'quaternary' may be unusual or learned for English readers, it is a basic school concept for Spanish readers. To what extent translators have licence to take such decisions is a legitimate subject for debate; when does 'improved relevance' become unacceptable intrusion or dereliction of duty? We submit, however, that sensitivity to the issue of relevance in text processing is a necessary part of the translator's skills.

The same principle can be used to throw light on a particular problem which affects French/English translating at the level of individual lexical items (on this point, see Chapter 10). It is a recognised text convention governing the field of discourse of news reporting/investigative journalism in French that a concept referred to in a noun phrase will not be expressed in the same way twice running in a text. Thus, *le dollar américain* will, in a subsequent lexicalisation, become *le billet vert; le Président de la République* will become, as well as the anaphoric *il*, perhaps *le chef de l'Etat* or even *l'Elysée*. A similar convention may be observed in English but the decision will be governed by different considerations to do with lexical cohesion. Indeed, unthinking translation, on an item-for-item basis, may produce unintended effects. In Text 5B, *M. Tricot* (line 219) is referred to in the immediately following co-text as *Le conseiller d'Etat* (line 221). No violation of the maxim of relation is involved here since, for ST users, the expressive device is entirely conventional:

> *M. Tricot = le conseiller d'Etat*

In English, however, the convention is not the same and a translation

> *Mr Tricot. . . The Councillor of State*

would appear to violate the maxim of relation, since neither co-text nor context provides evidence for the assumption that Mr Tricot is a member of the Council of State. Now, it is one of Grice's insights that, when a maxim is apparently violated, participants in conversation tend to infer some unexpressed content (implicature) rather than abandon the assumption that the principle of co-operation is being upheld. Here, readers might well assume that the Councillor of State was a person referred to in the Tricot Report rather than the author of the report himself. The translator has, of course, avoided the pitfall by replacing ST *le conseiller d'Etat* by the appropriate item for maintaining textual cohesion in TT, the anaphoric *He*.

QUALITY, RELEVANCE AND THE TRANSLATION OF IRONY

To end this chapter on the pragmatic dimension of context,

we shall consider another of the Gricean maxims, namely that of quality.

Do not say what you believe to be false.
Do not say that for which you lack adequate evidence.

By reference to this, Grice (1975) is able to provide an account of the rhetorical device of irony, since perceiving a statement to be intended as ironical involves perceiving that the first maxim of quality is being flouted: the speaker manifestly does not believe what he says. The implicature which is derived from this is that the speaker must be expressing an attitude towards the straightforward interpretation of the (apparently insincere) proposition. It is in this sense that Sperber and Wilson (1981, 1986) talk of 'second-degree interpretation', involving recognition that the speaker is echoing some (real or imagined) source from which he is dissociating himself by implication. The echo may be of some conventionally-held view which speaker B wishes to hold up to ridicule:

A: This Chernobyl thing really worries me.
B: Ah, but don't forget: it couldn't happen here.

or it may invoke some vague or imagined source:

A: You might even be appointed Managing Director.
B: Pigs might fly!

Sperber and Wilson criticise Grice's account of irony because such devices as ironic understatement do not in fact flout the maxim of quality. But we believe Sperber and Wilson's view of 'echoic second-degree interpretation' (i.e. echoing an imaginary person's view) is not inconsistent with an essentially Gricean view. Thus, ironic understatement, while it may not flout the maxim of quality, does involve apparent violation of the maxim of quantity ('make your contribution as informative as required'):

A (observing downpour): It seems to be raining!

In the same way, the ironic interjection 'You must be joking!', in violating quality, displays the implicature: 'I would prefer to believe you are not serious than that you really do subscribe to such a ridiculous view'.

In short, the account of irony which we retain here is that the apparent violation of a maxim implicates:

1. that speaker dissociates self from view expressed;

2. that speaker is echoing a point of view in order to display some attitude towards it (ridicule, indignation, exasperation, etc.);

and that drawing the appropriate inference involves a second-degree interpretation achieved by:

3. matching the view apparently expressed with any discordant view expressed co-textually; and/or
4. matching the view apparently expressed with what is assumed to be the case (mutual cognitive environment).

Now, it may occasionally be observed that a translation, while faithfully reflecting the propositional content of the source text, fails to achieve the degree of irony perceptible in the source text. In such cases, it will be difficult to point to mismatches in either denotative or connotative meaning. But the advantage of an account of irony such as the one outlined above lies in the light it may shed on the problem of achieving an adequate translation of irony. Text $5E_1$ is a formal translation of what Jean-Paul Sartre wrote, analysing the ills of the French economy in 1953.

Text $5E_1$

> Whose fault is it? you ask. Well, it's the Germans' fault because they were the ones who declared two ruinous wars on us. And it's the fault of the Russians who, in Moscow, are holding up the reconstruction effort. . .

Sartre was echoing a number of conventionally-held beliefs which he sought to ridicule. Contemporary readers of ST would have had no trouble in recognising the violation of the maxim of quality or the kind of view being echoed. However, since TT readers cannot be assumed to share the same cognitive environment as ST readers, the translator may feel the need to provide additional cues for recognition of the ironic intention, as for example in Text $5E_2$.

Text $5E_2$

> And whose fault is that? you might ask. Ah well, first of all, there are the Germans who declared two ruinous wars on us. And then there are the Russians who, far away in Moscow, are holding up our reconstruction effort. . .

It may be felt that Text $5E_2$ overplays the role and that fewer overt cues are needed. But successful translation will depend on whether or not TT readers are able to achieve second-degree interpretation with minimal extra processing effort. Recognition of ironic intention is, in all cases, crucial and will condition the translator's output.

Our review of pragmatic notions relevant to the translator has brought us a long way from atomistic speech-act analysis towards a more dynamic concept of the text as an evolving entity, a process whereby producers and receivers cooperate and communicate by making assumptions about a shared cognitive environment. We have also seen how language users establish relevance to each other's communicative objectives according to such principles as effectiveness and efficiency. But our consideration of the cultural environment and its impact on interaction in discourse has so far been schematic. It is to this essentially semiotic dimension that we now turn.

SIX

Translating texts as signs: the semiotic dimension of context

FROM PRAGMATICS TO SEMIOTICS

We have tried to provide a definition of context which is comprehensive enough to account for the complexity of actually occurring texts. With the translator in mind, we have developed an argument which rests on two basic premises. Firstly, lexical and syntactic choices made within the field (mode, tenor, etc.) of a given discourse are ultimately determined by pragmatic considerations to do with the purposes of utterances, real-world conditions, and so on. Secondly, in order to perceive the full communicative thrust of an utterance, we need to appreciate not only the pragmatic action, but also a semiotic dimension which regulates the interaction of the various discoursal elements as 'signs'. The interaction takes place, on the one hand, between various signs within texts and, on the other, between the producer of these signs and the intended receivers. It is only through this interactive semiotic dimension that language users can begin to do things with words, and values such as those of the field, mode and tenor begin to play a genuine role in communicative transactions.

To demonstrate the interdependence of pragmatics and semiotics in the practical pursuits of text analysis, let us consider the following discourse sample with which George Orwell in his essay 'Politics and the English language' (1945) invites us to 'consider. . . some comfortable English professor defending Russian totalitarianism. He cannot say outright, "I believe in killing off your opponents when you can get good results by doing so." Probably, therefore, he will say something like this. . .':

Text 6A

> While freely conceding that the Soviet regime exhibits certain features which the humanitarian may be inclined to deplore, we must, I think,

agree that a certain curtailment of the right to political opposition is an unavoidable concomitant to transitional periods, and that the rigours which the Russian people have been called upon to undergo have been amply justified in the sphere of concrete achievement.

Gregory and Carroll (1978:34) cite this text in order to illustrate how 'a specialized language can, of course, be misused and become a mask concealing what is really being said. . .'. With them, we can safely suppose that the 'masking' effect achieved by the text producer (real or fictitious) is a function of the use of 'pseudo-specialist jargon' (field), professorial authority and power (tenor) and the reflective orientation of the academic lecture (mode). Undoubtedly, all these factors will have contributed a great deal to the ultimate effect. However, other equally important factors are actively involved and this becomes particularly apparent when there is some reworking of text, as in translation. In order to achieve a satisfactory rendering, the translator will first of all ensure that the items listed below (List A) remain open to something like the interpretation contained in the pragmatic glosses in List B. These glosses will not, of course, appear in any actual translation. They serve only to indicate how sensitive the reader/translator should be to what the source text is 'doing' as well as 'saying'. For example, in translating the item *rigours* (List A), the translator has to ensure that the TL equivalent allows the allusion to be recovered by TT readers, without going so far as to make explicit what is deliberately being masked in the professor's discourse.

List A	**List B**
freely conceding	paying lip service
certain features	common pattern of behaviour
may be inclined to deplore	should categorically oppose
we must I think agree	I am telling you
a certain curtailment of the right	complete denial of the right
unavoidable concomitant	foreseen consequences
transitional periods	as long a period as necessary (indefinitely?)
rigours	physical hardships (torture, liquidation)
called upon	forced to

undergo	suffer
amply justified	convincing to those in power
concrete achievement	the ultimate goal of the State

Items in List A have assumed pragmatic values which turn them into what may be termed **intentional acts** whose sole purpose is to divert attention from the possible readings contained in List B. The process does not stop at individual words and phrases, however. It also reaches the higher levels of clauses and clause-sequences. For example, the subordinate clause

> While freely conceding that the Soviet regime exhibits certain features which the humanitarian may be inclined to deplore. . .

will act as a sign relaying 'weak conviction', even 'false concession'. It is a 'thesis cited to be opposed'. In terms of the Gricean maxims, this utterance may also violate the maxim of quality ('Do not say what you believe to be false. . .'), producing in the process the implicature of deflecting attention: 'let's not look too closely into. . .'.

Thus, in addition to the signs relayed by individual items, we find that whole sequences of text are also perceived as signs. That is, once features of field, mode and tenor are manipulated to relay special effects, these features inevitably convey intentional actions, and have potential as signs. In this way, they are able to interact with other signs in the text. The next element typifies the field of 'political propaganda':

> we must, I think, agree that a certain curtailment of the right
> to political opposition

Readers here perceive an intention which we can gloss as 'rebutting a thesis cited'. Such a reading, however, depends on a prior perception of the whole unit as a sign: 'having paid lip service to certain views, I now want you all to listen to mine'. What actually happens is that text users recognise a sequence which involves 'false concession' followed by 'opposition' followed by 'substantiation', as in Fig. 6.1.

Formats such as these are recognisable by virtue of being patterns of thinking characteristic of a given culture. In fact, we have entered the domain of semiotics in the context of Text 6A as soon as we perceive that 'our comfortable professor' is using language to tell 'lies', which we, as language users, can only do because we use linguistic expressions as signs. Recalling Peirce's

'false concession'
While freely conceding...

'opposition'
we must, I think, agree...

'substantiation'
. . . .

Figure 6.1   Sequence in Text 6A

definition of the sign ('something. . . which stands in place of something which is absent, which could even not exist. . .'), Eco (1973:1149) observes, rather amusingly, that

> This means that the fundamental characteristic of the sign is that I can use it to *lie.* . . (since everything that serves to tell a lie can also be used, in the right circumstances, to tell the truth).

The semiotics of context may thus be seen as an overall enabling dimension – the prime mover which pushes communication forward. It is the motivating force behind pragmatic and other contextual features. Our arguments so far find interesting echoes in recent semiotic research. Sebeok (1986:753) defines the interactional dimension in the following terms:

> . . . linguistic actions of other speakers participating in a communicative situation are the context of production of one's own discourse, acting with a similar productive power, and so forth. The interactional perspective completes the Austinian intuition of speaking as action.

Thus, the concept of 'interaction' is used here in the sense of what takes place between interlocutors. However, as we argued above, this sense of interaction implies the other sense in which we use the term: what takes place between signs. After all, a written text is a record of an exchange between the writer and some implied readers whose presence is inevitably felt throughout the process. What are being exchanged all the time are 'signs'.

SEMIOTICS-CONSCIOUS TRANSLATING

Languages differ in the way they perceive and partition reality.

This situation creates serious problems for the translator and all those who work with languages in contact. Rarely, if ever, do we find anything more than a superficial correspondence between the various categories and divisions which different languages impose on the thought patterns of their speakers. As we saw in Chapter 2, any strict interpretation of the Sapir/Whorf hypothesis would imply that the gap between views of the world held by different linguistic communities is almost unbridgeable. This in effect would exclude the possibility of successful translation.

There would be little point in denying the validity of some of the observations made by those who work within this hypothesis. It would, however, be futile to deny the possibility of translating. Cross-cultural communication through language takes place all the time and is generally successful. As observed particularly by those who work in Bible translation (e.g. Nida 1964; Nida and Taber 1969), where the emphasis is naturally on successful cultural encounter, there is sufficient shared experience even between users of languages which are culturally remote from each other to make translatability a tenable proposition. This position is also supported by research on language universals (see, e.g. Greenberg 1968).

A semiotic approach to text, context and translation supports the 'common ground' view. Lotman *et al.* (1975:57) define culture as 'the functional correlation of different sign systems'. These different sign systems operate both within and between cultures, and semiotics deals with the processing and exchange of information both within and across cultural boundaries. Translating can now be envisaged as the process which transforms one semiotic entity into another, under certain equivalence conditions to do with semiotic codes, pragmatic action and general communicative requirements.

THE SEMIOTIC ENTITY AS A UNIT OF TRANSLATION

Semiotic translation, we suggest, involves the translator in a number of important procedures.

Stage 1   Identification

The translator identifies a source-system semiotic entity. This will be a constituent element of a certain cultural (sub-)system. Consider for example Text $6B_1$, which is an idiomatic translation into English of an Arabic news report. The source text was used in the British Civil Service Arabic Competition (1987). The semiotic entity under discussion – an item referring to a religious ceremony well known in the Islamic world – is provisionally retained in transliteration to illustrate its semiotic potential.

Text $6B_1$

> The Iranian pilgrims began their demonstration during *al Tawaaf*, preventing other pilgrims from leaving or entering the shrine.

Stage 2   *Information*

The translator identifies an **informational core.** A suitable TL denotational equivalent for the sign *al Tawaaf* will be 'circum-ambulation'.

Stage 3   *Explication*

If the informational equivalent is not self-sufficient, the translator will seek to explicate by means of synonymy, expansion, paraphrase, etc. For a non-Muslim readership, 'circumambulation' will have to be modified. *Al Tawaaf* involves walking round the *Kaaba* (the Black Rock), and is performed as part of the pilgrimage to Mecca which every Muslim must perform at least once in his or her lifetime. In the expansion, at least some of this information will have to be included: 'walking round the Black Rock in Mecca'.

Stage 4   *Transformation*

Having retrieved the information core and carried out the necessary modification, the translator then considers what is missing in terms of intentionality and status as a sign. *Al Tawaaf* is a religious ceremony and it would be sacrilegious to violate it by engaging in unholy activities such as political demonstrations. The full translation might thus include at least the elements in Text $6B_2$.

Text $6B_2$

> The Iranian pilgrims began their demonstration during the sacrosanct ceremony of walking round the Black Rock in Mecca. . .

The semiotic entity which we have just discussed consisted of a discrete sign. But, as we suggested earlier, semiotic entities may be much larger, ranging from complete sentences to entire texts. One-line slogans (e.g. *Salford, the Enterprising City*), and entire political speeches in favour of the 'enterprise culture' are, each in their own way, a manifestation of a particular sign.

THE SIGN – A DEVELOPMENTAL HISTORY

Now that we have made a case for semiotics-conscious translating and the usefulness of the notion of the semiotic entity, it is perhaps appropriate to look back and reassess the origins of basic concepts such as sign and signification.

De Saussure

In the *Course in General Linguistics,* one of de Saussure's general assumptions was that linguistics would be taken as a model semiotic system and that its basic concepts would be applied to other spheres of social and cultural life. A shortcoming of this approach is that it places undue restrictions on the concept of the sign and related ideas. There are inherent risks in imposing a linguistic model on phenomena that are qualitatively different from language. De Saussure's basic definition of the sign as a junction of signifier and signified, when transferred to well-known social phenomena, becomes a futile exercise in nomenclature. To say that the signifier *al Tawaaf* (Text 6B$_1$) corresponds to the signified 'circumambulation' hardly improves our understanding of the concept. It ignores the connotative meaning of the term ('a sacrosanct ritual'), but, beyond that, it is also unable to cope with the term's place within a particular system of values which includes 'inviolability', 'immunity from worldly affairs', 'an apolitical stance', etc.

Similarly, the other basic Saussurean distinction – that between *langue* and *parole* – is problematic. The analyst is required to discern patterns in a 'system' (*langue*) which is the basis of speech (*parole*). *Langue* is viewed in terms of a code, whereas *parole* involves the exigencies of individual speech events. The opposition, however, seems too rigid. There is an implication that *parole* lacks structure, a characteristic which is restricted to *langue*. As recent work on communicative competence has shown (e.g. Gumperz 1982,

Stubbs 1983), this is untrue. There is now a vast body of work on the structure of conversations and the non-random nature of speech. In the domain of translation pedagogy, to take just one field of translation studies, the *langue–parole* distinction has given rise to views of translating as an operation carried out on *langue*. Hence there are manuals of translation which are based on language-as-system, with headings such as 'The translation of tenses' or 'The translation of adverbs'.

Finally, de Saussure's emphasis on the arbitrary nature of the sign has diverted attention from the important role of motivated signs in real communication. Motivated signs can be either linguistic (e.g. onomatopoeia, or even transitivity systems) or non-linguistic (e.g. a style of dancing). Within the Saussurean tradition, these are deemed to be impoverished in semiotic potential and therefore too unwieldy to be able to signify. Had this been the case, however, numerous fields of enquiry such as psychoanalysis, the study of ideology, literary investigation, theatre and drama, etc., would have been deprived of the insights which a broader conception of semiotics has undoubtedly brought them (see Silverman 1986). Semiotics transcends the study of language and looks at other ways of transmitting meaning in diverse cultures. Conversely, as de Mauro (1973:1180) points out:

> From a general point of view, verbal language can be specifically characterized only by comparing it systematically with other types of sign.

Peirce

Unlike de Saussure, Charles Peirce's approach (1931) advocates that we start with non-linguistic signs, then identify the status of language in them. It is true that these non-linguistic signs (e.g. social etiquette) do not readily lend themselves to straightforward and precise identification, and when they do (e.g. the tango or the foxtrot as styles of dancing), there seem to be no obvious implications for the study of language. Within a semiotic approach to activities such as translating, however, we feel that Peirce offers a way forward. His approach takes semiotics out of the narrow confines of the linguistic sign. Of course, there is a problem for the analyst with this kind of non-linguistic meaning. But the problem is not caused by some inherent imprecision in non-linguistic signs *per se*. Rather, it seems to stem from the imprecision of the linguistic terms we use to talk about non-linguistic meaning. In other words, it is a problem of metalanguage. The truth of the matter is that, in society, we are surrounded by signs of various descriptions. They are the essence of human interaction. What we need, so that we can impose order on this seemingly disorderly situation, is a set of coherent systems of classification.

In order to understand Peirce's position and be able to work with it, we must first of all recall that for Peirce all human experience is organised in such a way as to lead to the emergence of signs. The sign in turn is a triadic relation:

1. Whatever **initiates** identification of the sign (e.g. the colour gold in a Benson and Hedges cigarette advertisement).
2. The **object** of the sign (e.g. the product sample in the advertisement).
3. The **interpretant** or the effect the sign is meant to relay (e.g. the maxim in the advertisement). Generally speaking, the interpretant may be regarded as the meaning of the sign.

There is, however, no inherent association between an object and its interpretant. The link only occurs when it is so intended in some context. For example, the item *rigours* in the text we considered at the beginning of the chapter (Text 6A) is only associated with, say, 'liquidation' within a particular context serving a given ideological set of values. Likewise, the conventional sequence *I read with interest* can yield two different readings in two different contexts; 'I don't for one moment believe' in Text 6C and 'I wish to support' in Text 6D.

Text 6C

> Sir—I read with interest Dr A. M. Aly's review of *Islamic Medicine*, which appeared in a recent issue of *World Health Forum*. It was with some surprise that I read that "in no other major religion [except Islam] today is holy scripture being proposed, let alone applied, as the ethical and legal basis of medical practice."
>
> Judaism has dealt with the topic of medical ethics over many centuries. . . .

(*World Health Forum* 1984)

Text 6D

> Sɪʀ—I read with interest of the new development in village handpumps being carried out with the support of the IDRC, Canada.
>
> I agree with Sharpe & Graham that handpumps should be designed in consultation with the users, taking account of their needs and opinions. Here, in the Solomon Islands, I have been doing that. . . .

(World Health Forum 1984)

What is striking is that Text 6D is in fact a genuine endorsement of the Canadian experience, while *I read with interest* in Text 6C has a totally different value. In other words, expressions such as these interact semiotically with other text elements so that our perception of their meaning is closely bound up with the intended goal of the interaction. In addition to this **syntagmatic** association, there is inevitable association with other signs which could have been used but in fact were not (i.e. **paradigmatic** relations). This is the element of stylistic choice which assumes significance for translators in weighing up the value of signs in interaction. In Text 6C, *I read with interest* might have been replaced by *I totally reject, I cannot accept,* etc. The inappropriateness of these alternatives

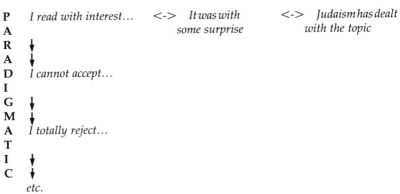

SYNTAGMATIC

P   *I read with interest...*   <-> *It was with*   <-> *Judaism has dealt*
A   *some surprise*   *with the topic*
R
A
D   *I cannot accept...*
I
G
M
A   *I totally reject...*
T
I
C
        etc.

Figure 6.2   Relations in Text 6C

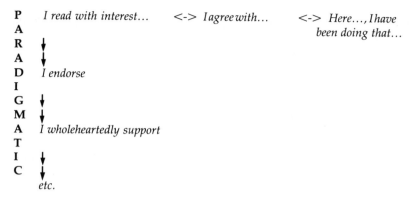

Figure 6.3   Relations in Text 6D

has to do with culturally determined semiotic constraints (i.e. the conventions of argumentation in Western culture). Figures 6.2 and 6.3 represent the paradigmatic and syntagmatic relations among signs in Texts 6C and 6D.

Peirce's interpretant, then, is primarily the meaning of the sign. As such, it is of necessity part of the paradigmatic set of meaning relations which help to define it. That is to say, the interpretant might be replaced by a number of other interpretants which are in a quasi-synonymous relationship with it. Translators pursue these interrelationships in an attempt to capture elusive shades of meaning and render sense across semiotic boundaries.

Barthes and myth

Peirce's 'interpretant' may be distinguished from de Saussure's 'signified', basically on the grounds that the interpretant is seen as having the quality of endless commutability, that is, it can constantly assume ever-wider meanings. The sign does more than simply elicit a concept. It is not an entity, but a correlation. That is, the sign, as the 'associative' total of signifier and signified, is potentially greater than merely the sum of its parts. A sign can thus consist of an expression ('roses'), and a signified ('a kind of flower'); in this case, the associative total may in some contexts be taken as the sign 'passion'. It is in this way that cultural beliefs are sustained. Indeed, whole myths can develop as a result. They may span centuries and cross generations, thus helping to define the value systems of entire cultures. Such proverbial notions as the myth of 'the white man's burden' or that of 'the noble bedouin' are examples of this cultural establishment of the sign.

Roland Barthes, particularly in his work on myth (Barthes 1957), pioneered investigations into what came to be known as **second-order semiotic systems.** These are systems which, in order to signify, build on other systems. Literature is an ideal example of such systems in the sense that, primarily through the element of 'creativity', it provides an alternative version of the real world. Thus, Beaugrande and Dressler (1981:185) define a literary text as

> . . . a text whose world stands in a principled *alternativity* relationship to the accepted version of the 'real world'.

But, by the same token, whatever semiotic factors serve to identify a text as literary also come into play in the identification of texts as being editorials, recipes, contracts, etc. In other words, as Lotman (1973) points out, all texts, fictional and non-fictional, have more than one organising principle at work: not only those of the 'primary code', but also one or more 'secondary modelling systems'. Thus, an editorial builds on a second-order system of persuasiveness, emotiveness, appeal, etc.

CONNOTATION AND DENOTATION

In introducing the notion of second-order systems, Barthes elaborates a signifying model which handles **connotation** as well as **denotation.** Here, the signifier and the signified work together to give rise to a sign which has denotative meaning. The resulting sign, however, acquires additional meaning. It becomes a new signifier in search of connotative meaning. Potentially, the process can be renewed several times, as additional connotative values are acquired. That is, signs are not static in the sense of saying, for example, a myth is merely a larger sentence or a wider concept. Rather, the myth is a qualitative reappraisal which shows that the sign, as the sum total of signifier and signified, can itself function as a signifier for a new signified. It is here that Barthes

SIG^r	SIG^d	
Col. Sanders	Military rank +Anglo-Saxon surname	

	SIG^r	SIG^d
LANGUAGE	SIGN = Brand name	The all-American idea, symbol of benign experience, reliability, retirement, gourmet-living,

	SIG^r, etc	
MYTH	SIGN	
	The secret of 'finger-lickin' good fried chicken	

Figure 6.4   Connotation in 'Col. Sanders Kentucky Fried Chicken'

does what Hawkes (1979:133) describes as taking us 'behind the scenes' of our social construction of the world.

By way of illustration, consider Fig. 6.4, which represents the routes by which a given myth finds its way into the collective mentality (modelled on Barthes 1959:115). Thus, a given sign may now be viewed not simply as the association of a word and a concept but as a self-renewing phenomenon which gradually establishes itself within the collective subconscious in a given culture. The case history of signs such as 'militant', (which, incidentally, may be translated into non-European languages as 'valiant' or 'extremist' depending on one's semiotic perspective), is a strikingly clear example of semiotic transformation and the development of myth. Such notions are central to the analysis of language and power (see Fairclough 1989; Kress 1985; Martin 1985).

What this implies for a semiotic theory of translating is that the concept of 'sign' is gradually giving way to that of 'semiotic entity' and, as in some recent formulations, to **sign**

function (see Silverman 1983). This arises from what happens when a given portion of reality (Hjelmslev's 'content plane') is subjected by the 'expression plane' to a process of segmentation. The resulting sign-functions are semantic units which, singly or collectively, constitute the filters through which a culture thinks, develops or decays. Figure 6.5 illustrates the process from the language of a current political issue.

EXPRESSION I

Islamic fundament-talists	A bunch of fanatics	Clandestine activities	Suicide attack	Death squad	Terrorist attack
SU1	SU2	SU3	SU4	SU5	SU6
	C O	N	T E	N	T
Party of God	Brothers in Islam	Prayer meetings	Martyrdom	Holy war	Self-denying act of heroism

EXPRESSION II

Expression I: Western media, etc
Expression II: Islamic media, etc
SU: semantic unit

Figure 6.5   Sign functions

BASIC ASSUMPTIONS OF SEMIOTICS

To bring to a close our discussion of the development of the notion of sign, we shall now attempt a résumé of basic assumptions underlying a theory of semiotics (see Sebeok 1986: 403–8). It is with these underlying principles that semiotics can hope to offer something to translators, interpreters and indeed all those who work with language.

1.   Signs refer to cultural structures

As Jakobson (1974) puts it, every sign is an act of 'referral'. This reminds us of the fact that Peirce's semiotic system differs from Saussure's most significantly in its emphasis on the 'referent'. On account of the triadic nature of the sign–interpretant–object relationship, signs do more than just elicit a concept. Eco (1973:1150) explains this phenomenon in the following terms:

> Independently of the ways in which they are used to designate objects or states, signs refer to the system of units in which the various cultures organize their perception of the world. . . cultural structures (the way in which a given society organizes the world which it perceives, analyzes and transforms) are semiotic structures and therefore systems of units each of which can stand for another.

2.   Semiotics transcends verbal language

Signification is not restricted to discrete elements within a given language, nor even to verbal language itself. It encompasses phenomena that may span the entire cultural universe. Within the remit of general semiotic enquiry, Eco (e.g. 1973) includes investigations not only of complex linguistic phenomena such as plot structures, categories of classical rhetoric, text typologies, etc., but also of all cultural phenomena (social structures and even economic relations).

3.   Basic mechanisms of signification are universal

The ultimate aim of a semiotics of culture is to isolate universal mechanisms of signification and discern patterns in the ways they operate. It is only by such means (entailing interdisciplinary effort) that semiotics can cope with the complex and varied types and functions of signs. This search for universal mechanisms will enable us to be more consistent in our description of seemingly disparate semiotic systems. Artificial intelligence, for example, has contributed in this respect by offering such concepts as **monitoring** (a mode of non-evaluative analytical exposition) and **managing** (which occurs when there is evidence that the discourse is manipulative) as universal semiotic structures which may be the basis for a typology of text.

4.   Context and co-text are crucial to the act of signification

Despite the universality of systems of signification suggested in 3, semiotics must constantly shift its focus of attention from single terms to co-textual and contextual factors. It is here that we can identify and attempt to remedy real problems of languages in contact and breakdowns in inter- and intra-cultural communication.

These and other problems have subjected sentence-oriented models of linguistic description to considerable strain. In this respect, semiotics offers an account of how particular modes of arguing, for example, are culture-specific and do not always achieve their goal across cultural boundaries (see Johnstone 1987).

SEMIOTICS IN TRANSLATING – SYNTHESIS

Our model of the process of translating must now be adjusted to incorporate the implications of this discussion of the scope of semiotics for the practical task of the translator.

Semiotic relations

Semiotics deals with syntactic, semantic and/or pragmatic properties of the sign. This means that the semiotic description of a given sign must include one or more than one of the following types of relation:

1. **Syntactic relations.** These obtain between one sign and other signs belonging to the same syntactic set. Linguistic expression provides clear examples of this kind of relation. Text $6E_1$ (a formal translation from Arabic) will be deemed less 'idiomatic' in English than Text $6E_2$ on semiotic-syntactic grounds.

Text $6E_1$

The President spoke to his people and assured his nation that . . .

Text $6E_2$

The President addressed the people reassuring the whole nation that . . .

In the source text, the possessive adjective *his* occurs twice to refer back to *President*. This degree of redundancy is not encouraged in English. The 'implicitness' and 'explicitness' of the pronominal reference in English and Arabic respectively are syntactic-semiotic properties of the signs in question.

2. **Semantic relations.** These obtain between the sign and those entities to which it refers in the real world. For example, whereas the English term 'propaganda' relays something negative that

one should beware of, the Russian equivalent refers to a legitimate and desirable function of government departments of information. We are here talking about semantic-semiotic properties of the sign, not only within but also between languages.

3. **Pragmatic relations.** These obtain between the sign and its users (senders or receivers). We can illustrate the point from the text fragment in Text 6F.

Text 6F

> . . . It is a curious system indeed which demands that tax-payers support private ventures when the latter should be generating not taking money.

To utter *it is a curious system indeed* and mean 'it is diabolical' can only be achieved in a context where the text producer is concluding an argument against a particular system. That is, it is only when two sides of an issue are identified, each displaying its own set of beliefs, that evaluative discourse materalises and pragmatic-semiotic properties such as 'understatement' are identified.

Two important points must be made clear at this juncture. Firstly, the description of a sign would be impoverished if it restricted attention to either the syntactics, semantics or pragmatics of the sign. To focus on one aspect is of course legitimate, but it should not be to the exclusion of other aspects. Overlap is inevitable. If we allow that intonation patterns form part of the syntactic arrangement of an utterance, the following example quoted by Gumperz (1977:208–9) is illuminating. At a major London airport, newly hired Indian and Pakistani women were perceived as surly and uncooperative when serving meat and asking 'gravy?' with a falling intonation pattern. This was perceived as an offhand statement instead of an offer which in English is usually made with rising intonation. Thus, in this communication breakdown, syntactic and pragmatic properties of the sign were involved.

Secondly, it is vital to appreciate that each of these sets of relations (syntactic, semantic and pragmatic) has a paradigmatic as well as a syntagmatic dimension. The do's and don'ts of TV interviews provide interesting examples of a semiotic grammar, semantics, etc., at work. (For an example that illustrates paradigmatic and syntagmatic semiotic relations, see Figs 6.2 and 6.3.)

SUMMARY

In this chapter, we have attempted to bring together the semiotic features of texts which are of relevance to translators. Let us recapitulate briefly. Taking the sign to be a triadic relation (initiator, object, interpretant, the latter being regarded as the meaning of the sign), we have seen how the sign involves connotative systems which ultimately lead to the development of myth as a cultural phenomenon. Let us look at a practical example of semiotic analysis along the lines suggested above. Text 6G is the opening sequence of a short story, translated from Bahasa Malaysia into English. A problem arises in the first sentence, to which we shall restrict our attention.

Text 6G

> In order to be blessed, Nyabung as head of the household, began the dance ceremony. He stretched out the long knife in his right hand and flapped the shield in his left. Suddenly, and simultaneously, a gunshot echoed at the west end of the hall. The *ngajat* (ceremonial dance) dance Nyabung was performing stopped abruptly.
>
> (Majod 1983)

The approach adopted by the translator in Text 6G may be summarised as follows:

1. In the process of identification of the sign as the first stage of semiotic translating, the translator perceives an initiator (*ngajat*), an object (a dance) and an interpretant (asking for the household to be blessed).

2. The next stage is to identify the essential information core which in this case is a 'ritualistic dance performed in order to bring blessing upon the household'.

3. Explication will obviously be called for since the relationship between 'dance' and 'blessing' is culture-specific.

4. In the process of transformation which follows, the translator opts for *dance ceremony* as the equivalent of *ngajat*.

But a problem remains. An essential aspect of this sign as myth is to relate 'a dance ceremony' to the act of 'blessing'. To convey such semiotic relations, signs interact with other signs in the source text. This interaction is bound to be manifested in the text by a variety of means, syntactic, semantic and/or pragmatic.

In Text 6G, however, the reader is left with the task of retrieving the cultural structure which relates 'dancing' to 'blessing'.

Syntactically, what is being asked of the reader of the translation is to establish a cataphoric (forward-pointing) relation between the subordinate group, *in order to be blessed,* and the main clause. But the relation is problematic. The syntactic arrangement does not entirely serve the purpose of the translation: viewed semantically, the link between 'dancing' and 'blessing' contained within the item *ngajat* is not paralleled by any TL equivalent. Pragmatically, the target reader is therefore prevented from participating fully in the cultural context which *ngajat* evokes.

Faced with problems of this nature, the formal options available to the translator could be listed as follows:

1. transliterate the initiator/signifier (*ngajat*);
2. relay information content only (dance ceremony);
3. give an indication of connotative value (the ritual of the *ngajat* for calling down blessing); and/or attempt to relay all or part of what participants in the source culture know of the sign as myth ('*ngajat*, which involves. . .').

While selecting option 1 alone is bound to leave an information gap, option 4 may not be efficient in certain contexts as a translation technique. The choice of one or more of these options will depend on a host of contextual factors including, most importantly, considerations of genre and discourse as well as knowledge of other texts.

In identifying what is appropriate in particular discourses and genres, one is automatically appealing to one's knowledge of other texts. This very important semiotic mechanism is referred to as intertextuality. In Chapter 7, we shall investigate intertextuality from the translator's point of view as an area where there is cross-fertilisation between semiotics and pragmatics.

SEVEN

Intertextuality and intentionality

INTERTEXTUALITY: ALLUSION AND REFERENCE

What knowledge does a reader need in order to make sense of Text 7A? How do readers call up their cultural background and knowledge structures in order to perceive subtleties of intended meaning?

Text 7A

> ### Terrorism was to become the keyword
>
> Not everyone feels immediately threatened by the Red Army, but every citizen gets on an aeroplane one day. There is every reason to think that the choice of 'terrorism' as the psychological theme was very carefully worked out. (After all, it has 57 varieties.)

(from 'No mistake: this *is* Reagan's foreign policy', *New Statesman*)

We have already seen how text producers and receivers exchange pragmatic and semiotic meanings. We have also seen how this activity takes place under all kinds of constraints – generic, discoursal and textual. An important principle which we have not so far investigated is the way we relate textual occurrences to each other and recognise them as signs which evoke whole areas of our previous textual experience. This is **intertextuality,** through which texts are recognised in terms of their dependence on other relevant texts. What is involved is much more than a simple process of text 'allusion'. Thus, as will become apparent, *57 varieties* in Text 7A above is in one sense a reference to a previous text ('Heinz 57 varieties'), but, in retracing the path to this reference, we are, to varying degrees, aware of a host of associations which have emerged from our previous experience (the way we have used the term or heard it used, including the implications of 'randomness', 'adhoc-ery', and so on).

APPROACHES TO INTERTEXTUALITY

Intertextuality provides an ideal testing ground for basic semiotic notions in practical pursuits such as translating and interpreting. It is 'semiotics at work'. In defining text, Kristeva (e.g. 1969) emphasises the process whereby a text goes back to what precedes it, adding to its ideologically neutral form the whole underlying volume of signification which accrues from experience, awareness, etc. This is in sum the function of intertextuality.

In current work on semiotic theory, Kristeva (1969) is the first to use the concept to refer to the existence of prior discourses as a precondition for the act of signifying, almost regardless of the semantic content of a given text. For example, the interpretation of seemingly simple references ('the token female', 'the fall guy', etc.) requires more than knowledge of semantic content. One needs to have experience of a body of discourses or texts which make up certain belief systems within Western culture.

THE INTERTEXTUAL CHAIN

To illustrate these introductory remarks, and establish a framework for presentation of basic notions of intertextuality, consider Text 7B, which is the entire stretch of discourse of which Text 7A is a fragment.

Articles from the British press regularly provide material for newspapers and magazines in other parts of the world and are often translated into other languages. Text 7A is no exception. But, one can imagine the problems faced by its translators. To make sense of it, text receivers must travel the whole distance from the 'ideologically neutral' denotation of language (i.e. usage) to the volume of 'signification' which underlies use. A chain of intertextual references will have to be pieced together and a thread identified, leading back from signals encountered later in the text to

Text 7B

> # No mistake: this *is*
> # Reagan's foreign policy
>
> *Washington*
>
> IN THE MOVIE version of Richard Condon's *Manchurian Candidate*, the poor sap who plays the Joe McCarthy figure gets all confused. One day he has to say there are 50 communists in the State Department, and next day his handlers order him to name 75. He fears that he may attract ridicule. 'You dummy,' says his ambitious wife, at breakfast, 'don't you realise? People aren't asking whether there are communists in the State Department any more. They're asking *how many* communists there are.' At this point, the husband's glassy eye falls on a bottle of Heinz ketchup. Cut to the next scene, where he solemnly announces that there are 57 enemies of the state holed up at Foggy Bottom....
> (*a few paragraphs later*)
>
> The chief ingredients of [Reagan's] doctrine can be, for convenience, numbered and placed in body bags:
> 1. Anti-communist subversion would no longer ...
> 2. Alliances with existing governments would be ...
> 3. The opinion of the press, of public opinion and ...
> 4. Terrorism was to become the keyword. Not everyone feels immediately threatened by the Red Army, but every citizen gets on an aeroplane one day. There is every reason to think that the choice of 'terrorism' as the psychological theme was very carefully worked out. (After all, it has 57 varieties.)

(*New Statesman*)

earlier signals and to the whole areas of knowledge being evoked, thus:

> terrorism's 57 varieties > > > solemn announcement:
> '57 enemies of the state' > > > Heinz 57 varieties
> > > > 75 communists, 50 communists, etc. > > >
> Joe McCarthy figure > > > McCarthyism > > > etc.

Schematically, the chain may be represented as in Fig. 7.1.

Three basic intertextual strands are on display here:

1. McCarthyism > > > paranoia, adhoc-ery, etc.;
2. Heinz 57 varieties > > > variety, randomness, etc.;
3. Reaganism > > > paranoia, random targeting of enemies.

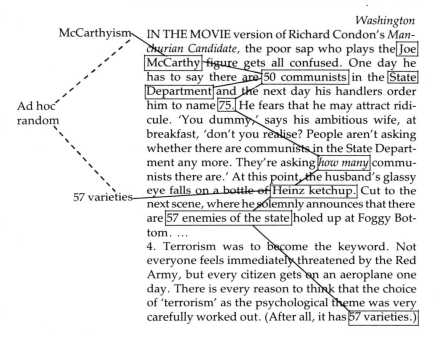

Figure 7.1   *Intertextual chain in Text 7B*

It is this intermeshing of at least three strands of reference to previous knowledge enshrined in texts we have encountered which confronts us as translators with a real challenge. A successful translation into any language, especially that of some non-Western community, is bound to be problematic. We shall consider possible solutions to some of the problems later on. For the moment, let us investigate further what is actually involved in intertextuality.

ACTIVE AND PASSIVE INTERTEXTUALITY

In the light of all this, we may safely discard the notion that intertextuality is some static property of texts, which in translating amounts to mere item-by-item replacement of a reference in the source text by one in the target text. On the contrary, intertextuality is best viewed in terms of semiotic systems of signification. In Text

7B, terrorism is seen as 'myth' (cf. Chapter 6). The producer of the text, in attempting to expose the myth, relates it to two other myth systems: McCarthy's ad hoc-ery and Heinz 57 varieties. Thus, readers' knowledge of previous texts is appealed to in order to achieve the producer's goal: seeing President Reagan's approach to terrorism as random.

The intertextual link is, in this case, strong, in the sense that it activates knowledge and belief systems well beyond the text itself. Intertextual functions, however, are not always as active. There are passive forms of intertextuality which amount to little more than the basic requirement that texts be internally coherent (i.e. intelligible). An example of this passive kind of intertextual thread would be the chain *poor sap* > > *confused* > > *dummy* > > *glassy eye* > >, which serves to establish continuity of sense. Awareness of such links enables translators to ensure that a similar network is reflected as far as possible in the target text. In other words, these are local solutions to local problems.

Translators have to learn to cope with the more passive forms of intertextuality. For example, reiteration of text items is always motivated. This form of passive intertextuality has to be considered by the translator in terms of its overall function within the text. Opting for a synonym or a paraphrase when what is required is verbatim reiteration can mar the communicative effect intended. During a televised face-to-face debate in the 1988 American Presidential election campaign, one of the candidates scored points over his opponent with the following incisive rebuttal:

> I knew John Kennedy. John Kennedy was a friend of mine. Senator, you are no John Kennedy. . .

Any translation which replaced the reiterated name by pro-nominal reference or variation such as 'the former president', 'Mr Kennedy', etc., would fail to capture the rhetorical effect.

Barthes (1970) extends this condition of intelligibility to include cultural and ideological significance, thus transcending the more neutral sense of the concept 'language code'. Intertextuality becomes more of a challenge when, as Barthes points out, cultural connotations and knowledge structures are incorporated into an intertextual reference. In this broader definition, intertextuality exercises an active function and entails the view that texts are never totally original or particular to a given author. They are always dependent on the prior existence not only of clearly identifiable texts but also of general conditions of appropriateness that may, for example, govern entire genres. Intertextuality in this sense makes it possible for us to situate a text in a system of relevant codes and conventions. It may take the form of imitation, plagiarism, parody, citation, refutation or transformation of texts. In the words of Kristeva (1969:146),

> every text is constructed as a mosaic of citations, every text is an absorption and transformation of other texts.

Text 7B is no longer seen only as a straightforward narrative, but occupies a new place in relation to codes and conventions governing the genre 'satire', perhaps even 'irony'.

TYPES OF INTERTEXTUAL REFERENCE

Lemke (1985) identifies two kinds of intertextual relationship that are over and above the passive–active distinction outlined above. Firstly, there are relationships which exist between elements of a given text, as when, for example, the argument of ten minutes ago is resumed or a reference (e.g. *57 varieties* in Text 7B) is taken up a few paragraphs later. The second type of intertextual relationship consists of those which exist between distinct texts. An example would be an argument resumed on a separate occasion, or, in Text 7B, re-using the original advertising text *Heinz 57 varieties*. Lemke suspects that the underlying principles regulating both forms of intertextuality may very well be the same. In other words, our recognition of co-reference within a single text is basically the same as our ability to classify one text in terms of another previously experienced text.

Such an approach to intertextuality would enable us to perceive relations between the functions of one discourse and those of other relevant discourses. It could be argued that these relations jointly contribute to the maintenance of such socio-semiotic structures as ideologies, power and cultural norms. Texts 7C and 7D are from annual reports of the Secretary-General of the UN in successive years (1986, 1987). What enables us to recognise a particular discourse in these two texts? How is an ideological structure defined and maintained? What are the intertextual relations that serve to ensure the continuity of particular social/ideological institutions?

Text 7C

> ## Report of the Secretary-General on the work of the Organization
>
> Regrettably, in marked contrast to sentiments expressed during the fortieth anniversary, 1986 has witnessed the United Nations subjected to a severe crisis challenging its solvency and viability. Precisely at the time when renewed efforts have been called for to strengthen the Organization, its work has been shadowed by financial difficulties resulting primarily from the failure of Member States to meet obligations flowing from the Charter. It is essential to lift this cloud so that the United Nations can, both now and in the longer term, be that strong constructive force in world affairs that is vitally needed in our increasingly interdependent world.

(9 September 1986)

Text 7D

> ## Report of the Secretary-General on the work of the Organization
>
> The United Nations has been an important catalyst for consensus on global problems and, at the same time is itself, I believe, the object of a greater commonality of view than when I last reported to the General Assembly. It remains prey to a financial crisis of very damaging dimensions. Yet, there has been a perceptible rallying to the Organization prompted, in part, by recognition that it was in serious jeopardy but, more decisively, I am convinced, by changes in the international political, economic and social situation which evidenced with persuasive clarity the need for, and the unique value of, the United Nations and other multilateral organizations.

(9 September 1987)

Both texts display a common discoursal thrust. At a time when the credibility of the UN is under threat, an attempt is being made to underline the need for continued support, both financial and moral, of the UN as an institution. The ideological stance being adopted is defence of institutions which cannot be expected to 'deliver miracles' or produce immediate short-term results.

In terms of intertextual relations, we can distinguish at least four different kinds of link. Firstly, there will be links to other parts (texts) of the same annual report. In this respect, it is interesting to note that both Texts 7C and 7D occur towards the beginning of each year's report, but only after a general statement of what the UN has achieved over the last year. Secondly, there are manifest links between Texts 7C and 7D as statements made on two separate occasions. They show the emergence and maintenance of the same ideological structure. Thirdly, there are subtle intertextual links between Texts 7C and 7D, on the one hand, and other non-UN annual reports, on the other, which all include expression of concern about financial viability. Finally, both texts relate to all such defences against pressures which push in the direction of assessing institutional viability in terms of tangible results only. (See also Fairclough (1989): for analysis of similar ideological structures.)

MEDIATION

Beaugrande and Dressler (1981:182) refer to the passive–active dimensions of intertextual reference in terms of greater or lesser **mediation.** Mediation is said to be

> The extent to which one feeds one's current beliefs and goals
> into the model of the communicative situation.

This is bound to occur when using knowledge of other texts relevant to the processing of the text at hand. When the distance between the current text and the previously encountered texts is great (through factors such as the passage of time), then mediation is said to be greater. For example, all that remains of some prototype of the 'comedy of manners' is the conventions of the genre itself. The perpetuity of genres or text types may be seen in terms of this extensive kind of mediation. Conversely, mediation is lesser in the case of quotes or references to well-known texts. Minimal mediation is also required in activities such as replying to, refuting or evaluating other texts in conversations.

The notion of mediation is a useful way of looking at translators' decisions regarding the transfer of intertextual reference. What is the degree of mediation involved in translating a Shakespearean reference, for example? Although it might be assumed that temporal remoteness is the overriding factor, there are other considerations which affect the required degree of mediation. The reference might involve minimal mediation by those who share, say, a Western culture, but maximal mediation for readers from other cultural backgrounds.

WHAT INTERTEXTUALITY IS NOT

It would be wrong to consider intertextuality simply as a mechanical process. A text is not merely an amalgamation of 'bits and pieces' culled from other texts. Nor should intertextuality be understood as the mere inclusion of the occasional reference to another text. Rather, citations, references, etc., will be brought into a text for some reason. The motivated nature of this intertextual relationship may be explained in terms of such matters as text function or overall communicative purpose. That is, one does more than just quote Shakespeare. One uses the Shakespearean utterance for one's own purposes. In the process, the utterance is bound to take on new values. Text 7E is a typical example of passing reference to Shakespeare in journalistic writing.

Text 7E

> Sir Terence Beckett, who as Director of the Confederation of British Industry might be expected to know, has called our precious stone set in the silver sea 'shabby and expensive'.
>
> (J. Mortimer, *Sunday Times*, 13.11.83)

Is the reference here intended merely to lend an element of authority to a committed piece of writing? The process is surely not so simple. Here, the citation . . . *precious stone set in the silver sea* has passed from one signifying system to another. In *Richard II*, it connotes values to do with patriotism. In Mortimer's text, however, it has taken on the added value of being satirical about the discourse of 'those who might be expected to know'. It is thus made to enter a new set of semiotic interrelationships including such oppositions as *expensive* ('not good value for money') vs *precious* ('good value') and *shabby* ('run down') vs *stone set in . . . silver* ('brilliant').

The intertextual process of citation, then, is not simply a question of association of ideas, something that is subjective and arbitrary. On the contrary, it is a signifying system which operates by connotation. It requires a social knowledge for it to be effective as a vehicle of signification. Each intrusion of a citation in the text is the culmination of a process in which a sign travels from one text (source) to another (destination). The area being traversed from text to text is what we shall call the **intertextual space.** It is in this space that sets of values attaching to the sign are modified. That is, the semiotic value of the source of the citation undergoes transformation in order to adjust to its new environment and, in the process, act upon it.

What is true of citations is equally valid for other types of intertextual reference. Intertextuality is a force which extends the boundaries of textual meaning. In *S/Z* (1970), Barthes describes texts undergoing this force as displaying through connotation a limitless 'perspective of fragments, of voices from other texts, other codes'. Indeed, the whole process may be seen as a kind of **code-switching.** There is, as it were, a shift from one sign system to another in response to a variety of socio-psychological circumstances dictated by particular communicative requirements. Text 7F is the full text from which Text 7E is taken.

From a semiotic point of view, the predominant 'code' here is that of the 'review' – objectively surveying a range of conceptual entities ('sayings of the week'). But in reviews, as writers and readers know, evaluation is ever-present in some form or another. Thus, there is another code vying for recognition. It is that of subjective assessment of what is being reviewed. At one level, the mere intrusion of an evaluative code is an intertextual process (cf. Texts 7C and 7D). In Text 7F, this manifests itself in the use of various evaluative devices such as *poor old, bad notices, charming and sensible.* Cited to enhance this evaluative tone, the Shakespearean reference may now be seen as part of the general strategy of subverting what could otherwise have been 'reviewed dispassionately'.

In assessing translations, the insight which all this provides is that

Text 7F

> POOR OLD Britain is reeling from a week of bad notices. Lord Lane, our charming and sensible Lord Chief Justice, seems to have suggested to a Cambridge audience that we have evolved into a nation of heroin addicts and pushers who spend our time watching video nasties and then rush out and commit the crime of refusing to co-operate with the police. Sir Terence Beckett, who as director of the Confederation of British Industry might be expected to know, has called our precious stone set in the silver sea "shabby and expensive". Mr Bernard Levin has said we are without enthusiasm. Mr Christopher Booker—"distinguished social commentator" according to the Daily Mail—has welcomed Lord Lane's "horrific picture of immoral Britain today". "There is", he writes, "a general blurring of boundaries which established right and wrong which is leading to a rapid erosion of family life".

it will be important to assess the extent to which the different codes have been maintained and how. Readers of translations need to be able to recognise what the reviewer's satirical stance is, especially in cases where the reviewer is less inclined to reveal his intentions than, say, John Mortimer in Text 7F. (For examples, see Texts $5E_1$ and $5E_2$.) Such important issues as the translation of metaphor and irony can also be seen in this light. We consider intertextuality to be a powerful tool for the analysis of all such problems.

CONTRATEXTUALITY

Social interaction by means of texts ensures that texts are related to each other in the cultural life of a community. Relationships are established and maintained, perpetuating socio-semiotic structures such as myth and ideologies. Systems that are capable of this 'assimilating' function, however, are also capable of doing the opposite: of preventing a particular text or group of texts from being seen as related to one another in any particular way (cf.

Lemke 1985). Thus, a politician may borrow an element from the discourse of opponents' ideology in order to strip it of what it genuinely stands for. This may be done through what at times amounts to play on words, as when the Conservative Party in Britain usurps a slogan of the Left such as 'Power to the People' and, in so doing, attempts to stifle opposing ideologies.

Translators and interpreters must always be aware of the motivation behind this kind of device. It is an important aspect of intertextual reference and, in view of the way it operates, can be referred to as **contratextuality.** The term covers all instances where speakers or writers systematically employ opponents' discourse (terms of reference) for their own purposes. Prominent figures in the Labour and Conservative parties in Britain, politicians from the pro- and anti-Sandinista camps in the USA, Christian and Muslim leaders in Lebanon, and so on, all attempt to 'hijack' each others' discourse in this way.

To sum up, the theory of intertextuality seems to be taking us in two different directions. On the one hand, it underlines the importance of the prior text, advocating that a literary text, for example, is not to be considered as an autonomous entity but as a dependent intertextual construct. On the other hand, by focussing on communicative intent as a precondition for intelligibility, intertextuality seems to indicate that the status of a prior text may only be seen in terms of its contribution to a code which evolves as the text unfolds.

It is this second orientation which, in our view, overcomes the limitations of a 'source and influence' concept of intertextuality. Coward and Ellis (   ) suggest what this new direction involves:

> Intertextuality thus becomes less a name for a work's relation to
> particular prior texts than a designation of its participation in the
> discursive space of a culture: the relationship between a text and the
> various languages or signifying practices of a culture and its relation
> to those texts which articulate for it the possibilities of that culture.

All these problems will be familiar to translators, who are, in any case, able to deal with intertextual problems independently of some theoretical precept. Individual solutions, however, tend to be instantaneous or idiosyncratic. In what follows, we endeavour to outline a more systematic procedure for solving problems of intertextual reference.

A FRAMEWORK FOR THE ANALYSIS
OF INTERTEXTUAL REFERENCE

A unified framework for analysing intertextual reference will primarily serve the function of identifying a number of *levels* within which intertextual reference is to be viewed. A convenient methodological device for handling intertextuality would be a hierarchy building up from the word, phrase, clause and clause sequence (as defined by Halliday, for example), and reaching the levels of text, discourse and genre (as defined within the applied semiotic model proposed here). In addition, a typology of intertextual signs needs to be developed and integrated within the descriptive framework suggested.

A TYPOLOGY

A typology of intertextuality, defined as 'the relation that the text maintains with those texts which have preceded it, inspired it, made it possible' (pre-texts) has been devised within literary studies. Intertexts are said to belong to one of the following categories (see Sebeok (1986) p. 829):

1. Reference, when one discloses one's sources by indicating title, chapter, etc.
2. Cliché, a stereotyped expression that has become almost meaningless through excessive use.
3. Literary allusion, citing or referring to a celebrated work.
4. Self-quotation.
5. Conventionalism, an idea that has become source-less through repeated use.
6. Proverb, a maxim made conventionally memorable.
7. Meditation, or putting into words one's hermeneutic experience of the effects of a text.

These categories do not, however, give the complete picture. They concentrate on discrete elements in the intertextual process instead of on the process itself. Lemke (1985) tackles the problem of intertextual typology on the basis of an additional set of criteria. The relationships which a community establishes between one group of texts and another may be described in a number of ways:

1. They can be generic (with genre membership as the basic criterion), e.g. reference to the 'committee meeting' genre.

2. They can be thematic or topical, e.g. reference to the bomb on Hiroshima.
3. They can be structural, displaying affinity of form, e.g. portmanteau words such as *Reaganomics.*
4. Finally, they can be functional, covering similarity in terms of goals, e.g. ways of saying 'I'm sorry'.

These categories, together with those listed above, provide us with a comprehensive system of classifying intertextual references. Nevertheless, it should be borne in mind that we are not talking about discrete instances but rather about sets of relationships that materialise only through semiotic interaction. It should also be remembered that the chain from pre-text (i.e. source) to host text is extended in the case of translating to include a target host text, into which the intertextual reference is to be rendered, as in Fig. 7.2.

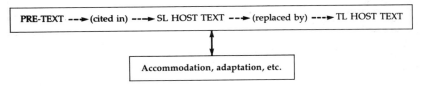

Figure 7.2   The intertextual chain

RECOGNITION AND TRANSFER OF INTERTEXTUAL REFERENCE

As we pointed out above, intertextuality is an aspect of both the reception and production of texts. Readers and writers wrestle with intertextual reference as an important aspect of text construction and deconstruction. In this final section, we shall trace the routes for recognising and transferring intertextual reference in the process of translating.

Translators encounter first of all what we will here term **intertextual signals.** These are elements of text which trigger the process of intertextual search, setting in motion the act of semiotic processing. An important property of these signals is that they are all tangible elements in a text. They do not constitute the intertextual reference as such but are crucial pointers to it (as in the case of *57 varieties* in Text 7B).

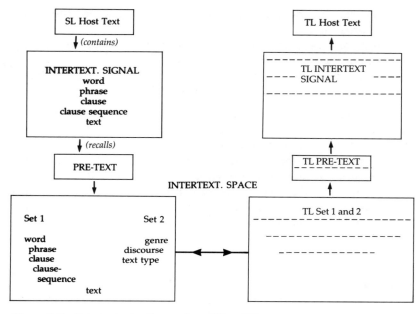

Figure 7.3   Intertextual reference from ST to TT

Having identified an intertextual signal, translators embark on the more crucial exercise of charting the various routes through which a given signal links up with its **pre-text**, or, as these routes are two-way systems, a given pre-text links up with its signal. Pre-texts are the sources from which intertextual signals are drawn, to which they refer, or by which they are inspired. In Fig. 7.3, we identify a number of types of pre-text. Set 1 comprises elements of the actual language system: word, phrase, clause and clause sequence. Set 2 includes units of a semiotic system: text, discourse, genre (see our definition of these phenomena in Chapter 4). In tracing an intertextual signal to its pre-text, the semiotic area being traversed is what we have called the **intertextual space**. It is here that text users assess the semiotic status of the intertextual reference. We suggest that answers to the following questions might form the basis of an inter-semiotic translation of intertextual reference:

1. What is the informational status of a given reference in the communicative transaction (features of field, mode, tenor, time, place, etc.)?

2. What is the intentional status of the reference in question as action?
3. What is the semiotic status of the reference as a sign 'interacting' with other signs?

The three questions may be put differently. Question 1 relates to the 'form' of the intertextual signal; question 2 relates to the 'function' of the signal; and question 3 assesses the priority of one over the other in the production of the sign. It is on the sign entity as a semiotic construct, however, that the ultimate decision bears: should the translator relay form, content or both, and in what proportions?

In other words, the principal aim is to evaluate which aspects of the sign are to be retained and which aspects must be jettisoned in the act of transferring that sign into another language. A hierarchy of preferences is developed which, in practice, seems to reverse the order of the three questions posed above: a translator's first responsibility is to the intertextual reference as a semiotic construct, which by definition involves intentionality. Bottom of the list of priorities would then be the informational, denotative status. For example, in Text 7E, whether the Shakespearean citation is rendered using an appropriate historical dialect, etc., is bound to be less important than relaying the intentionality involved. And, as we argued above, intention may be perceived adequately only within overall interaction.

The process is completed when the sign is subjected to a final, crucial procedure: a reappraisal of the contribution which that particular sign makes to the semiotics of the source text. This includes the description of the sign in terms of membership of a particular genre, discourse, or text. These membership values must be preserved as far as possible. If feasible, even the functional status of the reference as an item in the linguistic system must also be retained: is it a word, a phrase, a clause or a clause-sequence in the pre-text and/or SL host text? To sum up, the process of rendering an intertextual reference seems to be regulated by a number of procedures which we will illustrate from Text 7B.

In Text 7B, the first intertextual reference (Reference 1 in Fig. 7.4):

. . . *where he solemnly announces that there are 57 enemies of the state.* . . .

would probably be translated as something like 'reads out a random number, announcing that there were 57 enemies of the state in . . .'. Later, however, the rendering of the second intextextual reference (Reference 2):

After all, it has 57 varieties

may be rendered by whatever is the conventional way of denoting a random number (in French 36, in Arabic 60, etc.). The decision would in practice be tempered by the need to preserve the cohesive link between the two mentions of 57 in the source text.

With this example in mind, our suggested set of precedures may be presented in order of importance as follows:

1. Retain semiotic status: the sign 'variety' 'randomness' 'ad hoc-ery'.
2. Retain intentionality: the act of satirising the *ad hoc* nature of someone's decisions.
3. Retain linguistic devices which uphold coherence (e.g. Reference 1 <-> Reference 2)
4. Preserve, if possible, the informational status: the arithmetic of a given number.
5. Preserve, if possible, the extra-linguistic status: the genre of 'advertising'.

Schematically, the solutions to References 1 and 2 in Text B may be represented as follows. In Fig. 7.4, numbers refer to the above procedures, and a tick indicates that a given instruction can be observed.

It is important to note that procedures 1, 2 and 3 are basic in any rendering of an intextextual reference. Also of interest is the fact that, although the two solutions outlined above are not identical, the translator will have preserved not only the 'local' intertextual effects in References 1 and 2 but will also have upheld 'global' coherence within the text: in the same way as the second

	Reference 1	Reference 2
(1)	√	√
(2)	√	√
(3)	√	√
(4)	√	X
(5)	X	X

Figure 7.4   Translating the intertextual reference in Text 7B

mention of 57 varieties uses the first mention as a pre-text, the target text is able to maintain a link, albeit indirect, for example, between *60* and *random number*. Inevitably, the visual significance of the bottle of ketchup is lost in many TL communities, together with any other culture-bound evocations. But within the limits of translatability, semiotic status, intentionality and coherence have been preserved.

SUMMARY

The purpose of this chapter has been to look at a case of semiotics at work. The much-discussed concept of intertextuality, which has often been equated with mere 'allusion' to other texts, is now seen to be an essential condition of all texts. As users of texts, we all recognise and take part in the interaction of not only one text with another, but also one signifying system with another, both within the same language and across languages: the essential point of an intertextual reference is to analyse it in terms of the contribution it makes to its host text. In travelling from source to host text, the intertextual sign undergoes substantial modification of its code of signification. 'Variety' for Heinz turns into 'ad hoc-ery' in politics; 'patriotism' in Shakespeare becomes 'irony' in John Mortimer.

Consequently, no intertextual reference can be transferred into another language on the strength of its informational purport alone. In fact, intentionality normally outranks information content as it is the basis of the general semiotic description of a given reference. After all, what actually gets transferred is a sign that has brought with it across semiotic boundaries its entire discursive history including new sign values which it has gathered on the way. The translator in according priority to intentionality, will also make adjustments in the light of the fact that different groups of text users bring different knowledge and belief systems to their processing of texts. These are the issues which lie behind the translator's decisions.

EIGHT

Text type as the translator's focus

Many attempts have been made to set up a typology of texts, including some which have been used to form the basis of translators' decisions (e.g. Reiss 1976). But all attempts are beset by the same problems. Classifying texts according to criteria such as 'field of discourse' alone amounts to little more than a statement of subject matter, with examples such as 'journalistic', 'religious', 'scientific' text types. Defined in this way, text type, like register, is so broad as to have no predictive value. Yet when attempts are made to narrow the focus of description, we run the risk of ending up with virtually as many text types as there are texts.

Another approach based on an over-general notion of text 'function' leads to text types such as 'literary', 'poetic', 'didactic'. Again the categories are too broad and do not admit the possibility of a literary text being didactic and vice versa. In reality, far too many variables are at work for such all-embracing categories to be useful. The problem is that, however the typology is set up, any real text will display features of more than one type. This **multifunctionality** is the rule rather than the exception, and any useful typology of texts will have to be able to accommodate such diversity.

To account for the multifunctionality of texts, what is needed is a comprehensive model of context such as we have attempted to develop in earlier chapters. The most important feature of such a model is that it brings together communicative, pragmatic and semiotic values and demonstrates their importance for the development of text and the way in which communication takes place.

Thus, in looking at text types from the translator's point of view, we intend to examine the ways in which context determines the focus of any given text. We shall then see how this contextual focus is realised in the communicative plan of the text. The hybrid nature of texts proves amenable to a description of this kind. Shifts of text focus are motivated and our typology will allow for such fluctuations within an overall discoursal plan.

TEXT ACT IN INTERACTION

In Chapter 5, the new focus of pragmatic analysis was seen to involve realistic contexts of language use and to reflect users' intentions. These are preconditions for the appropriateness of a text to a particular discourse and genre. Ferrara (1985:140) defines the ultimate goal of text pragmatics as being the study of how entire sequences of speech acts

> are evaluated on the basis of higher order expectations about the structure of a text, and how they, being themselves coherent microtexts, contribute to the global coherence of a larger text.

Text, then, can now be seen as the bringing together of mutually relevant intentions. But, as we have argued in Chapter 6, perceiving the relevance of these intentions involves recognising their status as signs and the way these interact. Examples quoted earlier are good illustrations of this phenomenon which operates at word, sentence or even text level:

> 4% intended as 'a mere 4 per cent' (Text 4A, p. 55)

> *I read with interest* intended as 'I do not accept' (Text 6C, p. 109)

> John Mortimer's 'review of the week's sayings' intended as 'an indictment of those quoted' (Text 7F, p. 130)

Here, actual intentions are perceived as such only because of the status of the utterances as signs which are relevant to other signs in a given interaction.

The view we are putting forward here is compatible with the notion of the text act (see Chapter 5). The relevance of one set of intentions to another is established by relating them to an overall **textual strategy**. So, at any particular juncture in an interaction, a pragmatic focus is identified. The focus is likely to subsume a set of mutually relevant intentions and will define the type of text currently evolving. This is the basis of what we will refer to as **text type** – a conceptual framework which enables us to classify texts in terms of communicative intentions serving an overall rhetorical purpose.

For example, we described Text 6D (p. 110) as a genuine endorsement of the 'Canadian programme':

> I read with interest . . . Canadian handpumps

What, then, is the set of mutually relevant intentions which serve this overall rhetorical purpose? We can distinguish at least four:

1. to claim readers' attention;
2. to announce a topic;
3. to express support for a project;
4. to justify by argument.

Cumulatively, these intentions behave as signs which point to a single overall purpose. Despite the similarity to *I read with interest* which opens Text 6C, there is a clear opposition between the two texts as statements of rhetorical purpose. For practical purposes, we can posit a finite set of rhetorical purposes (e.g. narration) which we shall later put forward as our typology of texts.

TEXT IN RELATION TO DISCOURSE AND GENRE

The distinction between texts, discourses and genres was discussed in Chapter 4 in terms of the various semiotic constraints on the process of translating. Genres are viewed in terms of a set of features which we perceive as being appropriate to a given social occasion. It should not be assumed, however, that there is some simple one-to-one relationship between elements of lexis, grammar, etc., and the social occasions associated with particular genres. What have come to be known as 'found poems' (Porter 1972) provide evidence that genre membership of a given text is ultimately a function of users' intentions. The perceived meaning of Text 8A, for example, will differ significantly according to whether the text is intended as a note left on the kitchen table or a poem.

Text 8A

This Is Just To Say
I have eaten
the plums
that were in
the icebox

and which
you were probably
saving
for breakfast

Forgive me
they were delicious
so sweet
and so cold

(William Carlos Williams 1938)

Translators are aware of this multifunctionality and will seek to preserve in translation the generic ambivalence of Text 8A, thus allowing TT readers access to the poet's intentions.

Whereas the conventions of the social occasion are the key factor in determining genre, we have suggested that discourse is a matter of expression of attitude. Discourses are modes of speaking and writing which involve the participants in adopting a particular stance on certain areas of socio-cultural activity: racial discourse, scientific discourse, domestic discourse, etc. Discourses, therefore, are not independent of language, though they reflect non-linguistic phenomena. Work on ideology and power, to be discussed later in this chapter, has shown that certain syntactic and (far more commonly) semantic features correlate with certain discourses. In translating Text 8B, an extract from a speech by the British politician Enoch Powell, equivalence would be severely affected were we to ignore the specific discoursal values relayed by the italicised expressions.

Text 8B

Let us take as our starting point the calculation of the General Register Office that by 1985 there would be in this country 3½ million *coloured immigrants* and *their offspring* – in other words that the present number would have increased between two and three-fold in the next seventeen years – on two assumptions, current *rate of intake* and current *birthrate*.

(Enoch Powell, quoted in Sykes 1985; italics added)

This example of racially tendentious discourse may be compared with the italicised items in Text 8C below. It differs from Text 8B in terms of genre membership (not a political speech but a British-delegation reservation on the wording of a draft Programme of Action at a UN–sponsored conference), and also in terms of its discoursal values.

Text 8C

United Kingdom legislation seeks to ensure that *overseas workers* in the United Kingdom enjoy the same treatment in all appropriate fields as British nationals. This is, however, subject to certain limitations such as any sovereign State has the right to impose. The United Kingdom Government cannot recognize *family reunion* as a fundamental right, owing to considerations of public policy and national security . . .

Sykes (1985) discerns the dehumanising effects of certain lexical choices in Text 8B. Powell's systematic preference for the terms *offspring, immigrant*, etc. over alternative forms ('children', 'overseas workers', etc.) has the effect of degrading those referred to. The discourse is discriminatory. The discourse in Text 8C, on the other hand, may be described as 'non-discriminatory' (as defined by Sykes 1985:100) in that, it does not contain

any lexical or syntactic patterns that fairly systematically deny their human subjects the normal range of specifically human attributes.

Genre and discourse, then, reflect the social occasion and the attitude towards the occasion respectively. The social occasion is taken here to include how we do things with language when, for example, we write letters to the editor, letters of application for jobs or personal letters. Attitudinal meanings, on the other hand, emphasise the social significance of what we do with language when, for example, we write to the Press as 'antagonists' *vis-à-vis* a particular issue. Texts, finally, are perceived as divisions within discourses which signal shifts from one **rhetorical purpose** to another. Rhetorical purpose is here understood in the sense of the set of mutually relevant communicative intentions referred to earlier.

Consider Text 8D in terms of the interrelationship of text, discourse and genre and its implications for translation.

Text 8D

The influence of culture

[ABSTRACT]

A society's attitudes to health and disease are closely bound up with its culture. However, this culture is rarely static and can usually accommodate new ideas if they do not appear to threaten it. Whatever changes health workers introduce, they should always harmonize their activities with the culture in which they find themselves.

(*World Health Forum* Vol. 5 1984)

Translators of Text 8D must first perceive the social reality in terms of which the text is presented. This may be shown schematically as in Fig. 8.1.

ISSUE:	Can health workers introduce changes in traditional societies?
FOR:	Culture is not static
AGAINST:	The persistence of time-honoured medical practices in certain rural cultural environments is an insurmountable obstacle.

Figure 8.1   Social context of Text 8D

This particular issue could be presented in any one of a number of genres: an editorial, a scientific article or a political speech. But the choice is not entirely open (see Martin 1985). Some genres require 'commitment' in arguing for an issue while others demand 'impartiality'. The genre 'abstract', for example, normally requires that 'neutrality' be maintained. This will be apparent in the generic format and the distribution of content. Both the discourse and the text of abstracts, therefore, adhere to some principle of 'detachment' which ensures that generic meaning is conveyed. This may be illustrated by the way discoursal attitudes are relayed and the text is organised.

Within the domain of discourse of Text 8D, we have the items *closely* and *bound up* from the 'against' camp and *rarely static* and *accommodate* from the 'for' camp. Both sides are pitted against each other and the conflict resolved by the discourse of 'conciliation' towards the end. These several discoursal strands are organised into a coherent whole by the text, which serves a single rhetorical purpose. The issue presented and the case for and against are all brought together in a seemingly counter-argumentative format which in reality is neutral exposition. As will be argued later, had this text been a genuine counter-argument, we would have expected the case against to be developed and sustained before the text can reach a conclusion.

In the abstract, the view expressed in *however, culture is rarely static* is left largely unexplored and the reader is moved straight into the conclusion. This is consistent with the task of abstracting: to present the facts of the argument as they are. Any passionate appeal to either side, which would have been inevitable if one were to embark on a substantiation of a cited thesis, would compromise the overall effect. It will be recalled that in Chapter 4, the abstract, quoted as Text $4J_1$, p. 74, proved incoherent, in part because it violated generic and discoursal norms which adversely affected the cohesive progression of the text. Text 8D is a model abstract in that it upholds the standards of genre, discourse and text. From a semiotic point of view, generic, discoursal and textual considerations offer us distinct yet complementary perspectives on the process of communication. In what follows we shall focus on just one of these – the text as a unit of translation.

STANDARDS OF TEXTUALITY

In addition to factors which define textuality, such as intertextuality, a number of other principles regulate communicative behaviour. Beaugrande and Dressler (1981:11) identify these principles as 'efficiency, effectiveness and appropriateness'. As an abstract, Text 8D would not have been efficient had it involved the reader in a passionate appeal for or against a particular thesis. This would have entailed more processing effort than is needed in a text of this type. Similarly, Text 8D would have been ineffective had there not been an explicit means–end analysis to create favourable conditions for the perception of rhetorical purpose. Finally, the text in question would have been inappropriate if, instead of being a separate abstract, it had been intended to form part of the argument itself; it would have been too detached.

RHETORICAL PURPOSE

Our judgement of whether Text 8D is efficient, effective and appropriate is determined by our experience of having encountered texts of a similar kind. This heuristic procedure identifies what we have called rhetorical purpose, which is the hallmark of all texts. Text 8D, for example, is a summary of what was originally a fully fledged argument with the overall aim of 'convincing the reader'. But, while summaries are textual structures, activities such as 'persuasion' are essentially discoursal. Persuasion may be the goal, but in order to achieve it, a variety of rhetorical purposes may be employed: one can persuade by narrating, describing, counterarguing, etc. An entire argument, say in a newspaper article, is realised by a sequence of rhetorical purposes, each of which is implemented in a unit we shall label 'text'. As Kress (1985:12) points out,

> every text arises out of a *particular* problematic . . . [Texts are] the sites of attempts to resolve *particular* problems.

> (italics added)

The existence of a 'particular' problem is therefore a precondition for the identification of a rhetorical purpose. Upholding such a purpose guarantees what Halliday and Hasan (1976:1) identify as a property of all texts: namely that of forming 'a unified whole'. It should be noted, however, that rhetorical purpose, or the quality of 'being' a text, is not something inherent in a stretch of language but rather a property we assign to it in the light of a complex set of contextual factors.

DOMINANT CONTEXTUAL FOCUS

Rhetorical purposes, then, are located in text context. Werlich (1976:19), among others, bases a typology of texts on what he calls **dominant contextual focus**:

> Texts distinctively correlate with the contextual factors in a communi-

cation situation. They conventionally focus the addressee's attention only on specific factors and circumstances from the whole set of factors. Accordingly texts can be grouped together and generally classified on the basis of their *dominant contextual focus*.

The usefulness of this concept is that it helps to resolve some of the problems inherent in the multifunctionality of texts. It is sometimes claimed that texts are too fuzzy to yield distinct typologies, and that more than one purpose is always being attended to in a given text. However, although we recognise multifunctionality as an important property of texts, we submit that only one predominant rhetorical purpose can be served at one time in a given text. This is the text's dominant contextual focus. Other purposes may well be present, but they are in fact subsidiary to the overall function of the text.

For example, within news reporting, the dominant focus will always be on the sequence of events being related. Nevertheless, an evaluative strand will necessarily be present to a greater or lesser extent. The latter element is bound to remain subsidiary if the narration is not to drift into argumentation. Conversely, argumentation may, and often does, include a narrative strand (see, for example, Neubert 1985). In considering these elements as subsidiary, however, we do not seek to downgrade their importance. Indeed, the translator may in some contexts have to pay particular attention to the way a text's 'official' function is being manipulated.

THE HYBRID NATURE OF TEXTS

Texts, then, are units which are variable in nature, and text purposes may only be viewed in terms of 'dominances' of a given purpose or contextual focus. Beaugrande and Dressler (1981:184) point out:

> Some traditionally established text types could be defined along
> FUNCTIONAL lines, i.e. according to the contributions of texts
> to human interaction. We would at least be able to identify some
> DOMINANCES, though without obtaining a strict categorization for
> every conceivable example . . . In many texts, we would find a mixture
> of the descriptive, narrative, and argumentative function.

The hybridisation referred to here is of a fairly straightforward nature: a perceptible dominant focus is always present while other purposes remain subsidiary. There is a type of hybridisation, however, which is more problematic. It is what we may term 'intertextual' hybridisation. This is when, in subtle and highly intricate ways, a text is shifted to another type and made to serve another purpose without completely losing at least some of the properties of the original type. There will of course be cases in which the shift from one type to another is not so radical. These may be seen as borderline cases but the process of hybridisation is probably a continuum. This notion of a continuum is illustrated in Texts 8E$_1$ and 8E$_2$, both of which concern the French-Swiss writer J-J Rousseau.

Text 8E$_1$

> J-J Rousseau was the revolutionary, the impertinent who, for the first time, directly and effectively challenged the accepted rationalist view held by the enlightened century in which he lived. He made a real breach in that long tradition of reasonableness which, building up in North Italy before 1600, dominated the French and English academies in the seventeenth century and was carried on actively by Voltaire and the Encyclopedists in the eighteenth century . . .

> (from Bronowski and Mazlish
> *The Western Intellectual Tradition*)

Text 8E$_2$

> J-J Rousseau was one of the greatest of the European thinkers of the 18th Century whose writings inspired the leaders of the French Revolution and influenced what became known as the Romantic generation. As a philosopher, he tried to achieve a synthesis between Christianity and the Rationalist and Materialist thought of his time . . . In politics, his theory of 'social contract' went beyond both the economic liberalism of English thinkers and the Positivist attitude of Montesquieu . . .

> (from *Encyclopedia Britannica* 1974)

The essential properties of 'exposition' are in evidence in both texts: the first sentence in each sets a scene. However, each of these sentences proposes a different rhetorical purpose to be responded to in what follows. In Text 8E$_1$, the focus is on *the revolutionary* and *the impertinent*, which trigger the evaluative element in subsequent text. In Text 8E$_2$, on the other hand, subsequent text elaborates the concept 'great thinker' which creates the expectation that the various aspects of the 'greatness' will be listed.

Classifying Text $8E_2$ is not a problem in that the dominant contextual focus is clearly expository. Text $8E_1$, however, is hybrid. On the one hand, it bears a superficial resemblance to Text $8E_2$ and for that matter hundreds of other biographical notices, in that it relates who Rousseau was and what he did. On the other hand, there is already evaluation in the choice of how Rousseau is to be presented. Rather than *the greatest thinker*, Rousseau is *the revolutionary, the impertinent*, and these are the concepts which underpin the emotiveness of the subsequent text to such an extent that the dominant focus becomes in fact evaluative. Biographers or obituary writers, in their desire to uphold their commitment to the facts of the matter as well as to the subject of the biography or obituary, oscillate between factual writing and emotive partisan views. The dominant focus will depend on the degree of commitment the writer shows to his subject.

Translators and revisers, in seeking to reflect the dominant contextual focus as well as the other secondary purposes of Text $8E_1$, will appreciate the semiotic value of, for example:

X = *the revolutionary, the impertinent*
as opposed to
    X = (1) a philosopher
        (2) an educationist

What is in the first instance for the translator of Text $8E_1$ a problem of a definite article or a conjunctive 'and', has far-reaching implications. Important attitudinal values are involved. Here, as so often, a practical problem of translation brings to light issues which test existing models of language description. Descriptive categories have to be flexible enough to accommodate these real problems of hybridisation.

Hybridisation, then, is a fact of life and the very fact that it exists lends credence to the notion that we do indeed perceive texts as belonging to recognisable types. In the process of identifying a hybrid form, we are postulating a norm (i.e. a pure form) against which shifts of contextual focus (i.e. hybrid forms) may be studied. Text production is not entirely seamless.

TEXT-TYPE FOCUS

What we have been referring to so far as rhetorical purpose and contextual focus may now be conflated into a single term, **text-type focus**. This term stands for the means whereby a text is defined as a token of a type. The term subsumes the set of communicative, pragmatic and semiotic procedures which are followed when relating a text to its context. The basic assumption underlying a typology of texts is that

> texts in social communication always appear as manifestations of socially recognized *text types* (Schmidt 1977:54).

To illustrate these and other related matters, let us consider a case of breakdown in communication due to a misjudgement of text-type focus. Text $8F_1$, from an editorial appearing in *The Times*, was given as an on-sight translation assignment to a group of postgraduate translator trainees. The results of this case-study are presented in the subsequent discussion.

Text $8F_1$

The Cohesion of OPEC

. . .

Tomorrow's meeting of OPEC is a different affair. Certainly, it is formally about prices and about Saudi Arabia's determination to keep them down. Certainly, it will also have immediate implications for the price of petrol, especially for Britain which recently lowered its price of North Sea Oil and may now have to raise it again. But this meeting, called at short notice, and confirmed only after the most intensive round of preliminary discussions between the parties concerned, is not primarily about selling arrangements between producer and consumer. It is primarily about the future cohesion of the organization itself.

The Times

The majority of the twelve translator trainees tested in this exercise produced translations which could be faulted on the grounds that they misrepresented text-type focus. The result was a seriously flawed translation in which it was stated that OPEC's meeting was primarily about prices. Text $8F_2$ is a back-translation from Arabic of one of the erroneous versions produced.

Text $8F_2$

Tomorrow's meeting of OPEC is a different affair. It will undoubtedly be about prices and about Saudi Arabia's determination to keep them down. Undoubtedly, it will also have immediate implications for Britain . . .

To see how text-type focus informs the translator's decision-making in actual practice, it is best to consider the processing of texts on two levels which operate more or less simultaneously: macro- and micro-text processing.

Macro-text processing

As far as the reactions of our group of translators are concerned, misjudgement of text-type focus seems to have originated in a failure to appreciate the assumptions which readers normally bring to their processing of texts. For example, the title of the editorial (*The Cohesion of OPEC*) appearing in a publication which is independent of the organisation itself and at a time when OPEC was in fact in disarray (1981), should suggest that the central intention was to enquire into the organisation's claim to unity. Given these assumptions, a statement such as:

Certainly, it is formally about prices . . .

can only be an argumentative gambit, to be opposed in what follows. Figure 8.2 reflects the writer's intentions.

Field:	OPEC affairs as viewed by the editor of an independent national newspaper
Tenor:	investigative, non-official journalistic account
Channel:	*The Times* editorial
Pragmatics:	arguing that, contrary to common expectations, OPEC is meeting on this occasion to repair its internal disunity
Semiotics:	counter argument (as a sign)

Figure 8.2   Writer's intentions in Text 8F$_1$

Now compare the assumptions in Fig. 8.2 with the erroneous set of assumptions on which the faulty translations such as Text 8F$_2$ are based; these are presented in Fig. 8.3.

Naturally, we cannot assert categorically that Fig. 8.2 represents the precise and only assumptions which underlie the reading of Text 8F$_1$. Nor can we assert that our assumptions will always lead to correct inferences. The assumptions in Fig. 8.2 are no

Field:	OPEC affairs as viewed by the Public Information Department of the organisation itself
Tenor:	authoritative, official or semi-official views
Channel:	OPEC Bulletin
Pragmatics:	substantiating that, contrary to rumours, OPEC is as cohesive as ever
Semiotics:	official statement (as a sign)

Figure 8.3   Erroneous assumptions about the context of Text 8F$_1$

more than hypotheses to be confirmed or refuted, modified or jettisoned once reading begins and the realities of texts unfold. As Candlin (1976:250) reminds us,

> Interaction makes its own rules. We should therefore be cautious in asserting particular illocutionary forces, unless we are able to constrain the presuppositions sufficiently to make one reading most likely.

Micro-text processing

In terms of certain rules and conventions which regulate our knowledge of how the world works (the petroleum industry, the alleged disarray of OPEC, the nature of editorials, etc.), the headline of Text 8F$_1$ (which is probably the first element to be processed) opens up options for understanding the way the text is to develop:

Either:
   (A) question OPEC's claim to cohesion
Or:
   (B) expound OPEC's cohesion

The choice is made easier by our awareness of the title as a sign ('a cohesive OPEC?') and by our ability through intertextuality to compare it with the range of other possible signs (e.g. 'a cohesive team', 'NATO in disarray', etc.). Within the terms of the above option system, (A) is preferred. The title now reads as 'initiate a rebuttal of the claim that tomorrow's meeting of OPEC is about prices as usual'. A number of questions might cross one's mind at this stage. Why couldn't this title initiate an unbiased 'review of current trends within OPEC'? The answer to these and similar questions is provided by features of the communicative transaction that is taking place. These include the fact that the text is from an editorial and not a survey article, that the text appeared in *The Times* and not some OPEC-controlled propaganda sheet, and that, at the time, OPEC was in the news as an organisation in disarray. At the same time as pragmatic and semiotic values are perceived, communicative insights such as these are brought to bear on the micro-analysis of the text.

Let us now look at the particular portion of text under consideration to see how these expectations affect our interpretation:

Sentence 1:   *Tomorrow's meeting of OPEC is a different affair.*

To begin with, sentence 1 confirms the overall rhetorical purpose of the text which has emerged so far. As a topic sentence, it encapsulates the communicative strategy for the entire text (Werlich 1976). The key concept in sentence 1 which confirms the overall reading arrived at so far is the item *different*. The evaluative tone which this implies requires a substantiation: 'why or how?'. This is a rhetorical purpose which may be fulfilled in a number of ways. One way would be what we shall call the **through-argument**. This involves citing a thesis and arguing it through. Text $8F_1$ could be rewritten within this format as Text 8G.

Text 8G

Tomorrow's meeting of OPEC is a different affair. This time the meeting is primarily about the future cohesion of the organisation itself . . . .

In the actual Text $8F_1$, however, the process of substantiation is interrupted by a familiar argumentative device referred to in rhetoric as 'the straw man gambit'. This argumentative format corresponds to what we are calling the counter-argument. Here, a thesis cited to be opposed is followed by an opposition and finally by a substantiation.

Sentence 2:   *Certainly, it is formally about prices . . .*

This is set up as the straw man, a device which is used again in:

Sentence 3: *Certainly, it will also have immediate implications for the price of petrol . . .*

The argumentative gambit in sentences 2 and 3 now requires an opposition:

Sentence 4: *But this meeting . . .*

Figure 8.4 sums up the ways in which Texts $8F_1$ and 8G are developed.

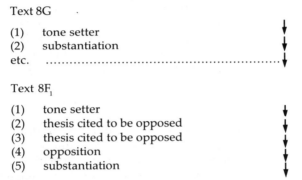

Text 8G

(1) tone setter
(2) substantiation
etc. ....

Text $8F_1$

(1) tone setter
(2) thesis cited to be opposed
(3) thesis cited to be opposed
(4) opposition
(5) substantiation

Figure 8.4   Development of Texts 8G and $8F_1$

The anticipation strategies at work in processing this portion of text are a good example of intertextuality. The signals are the actual items (*certainly*, etc.) which point to a hypothetical text type (counter-argument). Readers accommodate the intertextual reference on the basis of their previous experience of encountering this type of text. These anticipation strategies are particularly important in conference interpreting where text type provides an important indication of how the text is going to develop and an additional aid to better recall. Further research is needed into the psycholinguistic reality of these basic text formats and the ways in which conference interpreters automatically rely on them in producing simultaneous TL versions.

THE ARGUMENTATIVE TEXT TYPE

In general terms, the **argumentative** text type has as a contextual focus the evaluation of relations between concepts. Beaugrande and Dressler (1981:184) define argumentative texts as

> those utilized to promote the acceptance or evaluation of certain beliefs or ideas as true vs. false, or positive vs. negative. Conceptual relations such as reason, significance, volition, value and opposition should be frequent. The surface texts will often show cohesive devices for emphasis and insistence, e.g. recurrence, parallelism and paraphrase . . .

Text $8F_1$, for example, assesses the validity of the general assumption that all OPEC meetings are about prices. This assumption is contrasted with the facts of a particular meeting which is not about prices. Finally, to take one of the numerous cohesive devices used in the text, the repetition *it is not primarily about – it is primarily about* is particularly significant. It preserves the contrast iconically and thus functions as a sign of rebuttal which borders on irony. (On repetition, see p. 199.)

The serious mistake made by candidates in the translation test referred to earlier may be said to result from confusing the concessive *certainly, . . . but* with the confirmative 'it certainly is . . .'. This is more than a problem of English-language learning. In Arabic, the equivalent for English 'certainly . . .' as a concessive can be and often is used as a confirmative. It is only when text-type criteria are invoked that alternative ways of marking concession will be looked for, including syntactic as well as lexical means.

Readers abide by what Hörmann (1975:5) calls 'sense constancy':

> We expect what we hear [or read] to make sense, and we analyse the incoming message so as to conform to this criterion.

It also follows from this, however, that, whether initial assumptions about text development are right or wrong, readers tend to persevere with their initial hypotheses. Some of the translators of Text $8F_1$ forced the opposition (*But . . .*) to conform to their initial expectations by deleting the item *but*. (On this matter, see also Alderson and Urquhart 1985).

THE EXPOSITORY TEXT TYPE

Another basic text type is **exposition**. In this type, the contextual focus is either on the decomposition (analysis) into constituent elements of given concepts, or their composition (synthesis) from constituent elements (Werlich 1976). It would only take slight changes in Text $8F_1$ to turn the sample in question into well-formed exposition, a focus the students were probably trying to maintain. The difference between 'tomorrow's OPEC meeting' and 'previous meetings' could be objectively analysed in terms of a list of reasons, as in Text 8H.

Text 8H

> Tomorrow's meeting of OPEC differs from previous meetings in two ways. Firstly, . . . Secondly, . . .

Two important variants of this kind of **conceptual exposition** are descriptive and narrative texts. In place of 'concepts', description handles 'objects' or 'situations', while narrative texts arrange 'actions' and 'events' in a particular order. Whereas description and narration are generally easily recognisable, boundaries in other cases are more difficult to establish. What is of particular importance to translators is the distinction between argumentative texts (especially the 'through-argument' variant) and conceptual exposition. The difference between these two types can sometimes be subtle and therefore difficult to perceive. It is important, however, to distinguish between the two types; the following checklist of basic features may be helpful.

Monitoring and managing

In argumentation, the focus is on what is known as **situation managing**, i.e. the dominant function of the text is to manage or steer the situation in a manner favourable to the text producer's goals. In exposition, on the other hand, the focus is on providing a reasonably detached account, i.e a **monitoring of the situation** (Beaugrande and Dressler 1981).

Tone-setter and scene-setter

The topic sentence in argumentation 'sets the tone' and must be substantiated (as in Text $8F_1$). In exposition, on the other hand, the topic sentence 'sets the scene' and must be expounded (as in Text $8E_2$). Thus, through-arguments exhibit the pattern:

Tone-setter > Thesis substantiated

whereas exposition uses the pattern:

Scene-setter > Aspects of the scene expounded

In distinguishing these two categories, we have in mind the tendency of tone-setters to display such features as comparison, judgement, and other markers of evaluative texture.

Evaluative texture

Evaluativeness predominates in argumentative texts, realised by cohesive devices of emphasis such as recurrence or parallelism. More basic and less marked syntactic and semantic structures characterise expository texts. Other features which distinguish argumentation from exposition have to do with: reference to people, the semantics of the verb (perceiving, feeling, saying, and so on), frequency of certain syntactic structures (i.e. passivisation, transitivity, etc), lexical density of themes, modality, etc. (For more details of these and other features, see Martin 1985, Fowler 1985; and Chapter 10.)

THE INSTRUCTIONAL TEXT TYPE

One other basic text type to be identified in our typology is the **instructional** text type. The focus here is on the formation of future behaviour. There is an attempt to regulate through instruction the way people act or think. Two sub-types may be recognised: instruction with option (as in advertising, consumer advice, etc.) and instruction without option (as in contracts, treaties, etc.). We illustrate this type from another case of serious deviation in translation. Text 8I is a translation into English of a set of regulations. The translation shows that the text focus on 'instruction' is not adequately handled.

Text 8I

> IMPORTATION SHARE
> STATE PAVILION
>
> 1) State pavilions conforming to the conditions in these instructions are granted an import quota of ID 100.000 (One hundred thousand Iraqi Dinars) for Capital goods.
> 2) In order to obtain the quota mentioned in item No (1), it is a

condition to reserve an area not less than 200 sq m indoor or 500 sq m outdoor.

3) 'Likewise' is taken into consideration on granting important shares.

Apart from misuse of legal terminology (e.g. *likewise* for 'the principle of reciprocity'), Text 8I does not adhere to basic, conventional patterns of instructional text style in English:

1. *are granted* is not satisfactory in that it is interpretable either as 'have been granted' (which is informational and not instructional), or as 'shall be granted', 'are hereby granted', etc. (performative), an ambiguity which is unacceptable in this type of legal text.
2. *It is a condition to reserve an area* . . . would normally appear as 'an area must be reserved . . .' in an instructive text.

This kind of instruction without option may be compared with its counterpart, instruction with option, as in advertising. Here, structures similar to those found in sets of instructions are encountered. The focus, however, is on influencing opinions or behaviour and provoking action or reaction. For example, a slogan such as *Fly me – Air India* arouses interest and acts as an invitation. In this respect, instruction with option and argumentation have a lot in common. In fact, the two types are treated as one ('operative text') in the typology developed by Reiss (1976), who posits the following as the principles which all operative texts have to follow if they are to arouse the interest of the reader and succeed in persuading him or her:

1. Comprehensibility (use of short sentences, simple syntax, etc.).
2. Topicality (closeness to life, 'in'-words, topical allusions, etc.).
3. Memorability (rhetorical repetition, puns, rhymes, slogans, etc.).
4. Suggestivity (manipulation of opinions by exaggeration, value-judgements, implication, etc.).
5. Emotionality (anxieties and fears are played on, threats and flattery used; the associations of words are exploited).
6. Language manipulation (propaganda is disguised as information through means such as linguistic parallelism which is used to imply factual comparability).
7. Plausibility (appeals to authorities, witnesses, 'experts', etc.).

Despite these similarities, clearer patterns of logical thinking are more apparent in argumentative than in instructional texts.

Given discoursal as well as generic constraints, logical presentation tends to be part and parcel of the argumentative text format. These predominances need to be reflected in translation. If a counterargumentative pattern occurs in an advertisement, however, readers do not normally react to it by assessing its merits as an argument, but rather on the basis of its overall appeal, as illustrated by Text 8J.

Text 8J

Obviously the Legend Coupé does not boast quite the same devastating power as its racing relatives.

Nonetheless, its 2.7 litre 24 valve V6 engine will whisk you from 0–60 mph in 8 short but highly exhilarating seconds, with a top speed of 137 mph.

Enough acceleration, you'll agree, to satisfy even a Prost or a Piquet on his day off.

HONDA (UK) LIMITED, POWER ROAD, CHISWICK, LONDON W4 5YT.

(Reproduced by kind permission of Honda UK Ltd)

To sum up, the text typology proposed in the preceding discussion may be represented as in Fig. 8.5.

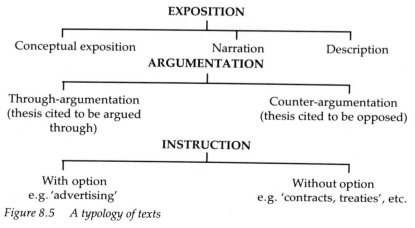

Figure 8.5   A typology of texts

THE PSYCHOLOGICAL REALITY OF TEXT TYPES

At two points in the discussion above, we have alluded to psychological factors involved in the identification of text types. The first is the language user's ability to recognise hybridisation by reference to some abstract, internalised patterns of text organisation. The second factor concerns the language user's ability to anticipate the subsequent development of text in line with these internalised patterns. In a sense we can spot the 'however . . .' that is to come, or the narration that will unfold.

It is no doubt in this sense that Werlich (1976:21) suggests that texts correlate with innate biological properties of the human mind:

> Texts, conceived of as assignable to *text types* primarily derive their structural distinctions (text structuring) from innate cognitive properties. Accordingly the five text types [description, narration, exposition, argumentation and instruction] correlate with *forms and ranges of human cognition*. They reflect the basic cognitive processes of contextual organization.

Figure 8.6 lists a number of cognitive properties associated with each of the text types.

Differentiation and interrelation of perceptions in **space** (description)

Differentiation and interrelation of perceptions in **time** (narration)

Comprehension of general concepts through differentiation by **analysis** and/or **synthesis** (exposition)

Judging: the evaluation of relations between and among concepts through the extraction of similarities, contrasts, and transformations (argumentation)

Planning of future behaviour (instruction)

Figure 8.6   Cognitive properties of text types

Beaugrande and Dressler (1981) build on Schank and Abelson's work on frames, schemata and plans by linking these global processing patterns to text types:

1. Description uses 'frames' of knowledge which state what things belong together in principle. Commonsense knowledge is promoted and no specific order for doing things is

emphasised (e.g. the frame involved in getting from A to B on the Underground).

2. Narration uses 'schemata' which establish a sequential order for the occurrence of events in terms of time proximity (e.g. narration of a particular journey).

3. Argumentation uses 'plans' which govern how events and states lead up to the attainment of a goal (e.g. criticising the inefficiency of the Underground system).

Although Beaugrande and Dressler do not deal with exposition separately, it is safe to assume that descriptive 'frames' or narrative 'schemata', envisaged in terms of 'situations' and 'causality' respectively, would be the patterns utilised in conceptual exposition. In the same way, 'scripts' (stabilised plans with pre-established routines) would be involved in the text type 'instruction'.

If these hypotheses are well-founded, the implications for translators and interpreters are obvious. Training programmes could do more to exploit these internalised norms, by organising programmes around basic types. It has been claimed (e.g. Reiss 1976) that each type calls on different sets of skills from the translator. The evaluativeness which predominates in argumentative texts, correlating with surface text forms such as recurrence, places different demands on the translator from, say, those of non-evaluative exposition. Further support for the psychological reality of text patterns has been forthcoming in recent years (e.g. Hörman 1975). But the precise structural distinctions in these patterns and the mechanisms whereby we recognise them are as yet insufficiently explored. Further research in this area might provide a sound basis for translation theory and translator training.

IDEOLOGY, TEXT TYPE AND TRANSLATION

Another fertile area of applied sociolinguistic research has been the study of text type in relation to ideology. Within our perspective, this warrants particular attention as the implications of the expression of ideology for translation are significant. Problems of text typology have obvious social implications. As Gulich and Raible (1975:147, translated in Schmidt 1977:54) point out:

> Linguistic barriers are probably less due to a lack of grammatical

competence than to the fact that certain speakers are unable to make use of certain text types, either actively or passively.

Martin (1985) reports on the results of a large-scale research project aimed at the analysis of factual writing among infants and primary school children in New South Wales, Australia. He notes the fairly prevalent preoccupation with narrative and expressive texts and adduces a number of ideological implications. Most important among these is the way genre is related to ideology. When ideology is challenged, Martin maintains, genres become implicated in a number of ways: which genres a group is able to use and which genres a group chooses to use. For example, a schooling system which does not expose children to a wide range of genres is unlikely to equip them to handle genres other than the most demonstrative. Translators and other professionals looking at language in terms of some of these complex social relations cannot fail to be aware of how language is implicated whenever the ability to use certain genres, discourses, etc., becomes an instrument of power.

Ideologies find their clearest expression in language. It follows, therefore, that the analysis of linguistic forms is enriched by the analysis of those ideological structures which underpin the use of language (Kress 1985, Fairclough 1989). In other words, behind the systematic linguistic choices we make, there is inevitably a prior classification of reality in ideological terms. The content of what we do with language reflects ideology at different levels: at the lexical-semantic level, and at the grammatical-syntactic level. To be meaningful, text features must be viewed within the necessary social embedding of all texts, since items considered in isolation will inevitably lack a significant ideological import. Whatever is said about the degree of freedom the translator has, the fact remains that reflecting the ideological force of the words is an inescapable duty. To illustrate this kind of language use, we return to Sykes's (1985) analysis of a speech by Enoch Powell. This time, our interest lies in the important translation problems which such a discourse entails. The extract is a continuation of Text 8B.

Text 8K

The first assumption is that the rate of net inflow continues as at present. It has not indeed diminished since the estimate was made, but I am willing to suppose that, especially with the substantially greater limitations which a Conservative government has undertaken to apply, the rate would be markedly reduced during the period in question. For the purposes of argument I will suppose that it falls at a steady rate from 60,000 in 1968 to nil by 1985. In that case the total of the latter year would be reduced by about half-a-million, that is to 3 million.

I now turn to the second and more crucial assumption, the birthrate . . . There are grounds for arguing that the immigrant birthrate is likely to rise during the next two or three decades; for instance the proportion of females must increase as dependants join male workers, so that a given total of immigrant population will yield more family units.

(Enoch Powell, quoted in Sykes 1985)

Working with a text such as this inevitably involves us in the various sign systems which it contains and the relations between the signs and their user. The various lexical and syntactic selections take on ideological significance by virtue of the way they participate in these pragmatic and semiotic systems.

Lexical choice

Sykes (1985) identifies a number of interesting lexical and syntactic features. The strategy adopted in the identification of discriminatory lexicalisation is to study the range of lexical items actually used in relation to the range of items that could have been used. Figure 8.7 assesses Powell's lexicon for

included	excluded
immigrants and their offspring	husbands
the offspring of immigrants	wives
immigrant offspring	mothers
children born to immigrants	fathers
children who have immigrated	parents
Asian and West Indian children	sons
of school age	daughters
females	families
dependants	etc.
male workers	
family units	

Figure 8.7   Lexical selections

family relationships in terms of items included (preferred) in the entire speech from which the extracts are taken and counterparts excluded (avoided).

The pattern of lexical choice which emerges from a study of these forms is one of using terms which denote only formal, legal or biological relationships and excluding those which relate more to family bonds.

Sykes also observes the tendency in Powell's speech to describe immigrants and immigration in terminology more suitable for inanimate objects: *current rate of intake, the rate of net inflow, the total, a given total of immigrant population, yield, family units*. These and other features of lexical choice demonstrate the discursive processes at work which reflect the ideological position of the users. It would indeed diminish the adequacy of the target text if the translator of Text 8K did not take into consideration the motivation behind the use of these lexical items. Translating the term *offspring* (Text 8B), for example, is a problem in that there may be no obvious equivalent. The apparent solution, to opt for 'children' as a synonym in another language, would ignore the whole point of the choice made in the first place.

Syntactic selections

A number of researchers have identified the expressive function performed by syntactic structures *vis-à-vis* their referents. Fowler (1985:66) maintains that

> . . . the major part of linguistic structure can be explained as responding to the needs of the society that uses the language – including, most importantly, the ideological needs . . .

This aspect of text constitution as a reflection of ideology can also be seen in Powell's speech. Sykes identifies a number of syntactic means by which the humanity of immigrants is minimised. This involves the use of constructions which allow the elimination of the human participants involved:

1. **lexical cohesion** established through the use of superordinate terms such as *number(s), total(s), proportions(s), rate(s)* as the subject of sentences;
2. the use of **nominalisations** with agent deletions (*inflow*).

If translators were to intrude by supplying the referents in 1 or opting for an active verb with immigrants as subjects in 2, they would inevitably compromise the ideological thrust of the source text. This should not be misconstrued as advice to translators to opt for preserving surface similarities of form (e.g. always retain passives, etc.). What is at stake here are coherence relations. So long as these are preserved, translators are free to avail themselves of whatever surface manifestations the target language offers them.

Choice of text type

In the expression of ideology, choice of which text type to employ becomes a crucial issue. Martin (1985:47) suggests that the use of

> Analytical Exposition tends to support the status quo, while Hortatory Exposition tends to challenge it.

But, given the hybrid nature of texts, there are interesting cases where one text type is used to mask the rhetorical purpose of another. What Powell seems to be doing in Text 8K is to use analytical exposition for the purposes of presenting as immutably given a set of contentious propositions. We normally expect contentious issues to be debated through argumentation. By the same token, we normally expect analytical exposition to relay the facts as they are. But expert arguers succeed in debating contentious issues through seemingly detached analysis. The deliberate ambivalence in this particular kind of hybridisation is clearly ideological. The subtle balance has to be reflected in translation, in the same way as the ideological import of individual lexical items. Awareness of text-type focus, therefore, is seen to be an important part of the translator's skills.

NINE

Prose designs: text structure in translation

PRINCIPLES OF COMPOSITION

Within the model of the translation process presented in this book, **text structure** refers to the hierarchical principles of composition. Text is composed of a series of sentences which together serve some overall rhetorical purpose. When we first approach a text, we identify series of words, phrases, clauses, etc., in the order in which they appear on the page. But the linear progression of these text elements does not tell the whole story. We are conscious that each element is active in fulfilling a rhetorical function. That is, each element enters into a discourse relation with other elements. The discourse relations enable us to identify **sequences** of elements which ultimately make up the unit text.

To illustrate the grouping of elements into sequences, let us consider Text 9A, which is an informative account of the activities of the Arab Monetary Fund.

Text 9A

The Arab Monetary Fund was set up by the Arab League states and is partly modelled on the International Monetary Fund (IMF). Its main aims are to provide soft credit to members with serious balance of payments deficits and to help in co-ordinating long-term Arab economic, financial and monetary policies. It does not finance development projects directly and uses its own currency, the Arab Accounting Dinar (AAD), for lending.

(*Arab-British Commerce* 1981)

We can characterise the individual elements of the text as in Fig. 9.1.

E1: establishment of the Fund (*The AMF was set up …*)

E2: establishment of the Fund (*… and is partly modelled …*)

E3: Aim (*Its main aims are to provide …*)

E4: Aim (*… and to help …*)

E5: mode of operation (*It does not finance …*)

E6: mode of operation (*… and uses its own currency …*)

Figure 9.1

The list of topics in Fig. 9.1, however, does not fully reflect the intended function of the various elements. We perceive a link between E1 and E2 which is quite different from the link between, say, E5 and E6. The mention of the Fund's own currency is closely related to the statement that the Fund does not finance projects directly. Taken together, these two elements realise a sequence which serves a single purpose: to explain the mode of operation. The discourse relation involved here is that of cause–effect. From the translator's point of view, it will be important to spot this relationship so that it can be relayed implicitly or explicitly in the target text. Figure 9.2 presents the three structural entities we have identified.

A different aspect of text structure is highlighted by texts such as $9B_1$ and $9B_2$. They illustrate that different structural norms operate in different languages and show how translators cope with the problem.

Element 1 AND Element 2	Sequence I	
Element 3 AND Element 4	Sequence II	Text
Element 5 SINCE Element 6	Sequence III	

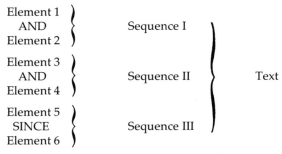

Numbers (1, 2, 3, etc.) represent the lowest level of individual elements (phrases, clauses, etc.). Roman numerals represent sequences of elements which display higher-order discourse relations.

Figure 9.2

Text 9B$_1$ (published translation from Arabic)

FRENCH INSURANCE COMPANY SUSTAINS HUGE LOSSES

I
- E1. Claims on the French Insurance Association, COFACE,
- E2. over exports to countries unable to discharge their debts,
- E3. with Poland at the head,
- E4. reached a record five billion francs,
- E5. according to statistics
- E6. issued on Thursday to the press by the chiefs of this association.

II
- E7. The state-controlled French Insurance Company for Foreign Trade
- E8. has paid out this sum in compensation . . .

III
- E9. It is known that the state controls COFACE,
- E10. which covers 30% to 40% of French exports,
- E11. 70% of which are to Third World countries.

(*Pragnell 1984*)

Text 9B$_2$: (suggested revision of Text 9B$_1$)

I   E1–E6 (as above)

II
- E7. This sum has been paid out in compensation
- E8. by the state-controlled French Company for Foreign Trade
- E9. which covers 30% to 40% of French exports,
- E10. 70% of which are to Third World countries

Our partial revision of Text 9B$_1$ bears on the structural status of 'background information' in English news reporting. Leaving aside other structural modifications which might be deemed necessary, let us concentrate on how sequence III in Text 9B$_1$ is incorporated into sequence II of Text 9B$_2$ as background information. Two different hierarchic designs emerge. But only that of Text 9B$_2$ is appropriate to the genre of news reporting in English. The inappropriate structuring of Text 9B$_1$ is of a kind commonly found in unrevised translated news reports from a range of languages. Payne (1987:147–9) provides a telling example of inappropriate structure in an expository text translated from Hungarian. Text 9C$_1$ relegates to the status of background information an element which properly belongs to an initial statement of topic. Text 9C$_2$ is Payne's suggested revision.

Text 9C$_1$

> Hungary's geographic situation is very unfavourable from the aspect of environmental protection. The majority of rivers are polluted when they reach the borders of the country, and atmospheric currents polluted by acid rain do not bypass the Danubian basin. Consequently, not only international economic relations are indispensable for Hungary, *which is a basin in East Central Europe.*

(italics added)

Text 9C$_2$

> Hungary is a basin in East Central Europe. Its geographical situation is therefore very favourable . . .

It will be apparent from these examples that the task of the reviser does not stop at tidying up terminology, clichés, etc., but includes an important element of text structure. In what follows, we shall be looking at how translators handle text structure in the light of their awareness of context in general and text-type focus in particular. We shall be asking the following questions:

1. What motivates a revising decision such as those taken in Texts 9B$_2$ and 9C$_2$?
2. What are the criteria upon which translators and revisers reconstruct text structure?
3. What modifications, if any, must be made, and how, in order to produce text structures appropriate to the target language?
4. What is the role of pragmatic and semiotic values in determining the appropriateness of a given structure?
5. How is the notion of text type used in attempting to convey subtle contextual differences?
6. Does the structural organisation opted for have an effect on cohesion and coherence?

These questions are germane to an understanding of the intimate relationship between context, structure and texture.

HOW CONTEXT INFLUENCES THE STRUCTURE OF TEXTS

It will be recalled that we defined context in Chapter 3 in terms of three basic dimensions, as in Figure 9.3.

communicative dimension (transaction)
field
mode
tenor

pragmatic dimension (action)
intentionality
speech act sequence
implicature
inference

semiotic dimension (interaction)
intertextuality
signs
genres
discourses
texts

Figure 9.3

These contextual factors are probably universal features of language use; ways of realising them, however, may not be. Cultural context is, then, an important factor in determining structural arrangement so that, for the translator, the important question will be: what is the status of any given structure in the actual process of translating. Where two languages do not share a structural pattern, what is the translator's room for manoeuvre in making modifications?

To answer questions such as these, we have firstly to consider the relationship between context and structure. In this book, following Hasan (e.g. 1985), we submit that use of any given structure is motivated by the way text users react to context. More specifically, users pursue a rhetorical purpose which becomes the focus of a particular text type. As we argued in Chapter 8, this focus reflects the way a given culture organises textual material in terms of signs. We recognise these signs within familiar generic, discoursal and textual structures. The underlying principle of this whole process is intertextuality, our ability to recognise and produce texts as tokens of a type.

Another factor involved in our choice of particular structures is intentionality. Together, the signs and the intentions behind their use ensure successful communication. For example, in courtroom interaction, the intention 'to raise an objection' is effectively relayed only when it is recognised as a sign. Activities such as 'objecting' display their own structural formats, and structure becomes an important indicator of what is going on in interaction.

CONTEXTUAL CONFIGURATION

How do the various contextual variables find expression in structure and, ultimately, in texture? As we suggested in Chapter 8, 'register' provides an ideal link between context and text structure. Hasan (e.g. 1977) introduces the term **contextual configuration** to refer to those values from the whole range of field, tenor or mode, actually selected in any particular instance of communication (text) within a particular discourse or genre. Thus, it is important to realise that the contextual configuration is a concrete representation, relevant only to one specific instance within a particular genre. By way of illustration, Hasan (1977:234) provides a characterisation of a text which begins with 'Good morning > Dr Scott's clinic > May I help you?'. This is reproduced in Fig. 9.4.

— good morning *(G)* Dr Scott's clinic *(I)* may I help you *(Q)*
— oh hello good morning *(G)* this is Mrs Lee speaking *(I)* I wonder if I could see Dr Scott today *(A)*
— um well let me see I'm afraid Mrs Lee I don't have much choice of time today would 6:15 this evening suit you *(O)*
— yes, that'll be fine *(C)*
— may I have your address and phone number please *(D)*
— 24 May Avenue, North Clyde and the number is 527.2755 *(D)*
— thank you *(D)* so that's Mrs Lee for Dr Scott at 6:15 this evening *(S)*
— mm yes thanks *(F)*
— thank you *(F)*

(from *Hasan* 1977:234)

Key: I = Identification, A = Application,
        O = Offer, C = Confirmation,
        G = Greeting, Q = Query,
        D = Documentation, S = Summary,
        F = Finis

Figure 9.4

Two basic characteristics of text structure emerge. Firstly, associated with each genre is a typical **format** (or **generic structure**) which is generalisable and which accommodates a number of actual structures (in the above instance, the format is: greeting > identification > query). Secondly, there are certain obligatory features which a text must display if it is to be recognised as belonging to the set of texts in question (in the above instance, while greeting may be optional, identification must be present for the text to be perceived as complete). As Hasan (1977:229) puts it:

> A text will be perceived as incomplete if only a part of some recognizable actual structure is realized in it; and the generic provenance of the text will remain undetermined if the part so realized is not even recognizable as belonging to the distinct actual structure.

Contextual configuration, then, is 'an account of the significant attributes of social activity' (Halliday and Hasan 1985:56). To be relevant to the analysis of text structure, however, the significant attributes must include such factors as how a social activity conforms to institutional norms. **Agent roles**, such as 'vendor' and 'customer', are relevant to the unfolding of communication and, consequently, must be included in any consideration of field of discourse. This institutionalisation of the social activity is also associated with the degree of **control** or **power** to be exercised (e.g. hierarchic vs non-hierarchic), as well as **social distance,** both of which are variables of tenor. All these factors affect the format of the text (see also Brown and Levinson 1978, on 'face-saving', 'hedging', 'imposition', etc.). Finally, notions such as **language role** (is language constitutive of or ancillary to the activity?) and **channel** (what is the vehicle of the message?) are fundamental to the analysis of text formats from the perspective of mode.

THE LIMITS OF STRUCTURE MODIFICATION

It is only within such a framework that the various signals of structure (optional elements, obligatory elements, etc.) become meaningful. In fact, these features and the way they are used are of central importance to the translator, who is constantly assessing the status of obligatory and optional elements as well as that of order and iteration. What, then, are the options the translator faces? We suggest they are as follows:

1. Is the element being translated obligatory or optional in the TL text format?
2. If it is obligatory, is the order in which it occurs appropriate for the TL text format?
3. If it is obligatory and the order is appropriate, will iteration, if there is any, be appropriate in the TL text format?

This assessment is carried out under all kinds of generic, discoursal and textual constraints. As an illustration of points 1 and 2, compare the italicised sentences in Texts $9D_1$ and $9D_2$.

Text $9D_1$

THE UNIVERSITIES AND HEALTH FOR ALL

> By common consent, the tripartite functions of higher education in most societies are those of education, research and service. *Academia in today's university has little difficulty in perceiving its obligations with respect to the first two.* Not so, however, the issue of service, which is often seen as a distraction . . .

> (*World Health Forum* 1986; italics added)

Text $9D_2$ (English back-translation of a rendering of Text D_1 into another language)

> By common consent, the tripartite functions of higher education in most societies are those of education, research, and service. However, *academia in today's university, which has little difficulty in perceiving its obligations with respect to the first two functions,* does not look at the issue of service in the same way. Indeed it often sees it as a distraction. (Italics added)

The interesting point about the translation is the structural modification involved in the italicised sequence. It affects the initial proposition (the 'citation of the thesis'), which in Text $9D_1$ is as follows:

I. {
1. *By common consent, the tripartite functions . . .* (thesis – general)
2. *Academia in today's university has little difficulty in perceiving . . .* (thesis – specific)

II.   3. *Not so, however, the issue of service . . .* (opposition)

Text 9D$_2$, on the other hand, displays the following structural arrangement of elements:

I.   1.   *By common consent, the tripartite function* . . . (thesis
           – general)

      2.   *However, academia in today's university, [. . .], does not
           look at the issue of service* . . . (opposition)

II.   3.   *[which has little difficulty in perceiving],* . . . (concessive
           parenthesis within the opposition)

What has happened in this translation is that an important part of the thesis (the specific thesis):

Academia in today's university has little difficulty . . .

has been downgraded to a parenthetic concession within the opposition which follows. That is, while Text 9D$_1$ deals with all concessions before the opposition is made, Text 9D$_2$ postpones an important concession and relegates it to the status of a mere circumstantial detail.

The translator, no doubt, has considered the sequencing of the ST element in question to be optional. It may, of course, be the case that a particular structural change is encouraged or even favoured by conventional TL structure formats. However, we submit that:

Although different languages may prefer different structural formats, ultimately, the limits on structure modification in translation are reached when the rhetorical purpose of the ST begins to be compromised. In such cases, the SL format must be considered the overriding factor.

We feel that this is what happened in Text 9D$_2$. The balance between opposing arguments is upset and a different message has emerged. In general terms, however, relatively little is known about the differences in the ways text structures develop in different languages. Further research in contrastive text structure is called for in order to determine the constraints on structural modification in translation between particular language pairs.

HOW ELEMENTS ARE GROUPED INTO SEQUENCES

We use the term 'element' to refer to one of the constituents of text structure. Rather than equating an element with any particular grammatical unit (phrase, clause, etc.), we prefer to see it as the smallest lexico-grammatical unit which can fulfil some rhetorical function, significantly contributing to the overall rhetorical purpose of the text. Each element marks a stage in the progression of a text. For example, *not so, however, the issue of service*, in Text 9D₁ above, constitutes an element in our sense of the term because it establishes an opposition.

Like all language users, translators work with aspects of both syntactic form and rhetorical function in dealing with a given element of text. It is this form–function interplay which defines the element in terms of its discursive relationships. Examples of the typical values which elements take on in different text types are illustrated in Fig. 9.5.

Narrative texts:	values related to	events
Descriptive texts:	" "	attributions
Conceptual expository texts:	" "	assertions
Argumentative texts:	" "	points in an argument
Instructional texts:	" "	steps in a procedure
		(based on Stratton 1971)

Figure 9.5

As Candlin and Saedi (1982:107) observe, the linear progression of elements within a text may obscure the non-linear interrelationship of rhetorical functions. For example, in Text 9B₁, concerning the French Insurance Company COFACE, the linear sequence of elements does not reflect the rhetorical relation between events and background information. As translators, we need to see beyond this linearity to discover how overall discourse relations are evolving. We now come to our second level of text organisation, namely **sequences**. A sequence is a unit of text organisation which normally consists of more than one element and which serves a higher-order rhetorical function than that of the individual elements in question. To illustrate how sequences are recognised, let us reconsider the translation problem identified in Texts 9D₁ and 9D₂.

In Text 9D₁, we classified

> *Academia in today's university has little difficulty in perceiving its obligations . . .*

as an element on the grounds that it constitutes a 'point' in the overall progression of the argument, thereby serving a rhetorical function ('specifying a general thesis'). In Text 9D₂, on the other hand, the element in question, although it still constitutes a point in an argument, has become part of a different structural component. The higher-order rhetorical function here is establishing the opposition to the thesis cited:

> *However, academia in today's university, which has little difficulty in perceiving its obligations . . .*

Thus, what we recognise as being a flaw in the translation depends on our ability to identify a sequence within the overall progression of the text. The structure of the source text follows a familiar pattern in argumentative texts which we illustrate in Fig. 9.6.

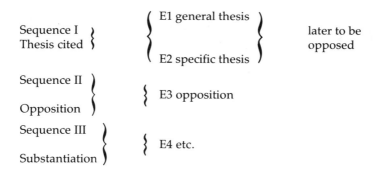

Figure 9.6   Elements and sequences in counter-argument

PERCEIVING BOUNDARIES BETWEEN SEQUENCES

How do text producers decide when one sequence is complete and the next sequence can be embarked upon? There is no predetermined limit, but people instinctively know when the rhetorical purpose of a sequence has been fulfilled. That is, they avoid going on too long (being redundant) or stopping before they have made their point (being incomplete). A sequence is as long as it needs to be in order to achieve its function.

The translator's concern is, of course, to relay the rhetorical purpose of the producer of the source text. Perceiving the plan of composition of sequences and of entire texts is an essential part of the task. In Fig. 9.6, sequence I in the familiar composition plan for counterarguments contains only two elements (general–specific thesis). But, frequently, a number of elements may be used to elaborate a given function within a sequence. (We shall refer to these elements as **enhancers**). In Text 9E, elements 2, 3, 4 and 5 may be seen to perform the ancillary function of enhancement.

Text 9E

The Verdict of Kahan and the Context

I

1. Much credit flows to the State of Israel for the vigour of the Kahan commission's enquiry and the rigour of its conclusions.
2. There is not another country in the Middle East, [. . .] where the rulers could be subjected to questioning of such a kind.
3. [and not too many beyond]
4. And in Lebanon, [. . .], the parallel enquiry has turned into a charade.
5. [at whose citizens' hands the massacres were committed]

II

6. The credit attaches to the state, though, and not the government
7. which at first refused to have its complicity attainted

(*Guardian* editorial)

To determine where one element ends and another begins is generally not a problem for the translator. What may be a problem, on the other hand, is recognition of where one sequence ends and another begins. In Text 9E, failing to appreciate the relative weighting of elements 2–5 (enhancers) in relation to element 1 (thesis cited), on the one hand, and in relation to elements 6–7 (opposition), on the other hand, can lead to serious problems in understanding or translating the argumentation involved. For one thing, a superficial reading of element 1 (*Much credit flows to the State of Israel* . . .) can easily lead to a target text which allows the reader to assume a pro-Israeli argument is about to be embarked on. And further, this misreading can be compounded by failure to appreciate and relay the true force of the oblique signal of opposition (*though*) in element 6.

TOPIC SHIFT

Having defined a sequence in terms of its contribution to some overall rhetorical purpose, we now turn to another useful indicator of structure within texts. **Topic shift** is to be understood as the point at which there is a perceptible change of topic between adjacent portions of discourse. Lexical and syntactic signals are always present to mark this shift (see Brown and Yule 1983:94), which may also at times correspond to paragraph boundaries. A closer definition of topic, however, enables us to identify boundaries not only between texts, but also between sequences and elements within a given text. Topic is a variable of field of discourse, but it also relates to discourse as action and as a system of signs. In this perspective, the topic shift between the initial sequences of Text 9E can be analysed as in Fig. 9.7.

Topic of Sequence I (E1–5):

Propositional meaning:	the soundness of judicial procedures in the State of Israel in comparison with neighbouring states
Illocutionary force:	considered praise (but only of the State), preparing the ground for a 'rebuttal'
Sign:	thesis to be countered

Topic of Sequence II (E6–7):

Propositional meaning:	distinction between *state* and *government*
Illocutionary force:	'opposition': exclusion of *government* from praise
Sign:	counterargument

Figure 9.7

The textual indicators of topic shifts complement the functional criteria for the perception of rhetorical purpose outlined earlier. In making selections related to lexis, syntax, cohesion, theme–rheme arrangement (see Chapter 10), and so on, translators are guided by this kind of analysis of topic. It is a useful additional guide to structural boundaries. In Text 9E, for example, the repetition in element 6 of the item *credit* from element 1 is a strong cohesive tie which links the thesis cited to the opposition.

PERCEIVING TEXT AS A UNIT OF STRUCTURE

We now come to the uppermost level of structure, namely text. It will have been apparent from earlier discussion that we are using the term not to refer to entire stretches of discourse (articles, books, etc.) but rather to subdivisions made within the undifferentiated whole. Text is a coherent and cohesive unit, realised by one or more than one sequence of mutually relevant elements, and serving some overall rhetorical purpose.

Just as it is important to perceive where one sequence ends and another begins, it is of vital importance for translators to identify text boundaries. It might at first be supposed that paragraphs (orthographic or conceptual – see Trimble 1985) are useful indicators of the limits of a text. Indeed, there is often a reasonable degree of correspondence between the paragraph, the topic of the text and its rhetorical purpose. But this is by no means always the case.

Of particular interest to the translator are the ways in which a text is made to progress towards a goal. A text will be deemed complete at the point where the rhetorical goal is considered to have been achieved. In other words, a boundary will come at a point where a sequence no longer commits the text producer to elaborate further in pursuit of an overall rhetorical purpose. More than one paragraph can realise a text, or, alternatively, more than one text can make up a paragraph. Consequently, any decision by a translator to modify paragraph boundaries should at least be consistent with the structure of the text.

To illustrate that text boundaries do not always coincide with paragraph boundaries, let us now analyse the structure of Text 9F (part of which was previously discussed in Chapter 4).

Text 9F

Oral health care does not have the makings of a dramatic issue. Very few people die of oral disease, and its effect on the economies of nations is insignificant. Yet very few people manage to avoid oral disease, and the two major variants—dental caries and periodontal disease—can and do cause irreversible damage. In the process, dental caries can cause some of the most severe pain that the average person is likely to experience in his lifetime. In 1978 a national survey in the United Kingdom, where 4% of the national health budget is spent on dental care, showed that 30% of the adult population was edentulous.

Yet the United Kingdom, like other countries with a long-established dental care system and the high levels of dental caries and periodontal disease generally associated with Western culture, now seems to be experiencing a minor revolution. Not only has the average dentition life expectancy increased by five years in the past decade but reports are now coming in of dramatic reductions in the prevalence of dental caries in schoolchildren in different parts of the country, some from fluoridated areas, some not. The United Kingdom is by no means unique in this respect. Similar observations have been reported in Australia, New Zealand, Scandinavia, and the U.S.A.

(*World Health Forum*)

From the point of view of the reader/translator, relying on paragraph boundaries alone can hamper understanding of the way a text is put together. For example, the initial sentence in the second paragraph expresses an opposition (*Yet . . .*). By our definition, this element cannot be text-initial. There has to be some statement of 'position' to which it can respond. The statement can be found at the end of the previous paragraph:

    I.   In 1978 a national survey in the
        United Kingdom, where 4% of
        the national health budget is

> spent on dental care, showed
> that 30% of the adult population
> was edentulous.
>
> II. Yet the United Kingdom, like
> other countries with a long-
> established dental care system
> and the high levels of dental
> caries and periodontal disease
> generally associated with
> Western culture, now seems to
> be experiencing a minor revolu-
> tion.

There is no suggestion that translators should necessarily change paragraph boundaries to match text structure. But, what is important is that the translation should reflect the kind of understanding which accrues from, say, viewing sequence II as a response to sequence I above, and not as initiating a new text with its own rhetorical purpose.

EQUIVALENCE: WORD LEVEL OR TEXT LEVEL?

Translators may directly or indirectly question the importance of text as a unit of translation: what is so magical about the unit 'text' as opposed to making do with lower-level units such as phrases or even words for purposes of translation? Isn't translation after all 'literal'? Questions such as these deserve consideration. There is no doubt that translators work with words and phrases as their raw material. Dictionary and reference work is bound to take place at this level. But, can equivalence be truly established at this level alone? Work in contrastive rhetoric has shown the importance of discourse structure at the paragraph and text level for determining equivalence (see, for example, Hartmann 1980).

At the decision-making stage, the appropriateness of particular items can only be judged in the light of the item's place within the overall plan of the text. The plan will involve a multitude of complex relations between texture, structure and the context of discourse. A striking example is to be found in Text 9F:

> Yet the United Kingdom . . . now seems to be experiencing a minor revolution.

Any decision taken strictly at word or phrase level on the item *minor revolution* might well result in the expression of a negative concept in many languages (*minor* = 'insignificant', 'negligible').

When, however, the item is seen as part of an opposition to an earlier thesis cited ('British teeth are in bad shape'), it can only be read as: *minor* = 'significant', 'noteworthy'. In other words, it contributes to the rhetorical function: '. . . but do not despair'. Even where a language closely related to English has an idiom equivalent to *minor revolution*, judgement must still be exercised as to whether the idiom can effectively fulfil the same function in the text.

BASIC TEXT DESIGNS

From the translator's point of view, what is particularly interesting about discourse relations is that they provide patterns which facilitate retrieval of rhetorical purposes. In Fig. 9.5, we identified the kind of values which different elements take on in different text types ('steps' in exposition, 'points' in argumentation, etc.). Nash (1980) identifies the relations obtaining between elements in a variety of text types. For example, the argumentative pattern is achieved by what Nash calls the **balance**. Here a shift between a proposition and counter-proposition is signalled, thus inviting the synthesis of conflicting claims. In the absence of explicitly marked relationships between the various units involved in such a pattern, translators have to ensure that text coherence is upheld through the perception of some underlying continuity. In Text $9G_1$ (a formal translation from Arabic), expression does not facilitate access to the rhetorical meaning of the source text. Coherence is relayed implicitly. Text $9G_2$, on the other hand, is a translation which attempts to render the relationships involved more explicitly for an English reader.

Text $9G_1$

> It is not surprising that the 'needle' by virtue of its shape, size and function (that of penetrating the flesh) takes on a flagrant symbolic significance. The more surprising fact is that the eyes also take on this significance.
>
> (Tarabishi 1984)

Text $9G_2$

> That the 'needle' by virtue of its shape, size and function (that of penetrating the flesh) takes on a flagrant symbolic significance is not

surprising. What is more surprising, however, is that the eyes are also accorded such significance.

(Tarabishi 1987)

Crombie (1985) suggests that readers accumulate evidence of the way a text is put together, forming a **macro-pattern** (e.g. situation –> problem –> solution –> evaluation). Within such patterns, discourse functions can be discerned such as 'making a concession and then countering it' (concession –> counter -expectation). Figure 9.8 illustrates a problem –> solution macro-pattern.

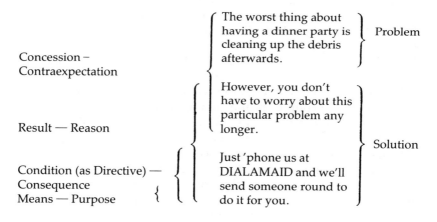

Concession –
Contraexpectation

The worst thing about having a dinner party is cleaning up the debris afterwards.   } Problem

Result — Reason

However, you don't have to worry about this particular problem any longer.

Condition (as Directive) —
Consequence
Means — Purpose

Just 'phone us at DIALAMAID and we'll send someone round to do it for you.   } Solution

(from Crombie 1985:61)

Figure 9.8

In essence, this formulation is comparable to our own model of structure, in which readers derive evidence for the way a text develops by assessing the interaction of the various elements and sequences within the text. Two basic structural formats can be identified. These are represented in Fig. 9.9.

The structural format of exposition is illustrated in Texts $9H_1$ and $9H_2$, which are examples of narration in Spanish and English respectively.

COUNTER-ARGUMENTATION

↓ Thesis cited to be opposed
↓ Opposition
↓ Substantiation
↓ Conclusion

EXPOSITION

↓ Scene-setter
↓ Aspect I of the scene
↓ Aspect II of the scene
etc.

[aspect is to be understood as event in narration, attribution in description, and assertion in conceptual exposition]

Figure 9.9

Text 9H₁

> 1   **H**ACIA 1515 un puñado de españoles encabezados por el Capitán Pánfilo de Narváez y Fray Bartolomé de las Casas establecieron la
> 5   penultima villa cubana en la costa sur de la actual provincia de La Habana. Pero aquel emplazamiento duró poco. Los fundadores emigraron hacia la costa norte acercándose al Estrecho de la Florida
> 10 cuyas rápidas corrientes favorecían la navegación. Así llegaron a un puerto de garganta angosta y bolsón desmesurado, bien protegido contra los huracanes por unas colinas.
> 15   En la orilla oeste de esa bahía quedó definitivamente fundada la villa de San Cristóbal de La Habana, en el mes de noviembre de 1519, un día del cual no se guarda recuerdo, pues las Actas del
> 20 Cabildo que van desde ese año hasta 1550 fueron quemadas por el corsario francés Jacques de Sores.
>   Cuenta la tradición oral que siguiendo la ...

Two interesting points arise here. Firstly, the translator has joined two paragraphs into one, in order to conform to the boundaries of the narrative text: there seems no need in English to break the

Text 9H$_2$

> 1   **S**OMETIME around 1515, a handful
>   of Spaniards led by Captain
>   Pánfilo de Nárvaez and Fray
>   Bartolomé de las Casas established a
> 5   settlement in Cuba on the southern coast of
>   what is now the province of Havana.
>   However, this settlement did not last long
>   and its founders moved to the northern
>   coast near the Straits of Florida, whose
> 10   swift currents were an aid to navigation.
>   They came to a harbour consisting of a
>   narrow inlet opening into a large bay, well
>   protected by hills against hurricanes. The
>   town of San Cristóbal de la Habana was
> 15   finally established on the western shores of
>   this bay in November 1519. The exact date
>   is no longer known since the records of the
>   municipal council covering the period from
>   that year to 1550 were burned by the
> 20   French pirate Jacques de Sores.
>   Oral tradition has it that, in accordance
>   ...

(UNESCO Courier July 1984)

paragraph before the narrative is complete. Secondly, whereas we have singled out items such as *however* (line 7) as important indicators of counterargumentation, their appearance in a text is not in itself enough to indicate text type. Here, the item merely serves to link two successive events in the narration.

Variation on these basic structural formats is always possible. For example, another argumentative text form (through-argument) is similar to the counter-argumentative format except that, instead of a thesis cited followed by an opposition, these two are conflated into a single 'statement of a point of view' to be argued through. The basic format is as in Fig. 9.10.

Text 9I shows how an argument can be constructed without an explicit reference to some opposite view.

THROUGH-ARGUMENT

↓ Thesis to be argued through
↓ Substantiation
↓ Conclusion

Figure 9.10

Text 9I

> **Education and society:
> follow the leader**
>
> In the United States, the schools
> have relatively little autonomy in
> terms of basic policy and the
> direction of education. Educational
> institutions basically follow the
> dictates of society in terms of policy,
> curriculum, standards and orienta-
> tions. When society's goals change,
> the schools must also change and
> the current 'crisis' reflects the fact
> that social goals have shifted from a
> stress on equity and the solution of
> societal problems through educa-
> tion which characterized the 1960s
> to a focus on academic and
> technological achievement to
> enable the nation to compete in an
> increasingly difficult world
> market. . . .

(from *Prospects* 1986:338)

In Text 9I, an evaluative note is stuck immediately (. . . *have relatively little autonomy*). Implicitly, this statement counters some unstated case (that 'in the US, schools are autonomous'). The initial thesis cited is then argued through in the rest of the text.

PUTTING TEXT DESIGNS TO USE IN SUMMARISING

Insights into the various designs explained above are important not only as an aid to better comprehension in general but also in activities such as summarising and reporting, which translators are often called upon to perform. The structure of the source text becomes an important guide to decisions regarding what should or should not appear in the derived text. It is noticeable that translator trainees often find summarising to be a process which has no clear rules. But, with closer attention to structural criteria, the skill should be amenable to much more systematic treatment.

It may be objected that translators often have to work with source texts which are far from being well constructed. Indeed, this is quite frequently the case. But, in order to be able to identify deviations, one has to have a clear idea of some norm. In deciding that a text is poorly constructed, the translator must have a notion of the conventions to which a text is expected to conform and it is only the intervention of the translator that will rid the target version from design shortcomings in the source text. This is yet another area where arguments about the translator's freedom can be seen in more realistic terms. The purpose of text structure is to serve a rhetorical purpose and, in striving to achieve equivalence, the translator seeks first and foremost to relay that purpose, making modifications accordingly.

TEXTS IN RELATION TO DISCOURSE

In this chapter, we have identified three units of structure: the element, the sequence and the text. Naturally, this raises the question of whether there is any larger identifiable unit than the text. Certainly texts concatenate within larger stretches of discourse. But, beyond the level of the text, it is difficult to perceive any regularly occurring patterns which would enable us to identify a unit of structure. Discourse is diffuse and can only be analysed by relating actual expression to the belief systems, power structures, etc., which underlie it. Translators find these to be important indicators of the attitudes to be conveyed. But, the attitudinal or ideological drift of a text is patterned in textual structures such as the ones we have discussed. These are the tangible linguistic units which guide the translator's work.

Even when, in certain cultures, a particular pattern is conventionally associated with a particular discourse and a particular genre, it will still be the textual structure which is the translator's focus. For example, the counter-argument has in Western cultures come to be regularly associated with 'contentious' discourse and occurs in a range of genres, including the 'Letter to the Editor'. But the format thesis cited –> opposition –> substantiation –> conclusion, which is of primary importance to the translator, is not peculiar to any single genre or discourse. Rather, it is a text structure. These textual structures are apparently not universal but vary from culture to culture. In non-Western cultures, as Text $9J_1$ clearly shows, the same genre (Letter to the Editor) and the same contentious discourse employ a wholly different text format from the standard counter-argumentative format of English.

Text $9J_1$

Sir. In the light of your Islamic activities which we all recognize, we would like you to pay greater attention than you have done so far to Muslim minorities, particularly in view of the fact that they are facing vicious attacks designed to divert them from the Islamic line which they have chosen for themselves.

These minorities desperately need assistance in various ways in order to be able to withstand these attacks and to raise the banner of Islam throughout the world.

Text $9J_1$ is characteristic of letters to the editor written in Arabic, just as the familiar counter-argument is characteristic of English. But in order to be maximally effective for an English-language target readership, a source text such as $9J_1$ must undergo considerable modification in translation, along the lines of Text $9J_2$.

Text $9J_2$

The activities of your magazine in promoting Islam are highly commendable. However, it would be greatly appreciated it you were to pay greater attention to Muslim minorities. They desperately need assistance of various kinds at a time when they are facing vicious attacks designed to divert them from the Islamic line.

In this version, the motivation for the reviser's changes is not the genre or the discourse but conventional text formats.

LIMITS OF THE TRANSLATOR'S FREEDOM

Structural modifications of the kind discussed above raise the question: how much leeway does the translator have in altering ST structure to make it readable in the TL? To answer this question, we tentatively propose the following working hypothesis. Placing the various text patterns on a continuum with maximally expository (non-evaluative) forms at one end and maximally argumentative (evaluative) forms at the other, we suggest that:

The less evaluative the text is, the less need there will be for its structure to be modified in translation. Conversely, the more evaluative the text is, the more scope there may be for modification.

The plausibility of this hypothesis finds support in an important concept from translation studies – namely, that of purpose of the translation. In all probability, consumers of translated expository texts (e.g. an analytic exposition of how the International Monetary Fund works) would expect maximum fidelity to structure. Rarely, however, would a consumer of a translated editorial, for example, make such demands; the consumer of such texts would be more interested in following the drift of the argument being put forward than in finding out how rhetorical conventions work in the source language. Text 9J clearly illustrates this point.

For instructional texts, a different kind of hypothesis may be put forward. Placing instructional text forms on a continuum, with maximally culture-bound texts at one end and minimally culture-bound texts at the other, we suggest that:

The less culture-bound a text is, the less need there will be for its structure to be modified. Conversely, the more culture-bound a text is, the more scope there may be for modification.

The notion 'culture-bound' may be defined in terms of the degree of 'universal currency' which the text in question enjoys. Thus, least modification seems to be called for in the translation of treaties, declarations, resolutions, and other similar documents. These forms are not culture-bound. They enjoy wide international recognition and therefore need to be made available for close scrutiny and cross-checking when translated. This may be illustrated by the almost universal formulaic layout of the Declaration as in Text 9K.

Text 9K

Declaration

The World Conference to Combat Racism and Racial Discrimination

Having met at Geneva from 14 to 25 August 1978 in accordance with General Assembly resolution 32/129,

Recalling that the Charter of the United Nations is based on the principles of the dignity and equality of all human beings,

Noting the vital need for the mass media to inform public opinion objectively about the liberation struggle in southern Africa,

Solemnly declares:

1. Any doctrine of racial superiority is scientifically false, morally condemnable, socially unjust and dangerous, and has no justification whatsoever;

(UN conference report)

Powers of attorney, marriage certificates, wills, etc., on the other hand, are specific to certain societies and may be considerably modified in translation. Consider Text $9L_1$ (formal translation of a court ruling on a will) and $9L_2$ (idiomatic translation of the same text) as examples of maximally restricted texts.

Text $9L_1$

In the name of God, the Merciful, the Compassionate

Sharia Court Department

TEXT OF JUDGEMENT

Issued on Monday 11.4.1985

I, . . ., Judge of the Sharia Court of . . ., have heard Case No 102/85 on 18.3.1985, brought by . . . against the heirs of the late . . . with regard to the entailment of the estate and have pronounced as follows:

The judgement of the court, issued in the presence of the parties is as follows:

1.   It is established that the late Mohammad Salman was from Al-Ain and that he died in London on 7.3.1985.

2.   His estate passes to his parents . . .

Text $9L_2$

In the name of God, the Merciful, the Compassionate

Sharia Court Department

Judgement Issued on Monday 11.4.1985

I, . . ., Judge of the Sharia Court of . . .,

Having heard Case No 102/85 on 18.3.1985, brought by . . ., against the heirs of the late . . ., with regard to the entailment of the estate,

Do hereby pronounce that the court is satisfied that:

(1)   Mohammad Salman of Al-Ain died in London on 7.3.1985.

(2)   His estate passes to his parents . . .

Again the notion of different translations for different purposes is relevant. Where a translation is for information only,
greater modifications are allowable to suit the needs of particular
consumers (e.g. translating a contract in order to inform a signatory
of what his or her obligations are). Where, on the other hand, a
translated text is to be legally binding, minimal changes may be
allowed (e.g. contracts in countries with more than one official
language, where legally binding documents often have to exist
in more than one language version).

ISSUES FOR THE TRANSLATOR

At the beginning of this chapter, we asked a number of questions
about text structure. They concerned the motivation behind any
structural changes made by translators and the limits on such
changes, the role of pragmatic and semiotic values and effects
on coherence relations. In response to these questions, we can
now summarise the salient points in our discussion.

Rhetorical purpose. We have identified text as the structural
unit which informs translators' decisions about lexical, syntactic
and other choices. In doing so, we have stressed the importance
of rhetorical purpose as the basis of the evolution of text
types. It is crucial that rhetorical purpose (and the lower-level
rhetorical functions which contribute to it) be identified. The
appropriateness of translations can be judged in the light of these
considerations. The whole matter of structural modifications and
the degree to which they are permitted needs to be considered
with the text producer's purpose in mind. In particular, degrees
of evaluativeness in the source text are of overriding importance
when it comes to deciding what structure to preserve and how.

Purpose of translation. An additional consideration is the purpose
for which the translation is intended. Particularly in the case of
culture-bound texts, the degree of intervention by the translator
will often depend on consumers and their needs. This matter is
not to be underestimated and may in certain cases even override
ST communicative intentions.

Global patterns. As a guide within the complex maze of decision-making, translators may also find it useful to refer to a recognisable set of global patterns to which texts conform in different languages. These are cognitive structures which help in the production and reception of texts.

But the world is changing. It is noteworthy that, whereas textual patterns and conventions are constantly modified when texts in less dominant languages are translated into English, the reverse is not the case. It seems that many of the world's languages are finding English rhetorical patterns creeping in as new norms. The degree of tolerance of foreign structures seems to be proportional to the relative prestige of a language. This is a fact of life, but it is also an interesting area of research and a necessary one if translation assessment is to be carried out in a more systematic fashion.

TEN

Discourse texture

Texture is one of the defining characteristics of text. It is that property which ensures that a text 'hangs together', both linguistically and conceptually. Under normal circumstances, we expect of a text that it should be coherent (i.e. have continuity of sense) and cohesive (i.e. display connectivity between its surface elements), and that it should display distinct patterns of thematisation (i.e. that it will be arranged in such a fashion as to draw attention to those parts of its content which are deemed most important – cf. Fowler 1986: 61). These expectations, and the ways in which they are met in the processing of actual texts, are what will occupy us in the present chapter.

'FORM' AND 'CONTENT'

In investigating this area of textuality, we shall inevitably be involved in studying the links between, on the one hand, the 'words on the page' (in the case of written texts) – the choice of lexis and its syntactic organisation – and, on the other, the negotiation of meaning between producer and receiver. The relation of the one to the other is problematic. Often referred to traditionally as 'form' and 'content', the perceived distinction has led to a simplistic view of text, in which a particular sequence of meaning is couched in a particular linguistic form according to the 'stylistic' preference (or, at worst, whim) of a given writer.

The use in linguistics and in translation theory of the terms 'message', 'encode' and 'decode' has not helped the situation. Partly through the influence on linguistics of information theory and cybernetics, the impression has been fostered that the process of transferring meaning into text is a mechanical one, in which lexical entries and syntactic patterns are 'mapped onto' a semantic core in the manner of a primitive machine-translation system. The inference is allowed that the 'message' is an invariant construct, a concrete entity which is conveyed intact from speaker/writer to hearer/reader as if by semaphore or morse code. Meaning, in other words, is being separated from expression, almost as if the two were unrelated but just happen to be fused into one in text.

TEXTURE AS MOTIVATED CHOICE

The model of text processing – and hence of translating – which we have presented in this book is essentially different. When texts are seen as social events, the links between text producer, text expression and meaning have to be considered not as random but as motivated. There are two points here which need to be elaborated somewhat before we can deal with texture in translation.

The first point concerns motivation. As observed earlier, it is crucial to the whole model of discourse context described in Chapters 3–8 that actual textual occurrences, though subject to the particular grammatical system of the language, are seen as being motivated by contextual factors. This view is not a deterministic one, in which speakers/writers are being deprived of their own free will and become linguistic prisoners of context (see, on this, the view of O'Donnell and Todd (1980): 61–83); it is rather that text producers make their choices in such a way as best to serve their own communicative ends and within an institutional setting which exerts its own influence on linguistic expression. In this way, text-type focus is a powerful motivating factor. A counter-argument demands different textural procedures from those appropriate for conceptual exposition, for example. Generic and discoursal constraints are also of obvious relevance to the study of texture. An example from spoken discourse should help to illustrate these points. Beaugrande and Dressler (1981: 54) cite the words of an American county supervisor, following a flash flood (reported in the *Gainesville Sun*, 20.12.78):

Text 10A

There's water through many homes – I would say almost all of them have water in them. It's just completely under water.

The repetition of the item *water* – a cohesive device which we shall refer to again as **recurrence** – may well have to do with what Beaugrande and Dressler identify as the 'short planning time' available in spontaneous speaking; but we would argue that it is probably not unmotivated. Reflecting the stress of the situation, the official is at the same time defending his position to the press and expressing his sense of being overwhelmed by events. The repetition responds to constraints of text-type focus, discourse and genre.

COHERENCE AS INTENDED MEANING

The second point relates to the nature of coherence. It has been argued that coherence is not something which is created by text, but rather an assumption made by language users that, in accordance with the cooperative principle, texts are intended to be coherent. In the view of Green and Morgan (1981: 173), ' "lexical patterns" are a symptom, not a cause, of coherence'. While there is indeed a sense in which interaction depends on the assumptions which users bring to it – assumptions which translators have to reassess – it seems unnecessarily extreme to limit coherence to a set of assumptions. For one thing, the utterances we hear/read do not all appear to us to be equally coherent. Yet we usually presume that they were intended to be coherent. In particular, such a view would undervalue the importance of the textual evidence (lexico-grammatical choice) which, apart from paralinguistic features, is the only evidence we can ultimately rely on. In other words, text producers intend meaning and receivers interpret it by virtue of the textual record. In Brown and Yule's (1983: 25) terms:

> what the textual record means is determined by our interpretation
> of what the producer intended it to mean.

There is nevertheless a danger that textual clues can be treated as an end in themselves. The various activities of translation criticism, translation assessment and revision all run the risk of concentrating on features of texture without relating them to the communicative process with engendered them. Texture needs to be seen as an integral part of what one is doing with one's language. For a simple illustration, let us recall Text 9E, p. 176:

Much credit flows . . .

. . .

The credit attaches to the state, though . . .

Like the recurrence of the item *water* in Text 10A, the recurrence of *credit* is not unmotivated. Part of the text producer's intention in this case is to channel 'credit' in a particular direction and the repetition corresponds to a counterargumentative strategy. In translation, the recurrence needs therefore to be relayed; replacing the second mention of *credit* by a synonym would compromise the overall effect of the text.

STANDARDS OF TEXTUALITY

Coherence can be defined, following Beaugrande (1980), as the procedures which ensure conceptual connectivity, including (1) logical relations, (2) organisation of events, objects and situations, and (3) continuity in human experience. It seems safe to assume that the sequence of coherence relations would, under normal circumstances, remain constant in translation from ST to TT. Such basic relations as cause–effect, problem–solution, temporal sequence, and so on, are universally fundamental to meaning and the way it is structured within a text. But the ways in which this underlying coherence is reflected on the surface of text – the **cohesion,** or sequential connectivity of surface elements – are much more likely to be language-specific or text-specific. There are many possible cohesive devices capable of relaying, say, a given relationship between propositions. And in a given language, some are likely to be preferred options. Both cohesion and coherence, then, may be said to be standards of textuality (Beaugrande and Dressler 1981); both need to be maintained if communication is to be successful.

SYSTEMS CONTRASTS

It will be important then to distinguish between those elements of intended meaning which can be represented in terms of universal coherence relations, and problems of translation arising because of the non-correspondence of grammatical systems, as discussed in Chapter 2. As we saw there, deixis – the relation of discourse to the spatial and temporal situation of utterance – is differently reflected in different grammatical systems. In English, there is a two-term set of demonstratives: *this/that*, whereas in Spanish the set comprises three members: *este/ese/aquel*, corresponding to [proximity to speaker], [proximity to addressee] and [remote from both] respectively. The North-West American language Tlingit, according to Levinson (1983: 81), has a four-term set, 'glossable as "this one right here", "this one nearby", "that one over there" and "that one way over there" '. In Bahasa Malaysia, as in many other languages, there are two categories of first-person plural subject pronoun, *kita* [inclusive of addressee] and *kami* [exclusive of addressee].

Potentially, such discrepancies between systems can lead to inevitable loss or gain of information in translation. In practice, however, translators experience relatively few actual problems ascribable to such causes (for an example, see Text 2B). Most of the real problems lie elsewhere. What concerns the translator is to assess a particular instance of deixis in terms of its significance for the emerging coherence and cohesion of the text.

For example, in a certain number of languages, including Japanese, there are explicit markers of topic (as distinct from case markers, such as subject and object). These are clearly deictic in that they relate the marked item to previous discourse. The translator's concern is then to reflect emerging coherence patterns, including topic prominence, in another language by means of word-order changes and so on. Elsewhere, the marking of pronouns for gender (e.g. French and German) allows a density of anaphoric reference which has to be sorted out in English. The following sentence from Marcel Proust (1914):

> *Il l'y a éveillée, mais ne la connaît pas . . .*

is formally equivalent to:

> *It has awoken it in it but does not recognise it . . .*

In other words, the first three items in the French sentence, *il/l(a)/y*, all theoretically equivalent to *it*, have three different anaphoric referents (corresponding to 'a cup of tea', 'the truth' and the author's 'mind', respectively). Coherence, once it has been retrieved from the ST, can easily be re-established in the TT (by using recurrence or co-reference), but not by the same pronominal means.

INFERENCE

The grammatical and lexical resources for conveying semantic relations between conceptual entities exist, no doubt, in all languages: they are universal phenomena. But in a particular communication process, the semantic relations will be realised in particular ways and the production of source text and target text are distinct, though related, processes. Consequently, instead of reviewing the various types of cohesion (listed in Halliday and Hasan 1976) or coherence relations (as in Crombie 1985), we shall work on a text (see Text 10B below), as a particular record of communication, in an endeavour to see how readers perceive intended meaning and underlying coherence on the basis of the textual evidence. As we shall see once again, inference is, in addition to textual cohesion, an essential property of the communication process.

Text 10B

> I am now more than glad that I did not pass into the grammar
> school five years ago, although it was a disappointment at the time.
> I was always good at English, but not so good at the other subjects!!
>
> I am glad that I went to the secondary modern school, because it was
> only constructed the year before. Therefore, it was much more hygienic
> than the grammar school. The secondary modern was light and airy, and
> the walls were painted with a bright, washable gloss . . . One day, I was
> sent over to the grammar school, with a note for one of the teachers,
> and you should have seen the mess! The corridors were dusty, and I
> saw dust on the window ledges, which were chipped. I saw into one
> of the classrooms. It was very untidy in there.
>
> I am also glad that I did not go to the grammar school, because of
> what it does to one's habits. This may appear to be a strange remark,
> at first sight. It is a good thing to have an education behind you, and
> I do not believe in ignorance, but I have had certain experiences, with
> educated people, since going out into the world.

(Muriel Spark 1958)

Field:	pseudo-autobiographical fictional account
Tenor:	informal, with occasional formality
Mode:	written to be read as if spoken monologue

Intention:	re-evaluation of speaker's educational background; promotion of esteem

Sign:	'the grammar school' as a sign; rebuttal of assumption that grammar school education is superior

Text-type focus: through-argument followed by counter-argument

Figure 10.1   Macro-context of Text 10B

Briefly, we can sum up the macro-context of Text 10B as in Fig. 10.1. Essentially, the intended meaning of the text appears to involve the projection of a particular world-view, slightly at odds with conventional assumptions. An analysis of structure, along the lines suggested in Chapter 9, would show how such a model of intended meaning gradually emerges.

As an example of fictional first-person narrative, Text 10B is distinct in terms of genre from most of those reviewed in earlier chapters. The relation of actual author to text is a complex matter which need not concern us here; let us behave as if the fictional 'I' were the actual text producer, and thus enter the fictional text world the actual author has created. In our analysis then, intended meaning relates to the subject of the narrative and not to the author, Muriel Spark.

Any prospective translator of Text 10B is faced with a number of problems, prominent among which will be the status of the culturally determined elements *grammar school, secondary modern school* as signs. In Text 10B, the distinction between the two kinds of schooling is crucial to the text world being developed and would have to be made explicit, perhaps through paraphrases or expansion. In an expository text on the history of the English education system, borrowing of the ST items into TT might be appropriate; but it would not be so here. By the same token, use of explanatory footnotes is acceptable in certain genres but not in others. So what should an expansion seek to convey? From the third paragraph of Text 10B, the inference is clearly allowable that, in the mind of the speaker, *an education* is something to be derived from a grammar school but not from a secondary modern school.

Consequently, the translation of the two items in question should seek above all to preserve the allowed inference and neither make it explicit nor delete it.

RECURRENCE AND CO-REFERENCE

In Text 10B, the element the *grammar school* occurs no fewer than four times while *the secondary modern (school)* occurs twice. The repetition of items with the same referent in a text is known as **recurrence.** As was noted in discussion of Text 10A, it is usually a symptom of intentionality (whether conscious or not) and as such is significant. Naturally, relative distance from a previous occurrence of an item may preclude the use of **pro-forms** (short substitute items of no independent status, such as pronouns or the item *so* in *I think so*), in which case recurrence is unavoidable. This is partly the case in Text 10B, as any attempt to replace the items in question by pronouns will show. But it is the strict recurrence of the same items in the same form which creates the effect; there is no attempt to use **co-reference,** that is, to activate the same content by using varied expression (e.g. *the other school, the (non) selective school*, etc.).

As noted by Beaugrande and Dressler (1981: 55), recurrence is 'prominently used to assert and re-affirm one's viewpoint'. In Text 10B, this impression is strengthened by the recurrence in the same co-text of *I am glad*, thus:

> I am now more than glad that . . .
> I am glad that . . .
> I am also glad that . . .

The strongly evaluative nature of these is a pointer to the real text focus of 10B; argumentation predominates, with description and narration as only secondary purposes. The iconic value of recurrences (iterations) such as *I am glad* for signalling rebuttal was noted earlier (Chapter 9, p. 178) and it is interesting to compare its use in Text 9E (*Much credit flows to the state of Israel . . . The credit attaches to the state, though . . .*) with the use here for the purpose of reaffirmation. It is now apparent that the cohesive devices at play are not random; they are motivated by overall rhetorical purpose. Assuming that recurrence is a universal rhetorical device, any attempt by a translator to vary TT expression at these points in the text is sure to detract from equivalence of text focus.

The point is valid not only in the case of literary translating. One of the concerns of revisers and assessors of translations is to ensure that patterns of lexical cohesion in texts are maintained, subject to the constraints of particular text norms in particular languages. It was mentioned in Chapter 5 (p. 97) that co-reference is a preferred strategy in fields such as news reporting in both English and French. In French, however, a more systematic, even exaggerated, use is made of this device. An example culled from the French regional press serves to illustrate the point. The co-referring items below from a news report about an incident of mugging are listed on the left, with formal translations of these items listed on the right.

deux jeunes Maghrébins	*two young North Africans*
voleur et complice	*the thief and his accomplice*
le fuyard	*the fugitive*
l'individu	*the individual*
le jeune voleur	*the young thief*
le mineur pénal	*the minor*
le jeune malfaiteur	*the young wrong-doer*
ce dernier	*the latter*

The degree to which an instance of recurrence or co-reference is motivated by text-type focus, as well as sanctioned by the conventions of the genre, will be a matter for the judgement of the translator or reviser concerned.

PARTIAL RECURRENCE

A further kind of lexical cohesion involves the repetition of items lexicalised in different word classes. This **partial recurrence** is illustrated in Text 10B:

(1) *dusty* → *dust* (*The corridors were dusty and I saw dust on the window ledges . . .*)

(2) *education* → *educated* (*It is a good thing to have an education behind you . . . but I have had certain experiences, with educated people . . .*)

Again, the cohesive ties need to be analysed. From the translator's point of view, one would have to ask whether the sequence referred to in (1) is glossable as (3) and if so, whether a translation calqued on (3) would be adequate:

(3)   *The corridors were dusty and so were the window ledges*

The judgement of most literary translators would probably be that it is not. The partial recurrence in (1) above is evidence of a number of possible features of speaker meaning, including: cataloguing of separate instances in support of an argument; obsession with cleanliness (for which there is no lack of co-textual evidence).

The partial recurrence in (2) is even more interesting. The cohesive tie supports the development of the counter-argument in which the thesis cited (*It is a good thing to have an education . . .*) relays weak conviction and prepares the way for the opposition (*but I have had certain experiences with educated people . . .*), in which the associative meaning of the item *educated* switches from positive to negative. Once more, the motivation is traceable to the text-type focus, which would be weakened in translation if the cohesive tie were lost.

PRO-FORMS AND ELLIPSIS

Anaphoric reference by pro-forms is a device which is subject to the restrictions on syntactic combinations in particular languages. It was mentioned earlier that, for example, languages in which nouns are marked for gender permit a greater density of pronominal reference than those such as English which are restricted to the single pronoun *it* for reference to all inanimate nouns.

But what is particularly interesting from our point of view is the use of pro-forms to activate not just the concept associated with a given noun but a whole idea. Text 10B provides two salient examples. Compare the straightforward use of *it* as a substitute for *secondary modern school* in the second paragraph with the use of the same pro-form in the following:

> I am now more than glad that I did not pass into the grammar school five years ago, although **it** was a disappointment at the time.

> I am also glad that I did not go to the grammar school, because of what **it** does to one's habits.

(emphasis added)

Halliday and Hasan (1976: 52) observe that the pro-form *it* can be used to refer to 'any identifiable portion of text', a phenomenon which they call **extended reference.** In the first example above, the presupposed text element is easy enough to identify as *that I did not pass into the grammar school* (although inferencing is necessary to arrive at this interpretation, involving the contrast signalled by *now* vs *at the time* and *glad* vs *disappointment*). But the second example is curious. On the face of it, there are three possible referents:

the grammar school?
going to the grammar school?
not going to the grammar school?

In fact, this surface ambiguity will be resolved by the normal inferencing process involved in interpretation: only the second of these options is fully satisfactory in terms of the coherence of the text world which is being developed as the text unfolds: 'going to the grammar school does something to your habits' (and not, presumably, something good). But the use of the cohesive device has not proved to be fully efficient in that extra processing effort has been needed to establish coherence.

In normative terms, both examples seem in fact to be slightly out of the ordinary, an impression which is strengthened by other features which relay an element of 'false formality': (*pass into, constructed, hygienic, going out into*, etc.). For the translator, then, there are two issues. One will be to ensure that continuity of sense can be recovered, that the potential ambiguity is not too disconcerting. The other will be to relay the impression of a slightly awkward or disconnected use of language. But this is a textual feature rather than one bearing on the use of the single pro-form *it*, so that the translator may resort to the familiar technique of **compensation,** that is, signalling an equivalent value but at a different juncture in the text. It matters less where exactly the impression is conveyed than that it is conveyed to an equivalent extent.

A simple example of the technique of compensation is to be found in the translation of cartoon strips, such as *Astérix*. Much of the humour depends on untranslatable puns. The translators abandon the attempt to relay the puns as such and, instead, compensate by inserting English puns of their own which are no part of the source text. But equivalence of intention has been maintained.

Occasionally, there will be instances where the translator elects actually to alter anaphoric reference for the sake of improved effectiveness and efficiency. An example from the field of film subtitling will serve to illustrate what is a legitimate, if infrequent, procedure. Text 10C is a fragment of dialogue from the French television soap opera *Châteauvallon*. The English subtitles, as they appeared in the British (Channel 4) television version, appear below as Text 10D. The field is a newspaper editorial meeting of a daily newspaper which goes in for sensationalism. The topic is whether or not an obituary which is to appear on page one should be written in a plain, simple style. From the context and the images on screen, it is clear that speaker A and speaker B do not agree with each other.

Text 10C

> A: Le plus vibrant hommage peut se rendre avec des mots simples. C'est pas la peine de rajouter la grosse caisse de l'emphase.
> B: De toute façon, c'est pas la tradition à *La Dépêche*.

Text 10D

> A: But the most touching tribute can be done in a few words. There's no call for heavy type.
> B: That's the *Despatch* tradition.

At first sight, Text 10D appears to be a mistranslation of speaker B in Text 10C, who declares that it is *not* the tradition at the *Despatch*. But analysis soon reveals that intended meaning has been faithfully preserved. It is difficult to identify a precise portion of the text which is represented by the pro-form *ce* in Text 10C (speaker B). It is rather the whole idea inferred from A: 'expressing emotion in a simple and sober fashion', which is said by B not to be in the tradition of the newspaper. This is an instance not of extended reference but of what Halliday and Hasan call **text reference**: the use of a pro-form to call up an idea or fact inferred from previous text.

The French televiewer would have no problem in interpreting the intended meaning and coherence would be maintained. But if B in Text 10D had read 'That's not the *Despatch* tradition' (formal translation of Text 10C, then the reader of the subtitle would be likely to identify *heavy type* as referent of the pro-form *That*. So the subtitler, whose task it is to make the text as easy as possible to process by the viewer, has opted to maintain the preferred cohesive tie with *heavy type* while deleting the negative in Text 10C (B) in order to preserve continuity of sense. Equivalence of effect is thus satisfactorily achieved. Our particular example has a lot to do with the constraints of subtitling (shift of mode, reduction of text, etc.) but it provides a real insight into the procedures of inferencing and identifying cohesive ties in the recovery of intended meaning in texts.

COLLOCATION

Achieving appropriate collocations in the TL text has always been seen as one of the major problems a translator faces. There is always a danger that, even for experienced translators, SL interference will occasionally escape unnoticed and an unnatural collocation will flaw the TT. In the usual case of translating into one's mother tongue (or language of habitual use), the danger is overcome by vigilance and by careful revising. Little more than this can be said, at least in the case of collocation narrowly conceived. But we would like to suggest that, as one of the devices of lexical cohesion, collocation is not purely mechanical, but provides powerful evidence of intentionality and text-type focus.

Let us begin by describing the process involved in collocation:

> In general, any two lexical items having similar patterns of collocation – that is, tending to appear in similar contexts – will generate a cohesive force if they occur in adjacent sentences.

> (Halliday and Hasan 1976: 286)

The key idea here is 'similar contexts'. It is helpful to see this in terms of the text-world and real-world models of text users. In other words, what is a natural collocation for one language user may be less so for another. In this sense, collocations perceived in texts can be pointers to an intended meaning which is not made explicit by other means. The collocational network built up over an extended length of text can, in itself, provide a model of speaker meaning at a level deeper than that of the surface text.

We now return to our analysis of Text 10B (Muriel Spark). The topic of secondary education is relayed by the progressive development of a network of simple collocations such as *grammar school – English – other subjects – secondary modern school – teachers – classrooms*, etc. As collocations, these are probably non-problematic in translation into most languages, although the more frequent the collocational pattern (as defined above), the more cohesive will be the resulting text. Examples of other simple collocations are *glad – disappointment; painted – gloss; education – ignorance*. But an interesting sub-topic soon emerges in the second paragraph, where the relatively unexpected item *hygienic* is highly informative (on this notion, see below). Collocations which then emerge are:

> *light – airy – bright – washable*

and:

> *mess – dusty – dust – chipped – untidy*

In terms of finding lexical equivalents, there is no problem and cohesion will be easily achieved. But the SL receiver of Text 10B is led to construct a text-world model which is presumed to reflect the world-view of the text producer. By inference, it is a model in which 'chipped paint' = 'a mess' = 'unhygienic' and even (although at one further remove), 'liable to encourage bad habits'.

The role of collocation in fulfilling a rhetorical purpose (whether explicit or unadmitted) is clear. Any attempt to mitigate in translation the unexpectedness of the item *hygiene*, for example, would lower its informativity, detract from the rhetorical purpose and from the overall text focus of argumentation. It follows that, in translation, the collocations should in general be neither less unexpected (i.e. more banal) nor more unexpected (i.e. demanding greater processing effort) than in the ST. It would be an understatement to say that such a balance is not always easy to achieve.

JUNCTION AND INTER-PROPOSITIONAL COHERENCE

Thus far, the cohesive relations we have reviewed are ones holding between various elements in a text. We now come to relations holding between propositions, in terms of both overt signalling (cohesion) and perceived intentions (coherence). **Junction** is a term used to refer to surface signals of relations among events or situations in a text world. Halliday and Hasan (1976: 238), while noting that no single complete inventory of types of conjunctive relations exists, propose four broad categories: additive, adversative, causal, temporal, including some of the relations which others (e.g. Graustein and Thiele 1983) list separately: alternative, explicative, conditional, concessive, instrumental, comparative, etc. Crombie (1985) describes many of these relations as **binary values** (cause–effect, condition–consequence, statement–exemplification, etc.) and lists some of the items which typify them (*because, so, if, for example,* etc.).

The consecutive interpreter is closely acquainted with these major relational categories for, whereas in natural discourse the relations may not be explicitly signalled, they are always inferrable and have to be made explicit in note-taking. This is so because the basic principle of note-taking, used as an *aide-mémoire* by consecutive interpreters, involves abbreviated or symbolic representation of propositions, arranged in a format which makes clear the relations between them. Training in this particular interpreting skill almost inevitably involves a form of discourse analysis and heightens awareness of inter-propositional coherence and the need to preserve it in translation.

To illustrate the process, Fig. 10.2 is a representation of a short extract from a trainee consecutive interpreter's notes. Discussion of note-taking techniques lies outside the scope of this book but what is of interest to us here is the clear marking on the left of the column of logical links between elements.

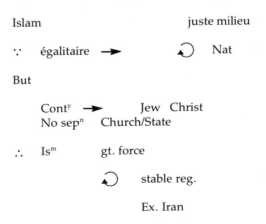

Figure 10.2

The interpreter's output from these notes was as in Text 10E.

Text 10E

In these various countries, Islam is perceived as the religion of the happy medium. Because it is egalitarian in character, it has sparked off several national revolutions. But, unlike the Jewish and Christian religions, in Islam there is no separation between Church and State and, consequently, it is a mighty force, capable of bringing down the most stable political regimes. Iran is a case in point . . .

EXPLICIT AND IMPLICIT RELATIONS

Exactly the same relations are involved in the processing of written discourse. The translator responds to signals in the ST in an attempt to maintain the same logical relations between propositions in the TT. But whereas translators seek to preserve the same coherent interpretation by relaying a universal binary value (such as cause–effect), they will be aware of a difference in the range of cohesive devices available in SL and TL for signalling that value. Explicitness may be required here but not there; a given conjunctive item (say, *and* in English) may have a greater range of signalling potential than mere 'addition'. One has only to consider translating into another language the relation between propositions in the following examples to see that there is no easy correspondence between surface signals and coherence relations:

I was sent over to the grammar school, with a note for one of the teachers, **and** you should have seen the mess.

It is a good thing to have an education behind you, **and** I do not believe in ignorance.

He says he hasn't got a penny **and** he's driving around in a new Porsche.

In each of these examples, the relation signalled by *and* is one which holds between propositions in the text world. Such relations are known as **internal** relations, as distinct from relations between events/processes in the real world, which are called **external** (see Martin 1983: 2, Halliday and Hasan 1976: 241). The role of *and* in the following sentence, signalling temporal sequence, is an example of an external relation;

She came into the room and sat down.

It will be apparent from these examples that the item *and* in English is versatile in its relational potential. Further, it is clear that inter-propositional relations need not be explicitly signalled. Compare, for example, the following sequence with the sentence above:

> She came into the room. She sat down.

Let us consider some examples of these processes at work. Fowler (1986: 67) notes that implicit causative relations are characteristic of the style of the novels of Raymond Chandler. The effect is that 'the reader has constantly to retrieve unstated assumptions to understand Marlowe's reasoning and motives'. But it is not only causation that is involved. The relations between all kinds of propositions are frequently left implicit, so that inferencing is continually required, thus involving the reader more closely in the text. Consider Text 10F as an illustration of this process.

Text 10F

> Down below the water there was what looked like an underwater flooring. I couldn't see the sense of that. I asked him.
> 'Used to be a boat landing before the dam was raised . . .'

> (R. Chandler, (1964) *The Lady in the Lake*)

Another writer might have preferred something like '. . . *I couldn't see the sense of that, so I asked him why it was there. He explained: 'Used to be . . .'*. But, the reader's participation would have been inhibited.

The translator of Text 10F, therefore, has the problem of reconciling the need to preserve the appropriate degree of inferencing with whatever are the requirements of junction in the target language. The fact is that in this area of cohesion, as in all others, textual procedures are motivated. And it is motivation which will be the deciding factor in the conflict between, on the one hand, the desire to improve the cohesion of the target text in conformity with TL norms and, on the other, the duty to reflect the 'style' of the source text.

In the light of these considerations, we now return for the last time to Text 10B. The third sentence in the text is an illustration of how cohesion may be used to create implications, allowing an unstated argument to emerge from the text. It is also an instance of conjunctive relations holding between more than a pair of propositions, a case of what Martin (1983) calls **range:**

> I am glad that I went to the secondary modern school, because it was only constructed the year before. Therefore, it was much more hygienic than the grammar school.

As cohesive signalling devices, the items *therefore* and *because* belong to the area of causative relations. Here, they both serve as encodings of the binary value reason–result (see Crombie 1985: 20, who points out that the reason member often follows the result member in English). Thus, in the first sentence above, 'recent construction' is advanced as the reason for 'gladness' and the coherence of this argument is supported by *because*. But the argument is perceived as unsatisfactory or incomplete: 'recent construction' does not, in a normal world, of itself create 'gladness'. Hence, the need for a further reason–result pair, in which 'recent construction' is said to be a cause of 'hygiene'. By inference, the reader constructs a model of the text producer's world-view, in which 'new' is 'hygienic', 'old' is 'unhygienic' and 'hygiene' is an overriding factor affecting choice. This model is borne out in subsequent text. By reference to the cognitive environment (world knowledge), the reader may then infer that what is a perfectly logical conclusion for the writer (*therefore* . . , *because* . . .) is not necessarily so for most people. Here, the explicit causation goes beyond signalling links between propositions and provides evidence of a whole world-view.

We can now appreciate how particular instances of junction may contribute evidence to the reader's model of the text producer's intended meaning. In this process, reference is constantly made to what are considered to be shared assumptions. As Beaugrande (1980: 19) suggests:

> coherence is upheld by continual interaction of text-presented knowledge with prior knowledge of the world.

In order to preserve intended meaning, the translator has to consider cohesion in the light of what constitutes assumed knowledge for ST reader and TT reader alike.

THEME AND RHEME IN TRANSLATION

Let us now briefly recapitulate on the discussion so far. We have considered cohesion as that aspect of texture which upholds textuality by making a sequence of sentences hang together as a coherent text. Cohesion and, ultimately, coherence may thus be taken as cover terms for the ways in which contextual values (including, most prominently, text-type focus) are relayed. That is, a cohesive and coherent text is one which successfully responds to indications of field, mode and tenor, pragmatic intentions, their value as signs and a specification of a given text-type focus. Translators relay the different kinds of meaning yielded by these contextual values, a process which we can illustrate by considering Text 10G.

Text 10G

Lebanon

For the tenth time
give us a chance

From our Levant correspondent
The latest peace plan for Lebanon, signed in Damascus on December 28th, has a slightly better chance of success than the nine previous plans hopefully pressed upon that sad country since the civil war began more than a decade ago. This is not saying much. One of the signatories has already just survived an assassination attempt by disgruntled people within his own following.

But there are reasons for hope. First, ...

(*The Economist*, 4.1.86)

Let us imagine a translator of Text 10G tackling sentence 1. The obliqueness of *slightly better* creates a problem of interpretation. Equally plausible at this stage are both the 'optimistic' and 'pessimistic' interpretations ('it really is better' or 'is only slightly better'). The transition to sentence 2, however, provides an ideal vantage point from which to view the way a given segment of text maintains a coherent point of view. Sentence 2 is a turning point at which a cohesive device (*this*) relates to previous discourse ('the pessimism is not unwarranted'). By now, intended meaning has become clearer; a concession is being made to those who subscribe to the 'pessimistic view'. Sentence 3 enhances the concession by providing concrete (but not conclusive) evidence. The entire sequence, therefore, reads as a thesis cited to be opposed. Sentence 4 ushers in the opposition. On this reading, the contextual description of sentences 1, 2 and 3 may be represented as in Fig. 10.3

Field:	journalist commentary on current affairs in Lebanon
Tenor:	semi-formal
Mode:	written to be read, with echoes of spoken hortatory discourse
Intention:	'concession to the pessimism theory'
Sign:	'provisional endorsement of the pessimism theory'
Text-type:	counter-argument
Structure:	thesis cited to be opposed, developed as thesis – enhancer – enhancer
Cohesion:	*this* as an anaphoric demonstrative pronoun; *saying* as lexical cohesion (general word to recap sentence 1)

Figure 10.3   Contextual description of Text 10G

The picture that emerges from the representation in Fig. 10.3 is, of course, idealised. In reality, due to the obliqueness of *slightly better*, perception of the intention and the sign involved is problematic. Even after sentence 2 has been processed, both 'optimistic' and 'pessimistic' interpretations are still equally plausible. But one of these must be selected. Some languages (e.g. Arabic) use two different lexico-grammatical representations to relay the 'optimism theory' or the 'pessimism theory'. The renderings in Arabic may be represented literally as (1) and (2) below:

(1)   'The latest peace plan enjoys a slightly bigger chance of success'
(2)   'The latest peace plan does not enjoy anything except a slight chance of success'

It may be contended that in translating a text such as 10G into closely related languages such as German or French, the need to mark the distinction between the two interpretations in question does not even arise. Of course, different languages resort to different surface solutions. The point at issue, however, is not what explicit surface devices are used to relay this or that coherence structure. Rather, it is the need properly to perceive how the text is developing and to avoid misconstruing the general drift of the argument. Clues for underlying coherence systems exist in every language. They are bound to be present in one way or another, even if they are not made explicit. Taking them into consideration is therefore a basic requirement for achieving the desired equivalence. In short, conditions of equivalence can only be met when elements of texture are analysed in terms of their basic function as reflectors of higher-level intentions and signs.

Cohesion must then be perceived as a set of responses to higher-level contextual indications. But is the analysis of cohesion alone sufficient to make clear the effect of higher-order semiotics on texture? We feel that it is not the case. Other variables of texture are in operation, relaying other, perhaps richer kinds of meaning and in the process establishing local and global coherence. It is our aim in the following discussion to shed light on some of these factors and establish how they function as support mechanisms for other aspects of text constitution. Two major systems will be discussed: (1) thematisation, manifested in the sequence of theme and rheme in the clause; (2) information, relayed by the sequence of 'given' and 'new' in the clause.

THEMATISATION: FUNCTIONAL SENTENCE PERSPECTIVE

One basic aspect of texture which works in harness with cohesion is **theme–rheme** arrangement. The organisation of the clause in terms of theme and rheme has come to be collectively referred to as **functional sentence perspective** or FSP (Firbas, Halliday, etc.). Sentence elements are seen to function within a certain perspective of communicative importance. Basically, this means that:

1. An order predominates in the sentence in which a theme precedes, and is commented on by, a rheme; for example, in *This is not saying much* (Text 10G), *this* would be theme, while *not saying much* would be rheme. (The item *is*, which for some would be included in the rheme, is labelled **transition** by Firbas and others, thus linking theme to rheme).
2. Thematic elements are 'context-dependent' and consequently of lesser communicative importance than 'context-independent'

rhematic elements; *not saying much* is communicatively more important than either *is* or *this*.

COMMUNICATIVE DYNAMISM

The Prague linguist Firbas (e.g. 1975) attempts to account for the relative importance of theme, transition and rheme in terms of their contribution to discourse. He uses the concept of **communicative dynamism** to refer to the quality which pushes communication forward. As the text unfolds, certain known, context-dependent elements contribute less to the advancement of communication than other context-independent elements occurring subsequently.

There is normally some relationship between the linear ordering of elements in a sentence and their FSP functions (that is, the subject of an English sentence tends to be thematic, the predicate rhematic, etc.) However, other considerations may override basic word order as when a later element is brought to the fore in a cleft sentence in English ('It's the presidency he's aiming for'). It is in cases such as these that linearity and function do not coincide. There will also be cases in which linear order is subordinated to other, quite subtle considerations. The same subject–verb–object word order in English can be used to quite different effects. For example,

> *Much credit flows to the State of Israel* (Text 9E)

is not rhetorically equivalent to

> *The State of Israel deserves credit* . . .

As a text-initial sentence, the first example is more likely to be followed by a rebuttal ('however . . .', etc.) whereas the second could set a scene for exposition of the merits of the State. In other words, communicative dynamism is, above all, a reflection of aspects of context such as intentionality and text-type focus, and not just of basic word order.

The Prague linguists view theme and rheme broadly as 'what the sentence is about' and 'what is said about it' respectively. The implications for translators of this conception of sentence texture may be illustrated by the following example. Text $10H_1$, is an idiomatic translation of an Arabic text. Text $10H_2$ is a version in which the importance of the theme–rheme arrangement in the ST has not been reflected, presumably on the assumption that theme–rheme ordering is random.

Text 10H₁

> The book provides an analytical historical exposition of the most important Islamic organizations in Egypt. These organizations – The Muslim Brothers, The Muslim Society and Al Jihaad – have all been involved in violent opposition to the government.

Text 10H₂

> The book provides an analytical historical exposition of the most important Islamic organizations in Egypt. The Muslim Brothers, The Muslim Society and Al Jihaad are the organizations which have all been involved in violent clashes with the government.

The divergence between the two versions of sentence 2 can be analysed in terms of theme and rheme, thus:

Text 10H₁

> Theme (*These organizations*) >>>> Rheme (*have all been involved*)

Text 10H₂

> Theme (*The Muslim Brothers*, etc.) >>>> Rheme (*are the organizations*)

In other words, two wholly different emphases emerge:

> 10H₁: 'these organizations have all been involved'
> 10H₂: 'X, Y and Z are the organizations which have been involved'

The first point to be made is that Text 10H₂ does not use the full potential of demonstrative anaphora: *these* in Text 10H₁ is a theme which reactivates a previously mentioned entity. The naming of the three organisations in 10H₂, by contrast, establishes a new entity as theme. Secondly, the rheme in 10H₁, sentence 2, has the illocutionary force of 'implicating these organisations in violence' whereas the rheme in 10H₂ 'tones down the involvement', relaying what amounts to a mere 'definition'. Two different rhetorical purposes are being served. But only the first of these is consistent with the text producer's intentions.

INFORMATION SYSTEMS: GIVEN–NEW INFORMATION

In addition to viewing theme–transition–rheme within a perspective of communicative importance, text users recognise another set of values accruing from the organisation of the clause into a message. The information structure of a text involves: (a) predictability and recoverability of information, (b) saliency of information, and (c) shared assumptions (see Prince 1981 for a detailed discussion of these concepts; and cf. Chapter 5 above). The three notions overlap: if speakers assume that a given unit of information is predictable, they must also assume that it is salient and that hearers share these assumptions.

Predictability and recoverability

Halliday (e.g. 1967) adopts the view that the clause as a message displays two kinds of information: **given** information, which the addresser believes is known to the addressee, because it is present in the textual or extra-textual environment; and **new** information, which is believed by the addresser to be unknown to the addressee. For example, in *This is not saying much* (Text 10G), *this* is recoverable from the preceding sentence and must be perceived as such. In Text 10H$_2$, one of the problems is that the thematic content of sentence 2 is not recoverable from available information in the preceding sentence. The reader is instead confronted with unpredictable information.

Saliency

Translators have to reassess hypotheses about hearers' beliefs and speakers' assessment of these beliefs in the text to be translated. Text 10H$_2$, however, not only involves a flouting of the readers' expectations but also a disregard on the part of the translator for the writer's hypotheses about the readers' beliefs. That is, the translator violates 'given' information, which in Chafe's (1976: 30) terms is:

> . . . that knowledge which the speaker assumes to be in the consciousness of the addressee at the time of the utterance.

The translator thus presents the reader with what Chafe would label 'new' information:

> . . . what the speaker assumes he is introducing into the addressee's consciousness by what he says.

The producer of the source text could not have made such an assumption since the information in question has already been presented as 'new' in the previous sentence.

The value of concepts such as recoverability and saliency is that they enable us to be more precise in speaking about translations. Very often, vague feelings of dissatisfaction with a translation are ascribable to subtle shifts in the saliency and recoverability of information.

Shared assumptions

The recoverability and saliency of *These organizations* (Text 10H$_1$, sentence 2) may also be seen in terms of 'shared assumptions'. This concept is explained by Prince (1981: 230) as follows:

> The speaker assumes that the hearer 'knows', assumes, or can infer a particular thing (but is not necessarily thinking about it).

This may again be illustrated from Text 10G. Sentence 3 (*One of the signatories . . .*) is inferrable as an instance of the pessimism relayed in the preceding sentence. By the same token, *this* (in sentence 2) is inferrable from the preceding sentence and *the latest peace plan* is inferrable from a wider context.

In formulations such as these, however, there seems to be no recognition of the active role played by producers as well as receivers in assessing 'givenness' in terms of a text plan. A plan puts into operation the requirement that speakers seek to maintain a coherent point of view and orchestrate their discourse accordingly (see Grimes 1975, who refers to this as 'staging'). This is the principle on which speakers decide whether or not to present a particular item as given. In other words, the choice is not *ad hoc*; it is motivated by knowledge, hypotheses and assumptions on the part of speakers and, far more importantly, it is related to intentionality. There will always be textual evidence of speakers' judgement (cf. the notion of 'textual indices', referring to signals of intended meaning, in Candlin and Saedi 1983).

Assumed familiarity

As mentioned in Chapter 5, Prince (1981) prefers the term 'assumed familiarity' to that of 'shared knowledge'. This notion refers to the assumptions which a speaker/writer makes about the hearer/reader and which have a determining effect on the form of the text being produced. Prince's (1981: 245–6) purpose in distinguishing between new entities and inferrables is to show that where possible

> hearers do not like to make new entities when old ones will do and speakers, if they are cooperative, form their utterances so as to enable the hearer to make maximum use of old entities.

Thus, Text 10H$_2$ is inadequate in that it does not make use in sentence 2 of entities evoked in sentence 1. In other words, the text violates Prince's maxim concerning making use of 'old' entities.

This analysis enriches our understanding of notions such as predictability, recoverability and saliency. But what is of interest to the translator is to know more about the motivations behind subsequent re-use of an entity, according to a given discourse plan. There can be no doubt that the entities and the plan are related.

THEMATIC PROGRESSION

What we are suggesting, then, is that thematicity or givenness is a discoursal phenomenon, rather than merely a property of the sentence. The reason why text producers develop particular theme–rheme or given–new patterns in whole texts has attracted relatively little attention (cf., however, Daneš (1974), Scinto (1977), etc.) Most work has been carried out on the internal arrangement of individual sentences.

When theme and rheme analysis remains restricted to the boundaries of the sentence, however, it is naturally unable to bring out the function of these elements within texts. Yet, if theme–rheme analysis is to have any relevance to translators, it must provide an account of thematic progression in the service of particular rhetorical purposes. We shall use Daneš's term **thematic progression** to refer to the way subsequent discourse re-uses previous themes or rhemes according to an overall text plan. Thematic progression relates the way themes and rhemes concatenate within a text to the hierarchic organisation of the text and ultimately to rhetorical purpose. According to Daneš (1974: 113):

> By [thematic progression] we mean the choice and ordering of utterance themes, their mutual concatenation and hierarchy, as well as their relationship to hyperthemes of the superior text units . . ., to the whole text, and to the situation.

Given the specifications for Text 10G presented in Fig. 10.3 above, the thematic pattern presented in Fig. 10.4 emerges.

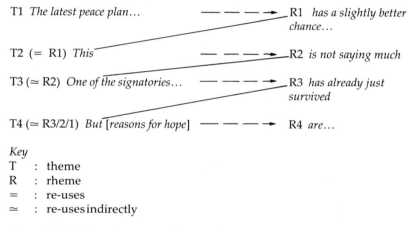

Key
T   : theme
R   : rheme
=   : re-uses
≈   : re-uses indirectly

Figure 10.4   Thematic pattern of Text 10G

The emerging pattern for the text may be described as 'zig-zag', relaying an element of evaluativeness which we believe to be compatible with the overall 'hortatory' function of the text in question. Some aspects of re-using rhemes as themes in Fig. 10.4 may seem erratic; there is less than total identity between T3 and R2 and between T4 and R1/2/3. But there is no need for the link between themes and rhemes to be explicit. The association is often perceived on cognitive grounds as part of text comprehension, as recognised by Scinto (1977), who develops a typology of 'rheme thematisation' (i.e. cases where rhemes are picked up as themes in the subsequent discourse):

T1   >>>> R1 ⎫
                    ⎬ consequence   ⎰ John drank the poison.
T2 (=R1) >>>> R2 ⎭   ⎱ Death followed quickly.

T2 (=R1)   derived by implication ⎰ He paid the workers. The
                                  ⎱ wages came to not very much.

T2 (=R1)   illustration ⎰ John didn't like Bill's bad habits.
                         ⎱ His lying was pathological.

T2 (=R1)   reason, backing ⎫ ⎧ Leander couldn't sleep that
           or explanation ⎬ ⎨ night. Losing gracefully was just
                           ⎭ ⎩ not in his nature.

T2 (=R1)   conclusion ⎰ John ran in the third race.
                       ⎱ Winning was very satisfying.

Scinto also illustrates this kind of permutation from cases of 'theme repetition'. This is when themes are picked up as themes in the subsequent discourse, a pattern which, we maintain, tends to be characteristic of conceptual exposition as a text-type focus:

T1   >>>> R1 ⎫
                    ⎬ partial identity (a party = good time)
T2 (=T1) >>>> . . . ⎭

T2 (=T1)   member of a set (the boys = John)
T2 (=T1)   a particular instantiation (a large car = the Rover)
T2 (=T1)   the contrary or opposite (boy = girl)

Finally, Scinto mentions that themes or rhemes may be derived from metalinguistic context or setting, time or circumstance. In fact, extending Scinto's taxonomy, one may go as far as to say that when themes and rhemes are redeployed, there need only be some affinity at the higher level of the signs involved. In Text 10G, for example, *one of the signatories narrowly escaping assassination* is located within the same semiotic sphere as 'the realistic but pessimistic view of the future of Lebanon'.

There is a need for analysis of thematic progression in different languages over a range of text types. We know little about what patterns there are and how equivalence could be achieved between them. One thing of which we can be confident, nevertheless, is that the patterns are always employed in the service of an overriding rhetorical purpose. This is an aspect of texture which is of crucial importance to the translator.

THEME–RHEME IN RELATION TO GENRE AND DISCOURSE

Considerations of text structure and overall context are not static; 'zig-zag' patterns, for example, do not always and inevitably represent argumentation. Rather, there is a preference for a given pattern in a given text plan. Context sometimes admits subtle variations which entail certain adjustments on the part of text users. A case in point is the phenomenon of hybridisation (discussed in relation to text type in Chapter 8).

To illustrate the kind of discoursal and generic constraints on theme–rheme patterns, let us consider Text 10I.

Text 10I

> Britain has uncovered a plot by Israel to use forged British passports for Mossad secret service hit-men to attack opponents abroad. The discovery has led to a furious diplomatic row, and an Israeli apology and assurance that it would not use British cover again.
> The eight forged passports were discovered by chance last summer in a bag inside a telephone booth in West Germany. The bag also contained a genuine Israeli passport and envelopes linking the document with an Israeli Embassy. All the papers were handed in to a British consulate-general and brought back to London.

> (*Sunday Times* 15.3.87)

Text 10I is an Expository text made to display features of argumentation. The theme–rheme pattern that emerges is shown in Fig. 10.5.

The 'zig-zag' theme–rheme pattern, characteristic of argumentation, is unmistakable. Yet Text 10I is an instance of news reporting. This form of thematic hybridisation may be explained in terms of discoursal and generic constraints. The discourse of

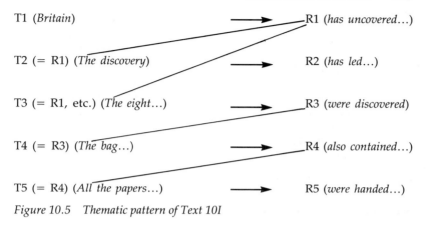

Figure 10.5   Thematic pattern of Text 10I

'sensationalising' news (as opposed to simply reporting it) and the genre of 'the scoop' (as opposed to mere news reporting) play a vital role in revealing the 'real' intention of the text producer. The scoop is an ideal genre which tends to entail two discoursal functions: reporting events and evaluating them. Translators will have to be vigilant: while preserving these discoursal and generic values in whatever is the appropriate TL form, they will have to avoid the pitfall of, on the one hand, turning the text into an instance of bland news reporting or, on the other, of 'editorialising'.

In Text 10I, the *Sunday Times* is not so much concerned to argue an ideological case but rather to sensationalise the events. Furthermore, the journalists producing the piece must have been careful not to operate within a 'propagandising' editorial genre, but merely to promote their own 'scoop'. Unawareness of these subtleties can lead to serious problems such as those faced by a group of translator trainees given the text as a translation assignment. Figure 10.6 illustrates the deviant renderings produced.

More neutral alternatives were available. The majority of the students, however, felt that they were genuinely evaluating the discovery for an Arab audience, from an anti-Israeli point of view. In short, because of their own cultural and ideological predilections, they were operating within the discourse and genre appropriate for an argumentative text (e.g. an editorial), in which such a theme–rheme pattern would be expected.

Items from Text 10I	Back-translation of student renderings into Arabic
uncovered	unmasked
plot	conspiracy
forged	distorted, faked
hit-men	death squad
attack	liquidate
opponents	dissidents
row	clamour

Figure 10.6   Semantic deviation

TEXTURE – A FINAL WORD

The basic argument in this chapter has been that texture provides the means for the realisation of discourse intentions (context) and the implementation of a given text plan (structure). Our account of texture has been an attempt to chart the routes through which context (most prominently, text-type focus) is made more accessible and structure (hierarchic organisation) more transparent. For the translator, therefore, negotiation of texture marks the transition from the stage of forming hypotheses about an ST to the crucial stage of making lexical and grammatical choices for the TT.

To test these hypotheses, we have attempted to relate the various manifestations of texture to higher-order contextual values. But, as we have frequently suggested, more work in this area of text constitution is needed. So far, the evidence which has accumulated (see Prince 1978 for an example) suggests that texture is almost causally determined by text structure and, ultimately, by overall context.

Thematic organisation also appears to be an area which language users exploit in establishing a coherent point of view. Perfetti and Goldman (1974) suggest that placing the main referent in subject position (that is theme 1 becoming theme 2, and so on) is a method favoured by those who prepare encyclopedia entries, obituaries and children's books. In a similar vein, Brown and Yule (1983) point out that a detective novel constantly thematises time adverbials, while a travel brochure systematically uses place adverbials as themes. These questions are germane to the work of those involved in the study of language and culture as, no doubt, different societies avail themselves of different means of structuring their discourse.

ELEVEN

The translator as mediator

In this book, our concern has been to show that speech and writing are not random activities; that texts provide evidence of how speakers/writers intend meaning and hearers/readers infer meaning, in terms of what both parties perceive as being relevant to a particular context. In broad terms, we would say that context exerts a determining influence on the structure and, ultimately, the texture of discourse. Accordingly, we have traced the paths which lead from analysis of context (Chapters 4–8) to study of the structural patterns of texts (Chapter 9) and the motivated lexical and syntactic choices which serve overall rhetorical purposes (Chapter 10).

We hope to have shown that the translator stands at the centre of this dynamic process of communication, as a mediator between the producer of a source text and whoever are its TL receivers. The translator is first and foremost a mediator between two parties for whom mutual communication might otherwise be problematic – and this is true of the translator of patents, contracts, verse or fiction just as much as it is of the simultaneous interpreter, who can be seen to be mediating in a very direct way.

TWO KINDS OF MEDIATION

What, then, is involved in this process of mediation? Most obviously, the translator has not only a bilingual ability but also a bi-cultural vision. Translators mediate between cultures (including ideologies, moral systems and socio-political structures), seeking to overcome those incompatibilities which stand in the way of transfer of meaning. What has value as a sign in one cultural community may be devoid of significance in another and it is the translator who is uniquely placed to identify the disparity and seek to resolve it.

But there is another sense in which translators are mediators; in a way, they are 'privilege readers' of the SL text. Unlike the ordinary ST or TT reader, the translator reads in order to produce, decodes in order to re-encode. In other words, the translator uses as input to the translation process information which would normally be the output, and therefore the end of, the reading process. Consequently, processing is likely to be more thorough, more deliberate than that of the ordinary reader; and interpretation of one portion of text will benefit from evidence forthcoming from the processing of later sections of text. This benefit of hindsight is something which the written translator shares with the consecutive interpreter but not with the simultaneous interpreter, whose processing of incoming text mirrors more closely that of TL receivers.

Now, each reading of a text is a unique act (cf. G. Steiner 1975, Beaugrande 1978: 30), a process subject to the particular contextual constraints of the occasion, just as much as the production of the text is. Inevitably, a translated text reflects the translator's reading and this is yet another factor which defines the translator as a non-ordinary reader: whereas the ordinary reader can involve his or her own beliefs and values in the creative reading process, the translator has to be more guarded. Ideological nuances, cultural predispositions and so on in the source text have to be relayed untainted by the translator's own vision of reality.

In this final chapter, we propose to study this process of mediation at work. Taking a text which has been translated into many languages, we shall look at the way translators act as intermediaries between ST producer and TT receivers. We have chosen as our sample text the opening paragraphs of J-J Rousseau's *Emile* – a text which is not particularly culture-bound (i.e. inaccessible through cultural specificity) and which purports to be fairly universal in the message it conveys. Text 11A is the source text, first published in 1762, as it appears in the Pléiade edition (Rousseau 1969); Text 11B is the English translation by Barbara Foxley (Rousseau 1911).

Text 11A *Emile*, Livre I

Tout est bien, sortant des mains de l'auteur des choses: tout

dégénére entre les mains de l'homme. Il force une terre à nourrir
les productions d'une autre; un arbre à porter les fruits d'un autre.
Il mêle et confond les climats, les élemens, les saisons. Il mutile
5 son chien, son cheval, son esclave. Il bouleverse tout, il défigure tout:
il aime la difformité, les monstres. Il ne veut rien tel que l'a fait
la nature, pas même l'homme; il le faut dresser pour lui comme
un cheval de manége; il le faut contourner à sa mode comme un
arbre de son jardin.

10 Sans cela tout iroit plus mal encore, et nôtre espéce ne veut pas
être façonnée à demi. Dans l'état où sont desormais les choses, un
homme abandonné dès sa naissance à lui-même parmi les autres
seroit le plus défiguré de tous. Les préjugés, l'autorité, la necessité,
l'éxemple, toutes les institutions sociales dans lesquelles nous nous
15 trouvons sumergés, etoufferoient en lui la nature, et ne mettroient
rien à la place. Elle y seroit comme un arbrisseau que le hazard fait
naitre au milieu d'un chemin, et que les passans font bientot périr en
le heurtant de toutes parts et le pliant dans tous les sens.

C'est à toi que je m'address, tendre et prévoyante mére, qui sus
20 t'écarter de la grande route, et garantir l'arbrisseau naissant
du choc des opinions humaines! Cultive, arrose la jeune plante
avant qu'elle meure; ses fruits feront un jour tes délices. Forme
de bonne heure une enceinte autour de l'ame de ton enfant: un
autre en peut marquer le circuit; mais toi seule y dois poser la
25 barriére.

Text 11B *Emile* Book I

1 God makes all things good; man meddles with them and they
become evil. He forces one soil to yield the products of another,
one tree to bear another's fruit. He confuses and confounds time,
place, and natural conditions. He mutilates his dog, his horse, and
5 his slave. He destroys and defaces all things; he loves all that is deformed
and monstrous; he will have nothing as nature made it, not even
man himself, who must learn his paces like a saddle-horse, and
be shaped to his master's taste like the trees in his garden.

Yet things would be worse without this education, and mankind
10 cannot be made by halves. Under existing conditions a man left
to himself from birth would be more of a monster than the rest.
Prejudice, authority, necessity, example, all the social conditions
into which we are plunged, would stifle nature in him and put
nothing in her place. She would be like a sapling chance sown

15 in the midst of the highway, bent hither and thither and soon
   crushed by the passers-by.

   Tender, anxious mother, I appeal to you. You can remove this
   young tree from the highway and shield it from the crushing
   force of social conventions. Tend and water it ere it dies. One
20 day its fruit will reward your care. From the outset raise a
   wall round your child's soul; another may sketch the plan, you alone
   should carry it into execution.

As an illustration of the notion of the translator as privileged
reader, let us consider Text 11A, lines 2–3:

   Il force une terre à nourrir les productions d'une autre . . .

At this early stage in the reading process, there will be uncertainty
in the reader's mind as to the real import of this element: is it to
be understood as:

1. a whole-hearted condemnation of 'man meddling with the
   good things God has made'?
2. a not-so-whole-hearted condemnation, after all?
3. a counter-example to the initial proposition?

Of course, once reading has advanced beyond a certain stage,
readers conclude that it is option 2 which was intended by the
writer, given the overall rhetorical purpose of the text. But whereas
most readers are content to follow the thread of discourse as it
proceeds, translators are constantly aware of the need to reconstruct
the entire 'gestalt' of the text from the individual fragments. Then,
and only then, are translators in a position to mediate between ST
producer and TT reader. So how do translators resolve their initial
uncertainties and arrive at a reading on the basis of which they can
re-create intended meaning?

Reading is a two-way process. On the one hand, readers
bring to texts their own sets of assumptions based on previous
experience of the world, so that each successive portion of text
is processed in the light of these assumptions, and predictions
are made about the likely development of the text. On the other
hand, text items are analysed in themselves and matched against
each other, a process of syntactic and lexical decoding which
results in the gradual building-up of composite meaning as reading
proceeds (see Alderson and Urquhart 1985). In the field of artificial

intelligence, these procedures are known respectively as **top-down** and **bottom-up processing** (see Brown and Yule 1983: 234). Both, of course, take place simultaneously and there is constant interaction between the two. Top-down analysis informs, and is constantly being informed by, the bottom-up analysis. But whereas the activity of translation criticism has more often than not adopted a uniquely 'bottom-up' approach – identifying discrepancies between ST and TT at word or phrase level and only then relating the problem to contextual factors – we propose in what follows to encompass both procedures. That is, while not losing sight of the micro-analysis which is constantly going on in the translator's mind, we shall trace the path from context, through structure, to texture in order to bring out the communicative, pragmatic and semiotic values which influence translators' decisions and to relate all discussion to producers' and receivers' motivations and expectations.

READER ASSUMPTIONS AND EXPECTATIONS

In our analysis of Texts 11A and 11B, the first thing to point out is the obvious differences in the profile of the target reader groups of ST and TT. Rousseau might be said to have been writing for 'un public "philosophe" ' (Rousseau 1969: 1288), many of them aristocratic, within the context of eighteenth-century Europe. In translating the book for a twentieth-century English-speaking readership, the translator would be bound to assume that readers would be well educated, motivated enough to read an eighteenth-century treatise, perhaps with a professional or academic interest in education, the topic of *Emile*. But the twentieth-century reader would expect to read what appears to be an eighteenth-century text, even if the translation is a modern one. It is here that the user variable of temporal dialect is relevant; the existence in Text 11B of such items as *highway, hither and thither, ere*, show how the translator has responded to this clearly felt expectation.

As reading proceeds, another set of assumptions are involved in defining the text as a communicative transaction (cf. Chapter 3). Figure 11.1 offers a summary of the kind of specification which emerges. To this we can add the pragmatic dimension, involving a text act which could be summarised as: a statement of ideological commitment to a particular version of reality. Finally, semiotic interaction defines the text as a sign among other signs,

Field:	social/educational philosophy (within a genre which no longer exists as such)
Tenor:	formal; addressed to educated reader on an equal-to-equal basis, but with characteristics of didactic, authoritative discourse
Mode:	written to be read reflectively, but reminiscent of spoken mode as in sermons, etc.

Figure 11.1   Text 11A as a communicative transaction

acquiring significance within a cultural context. Thus, the text is recognisable as an instance of a given genre (the academic treatise) and as an expression of the discourse of evaluativeness, half-way between the reasoned account and the provocative polemic (cf. Chapter 4).

SELECTING BETWEEN OPTIONS

How do indications such as these influence the reading process? It was seen in Chapter 8 that all such values help collectively to define an overall rhetorical purpose which in turn defines a text-type focus. And it is within the framework of a particular text type that structural and textural patterns emerge. For example, the initial proposition of Text 11A, lines 1–2:

> *Tout est bien, sortant des mains de l'auteur des choses:*
> *tout dégénére entre les mains de l'homme*

may be perceived as a sign representing either:

1. a thesis stated and to be substantiated; or
2. a thesis stated and to be enhanced, but eventually to be opposed.

We stress, however, the 'hypothetical' nature of these readings, which are to be confirmed, modified or altogether discarded and replaced, once micro-reading is under way.

The second sentence in Text 11A (lines 2–3: *Il force une terre . . . les fruits d'un autre*) is likely to be considered initially as consistent with the ultimate goal of option 1 above: 'maintaining that it is Man who meddles', thus upholding the sequence which emerges from the 'thesis cited' in the first sentence. The following sentences (lines

3–9) confirm this initial reading, serving to enhance the 'Man as meddler' thesis. Yet somehow the more the thesis is reinforced, the weaker the conviction it relays; the picture being painted is too black. Our general assumptions as readers, including what we know of Rousseau and what we recognise as conventional modes of argumentation, lead us to withhold judgement as to the writer's real purpose.

With sentence 7, line 10 (*Sans cela tout iroit plus mal encore . . .*), a problem is encountered and option 1 above becomes no longer tenable. At this stage, readers back-track on the model of writer's intentions they have been working with and revise their initial hypotheses. The first sequence (lines 1–9) now reads 'No doubt Man has committed all these sins' but, with line 10, the text continues as 'However, this has not been entirely inopportune'. The intention is still perceived as 'to convince', but is now understood as 'to convince by putting mens' sins into the perspective of how much worse off we would all be without them'. Consequently, option 2 above is selected and the interaction is now seen as serving rhetorical purpose: that of counter-argument.

INTERACTION OF SIGNS WITHIN THE TEXT

Reading, as an interactive process, is both retrospective and prospective. As Haslett (1987: 17) puts it:

> Ongoing talk can retrospectively recast the interpretation of preceding turns as well as prospectively shape opportunities for future interaction.

The key concept here is interaction. We suggested in Chapter 6 that interaction is a process which takes place not only between participants (ST author, translator, TT reader), but also between the signs which constitute texts and between the participants and those signs. Thus, sentence 2 in Text 11A acquires interactive status only after it is seen, on the one hand, as an enhancer of a thesis cited to be opposed (lines 1–2) and, on the other hand, as part of a sequence which stands in a concessive relationship with the following sequence which is the opposition. Perception of this interaction of signs within the text constitutes the basis of micro-text processing, namely, discovering the hierarchic organisation – or structure – of the text.

The full structural format which emerges from the reading of Text 11A is, then, that of the counter-argument:

> Lines 1–9 **Thesis cited to be opposed,** followed by a set of enhancers lending interim support (discourse = 'Man is a meddler', portrayed so negatively that some redeeming feature must be expected).

> Lines 10–13 **Opposition** (discourse = 'But without Man's meddling, things would be worse')

> Lines 13–18 **Substantiation** (discourse = 'The corruption of social Man'; impassioned polemic)

> Lines 19–25 **Conclusion** (discourse = 'The need to protect natural Good'; didactic)

INTERACTION WITH OTHER TEXTS

Intertextuality is of course involved here in the identification of a text as a sign (cf. Chapter 7). The format listed above is a familiar one, at least within the intertextual conventions of the Western world. But, signs are not always simple instances of a general type; other rhetorical functions may be present which make for a hybrid format. While the overall purpose of Text 11A is definitely counterargumentative and the opposition in lines 10–11 constitutes the fulcrum of the text, the opening sequence (lines 1–9) has the makings of a through-argument rather than a thesis cited to be opposed. On first reading, it does not appear as a concessive ('Certainly it is true that Man is a meddler, yet . . .') but rather as making a case ('Man meddles; for one thing, he . . . Secondly, he . . .'). However, as suggested earlier, we respond to it as preparing the ground for an opposition because of the very vehemence of the condemnation; the list of Man's sins goes on and on and the discourse is impassioned (*Il force, il mutile, monstres,* etc.). This ambivalence of the opening sequence is a feature which must be relayed in translation.

In a similar manner, the conclusion is a hybrid form. Instead of a simple statement of the conclusions derived from the preceding argument, the use of imperatives marks a shift to an instructional text format, but still with the intention of concluding from the 'Man as meddler' argument. The result is that the argument becomes more directly operative (cf. Chapter 8, p. 157): the reader is invited to take action.

PROBLEMS OF COHESION

Armed with this complex structural outline, the translator makes choices at the level of texture in such a way as to guide the TT reader along routes envisaged by the ST producer towards a communicative goal. That is, items selected from the lexico-grammatical resources of the TL will have to reflect the overall rhetorical purpose and discoursal values which have been identified at any particular juncture in the text. How are these values relayed by the English translator in Text 11B? We have seen that the hybrid form of sequence I requires a 'blacker-than-black' picture to be painted of Man. Among the items which relay this discourse of condemnation are *CONfuses, CONfounds, DEstroys, DEfaces, DEformed*. It might be thought that these are merely literal renderings; but the expressive repetition of these prefixes (not paralleled in the ST) serves to reinforce the discoursal values which have been identified. A coincidence, perhaps? For supporting evidence, we turn to the German translation of Text 11A (Rousseau 1963):

> Er **ver**mischt und **ver**wirrt Klima, Elemente und Jahreszeiten. Er **ver**stümmelt seinen Hund . . .

> (emphasis added)

Clearly, exactly the same need is felt to respond in some way to the rhetorical value of the ST sequence.

We have also suggested that in sequence I, the ground is prepared for the subsequent opposition by the very length of the list of Man's misdeeds. In the ST, this enumeration is achieved largely by piling up one instance of 'meddling' on another, without any connectives, until saturation point is reached. In English, the same effect ('overwhelming evidence') is achieved by the insistent repetition of the conjunctive *and*. There is in fact, in Text 11B, conjunction by *and* no fewer than seven times (as opposed to one occurrence only of the item *et* in Text 11A). It is in subtle ways such as these that rhetorical functions are relayed, within generic and discoursal traditions which vary between source and target languages.

In Text 11A, the transition to sequence II (Opposition) occurs in line 10. It is not explicitly signalled, except indirectly by the use of the comparative form *plus mal encore*: 'even worse'; in French, the opposition to sequence I is clear enough, without the need for an explicit marker of the adversative relation. Similarly, the German translator is able to relay the opposition implicitly:

Ohne das wäre alles noch schlimmer . . .

and in English, we might have had:

Without this, everything would be even worse.

In Text 11B, however, the translator, motivated no doubt by the perceived rhetorical purpose, has felt the need to signal the opposition explicitly:

Yet things would be worse . . .

This rendering is entirely consistent with the perceived intentions of the ST author and supports the structural pattern of the text. It also conforms closely to generic conventions in English.

Cohesive relations are also involved in the translation of *Sans cela* (literally 'without that'; Text 11A, line 10) by *without this education* (Text 11B, line 9). Potentially, the ST pronoun could be taken to refer to all the processes referred to in sequence I, including 'mutilation of dogs', etc. Here, the translator has chosen to restrict the anaphoric reference to 'what Man does to Man' (Text 11A, lines 7–9), and to take the opportunity of heralding the actual topic (*education*) of the stretches of discourse which are to follow. This is, no doubt, a bolder move on the translator's part, and one which is not made by the German translator (*ohne das* . . .). It reduces the ambiguity of the anaphoric reference but imposes a particular reading of Text 11A.

Lexical cohesion is involved in a problem of collocation which arises in the translation of Text 11A, lines 22–5:

Forme de bonne heure une **enceinte** autour de l'ame de ton enfant: un autre en peut marquer le **circuit;** mais toi seule y dois poser la **barriére.**

(emphasis added)

The cohesive chain which is formed by the collocation of the three emphasised items ('enclosure' – 'circumference' – 'fence') in this portion of text is, of course, figurative. The metaphor is, however, vague and coherence is established only by tracing the collocational link between the three lexical items. This constitutes a pitfall for translators: any literal rendering is likely to result in a set of low-frequency collocations and coherence will thereby be more difficult to recover. Let us consider the solutions adopted by our translators:

English
> From the outset **raise a wall** round your child's soul; another may **sketch the plan,** you alone should **carry it into execution.**

German
> **Friede** beizeiten **die Seele** deines Kindes **ein;** ein anderer mag **den Umkreis abstecken** wollen, aber du allein muß **die Schranken setzen.**

It will be seen that, whereas the English translator has opted for a more concrete, architectural metaphor ('wall') and altered subsequent collocations to match, in German each item attempts to match as closely as possible the individual values of the French words ('fence in', 'mark out the radius', 'set the limits'); but the contrast between the second and third phrase ('mark out the radius' – 'set the limits') is not clear and consequently, the coherence of these last two elements is weakened. In this respect, the English text has greater clarity.

Solutions to problems of translating metaphor should, in the first instance, be related to rhetorical function. We have maintained throughout the book that texture – the selection and arrangement of items appearing in texts – finds its motivation in higher-order considerations of context and structure. The extended metaphor we are considering is located within a sequence whose purpose is to conclude an argument on 'the need to protect natural Man from the corruption of social Man'. If the function of the metaphor is to relay this rhetorical purpose, then the English (*you alone should carry it* [i.e. the plan] *into execution* for the ST 'You should set the fence/gate') does not fully meet the requirement. The image of 'protection' must be paramount. An alternative rendering, which maintains the collocation and supports the rhetorical function, might be something like: *Raise a wall . . . another may sketch the plan but you alone must be its builder.*

THEMATIC PROGRESSION

In Chapter 10, we saw that theme/rheme arrangement is not random. Thematicity, or givenness, was said to be a discoursal phenomenon, rather than just a property of the sentence. It follows from this that, if thematic progression is to be altered in translation, it should not compromise in any way the rhetorical purpose of the SL text. Changes will not normally be unmotivated.

In the light of these considerations, let us compare the opening sequences in Texts 11A and 11B. Figure 11.2 represents the thematic progression of the two passages.

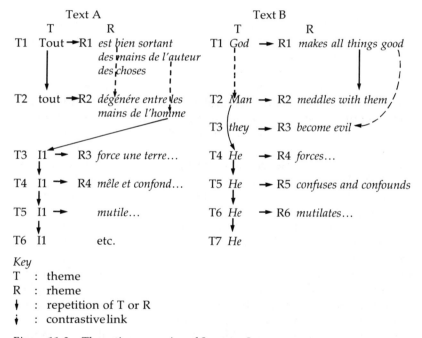

Figure 11.2   Thematic progression of Sequence I

The most significant shift in translation is to be found in the Thesis Cited, where the contrast between *God* and *Man*, which is rhematic in Text 11A, is made thematic in Text 11B. The change may well be motivated by the feeling that, by convention. English prefers to establish the contrast in thematic position. But whereas in the French, the Thesis Cited provides a rheme which is then re-used by the succession of Enhancers as theme, the English establishes 'man' as theme early on; indeed, there is indirect repetition between T1 and T2: although God and man are contrasted, they are both seen as 'makers' (cf. Scinto's list, p. 219). Thus, the 'zig-zag' transition from Thesis Cited to Enhancers is not marked in the translation (although there is an echo of it in T3 = R2: *man meddles with them and they become evil*). A more important point, however, concerns the loss of the thematic link between Sequences I and II, represented in Fig. 11.3.

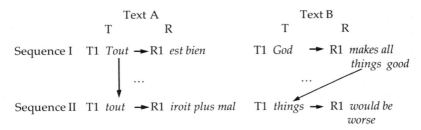

Figure 11.3   Thematic link between Sequence I and II

The repetition of T1 as the first theme of sequence II establishes it clearly as an opposition to the initial thesis cited; this link is less explicit in the English of text 11B.

As the Opposition sequence proceeds, a clear 'zig-zag' pattern emerges, characteristic of the evaluative nature of the counter-argument. A similar thematic progression is followed in translation. But an interesting comparison is to be made at the beginning of the conclusion sequence. In Text 11A, 'You' is placed in theme position by the cleft *C'est à toi que . . .* ('it is to you that'), thus establishing the hypertheme of this particular sequence. The German translator is able to parallel this theme/rheme arrangement: *An dich wende ich mich . . .* In Text 11B, the English translator prefers to avoid the cleft 'It is to you that . . .' but is nevertheless able to preserve the hypertheme by placing the vocative *Tender, anxious mother* in theme position. In this way, the 'operative' intention of the conclusion, mentioned earlier, is retained, even though the item *you* has become a post-posed indirect object.

Much more could be said about Texts 11A and 11B, about

actual and possible translations, their relative adequacy and the problems involved. For example, the rendering of the oblique *auteur des choses* by the direct *God*; the optional use of the feminine pronoun *She* to refer to *Nature*, a personification which helps to support Rousseau's theme of 'natural good'; the use, in the published Arabic translation, of the more specific 'castrate' for the more general *mutile* of Text 11A. But our analysis is intended as illustrative rather than exhaustive.

We have deliberately excluded from our analysis a clear case of mismatch between ST and TT meaning (Text 11A, lines 19–20: *qui sus t'écarter de la grande route;* Text 11B, lines 17–18: *You can remove this young tree from the highway*). It is not that the mismatch is unimportant; rather that it is not a problem of translation as such but more a reflection of a translator's attitude towards a source text, a case of translator's 'licence' which we would not wish to follow. But our purpose in this chapter has been to show our own model of analysis at work, an application of context-sensitive linguistics to the translator's work.

CONCLUSIONS – THE TRANSLATOR AT WORK

In this book, we have attempted to show how translators grapple with the complex web of discourse. To conclude, we shall now highlight some of the main insights into the translation process which have emerged from the text analysis that we have outlined. Figure 11.4 serves as a reminder of the major principles involved. These are essentially **communicative, pragmatic** and **semiotic.** From the translator's point of view, they can be stated as a set of procedures which place the translator at the centre of communicative activity. Within this perspective, the translator takes on the role of mediator between different cultures, each of which has its own visions of reality, ideologies, myths, and so on.

Communicative transaction

As far as different fields of discourse are concerned, the problem of terminologies (to which discussion of translation is often reduced) stands out as particularly acute. Terminologies are not merely a matter of one-to-one equivalence. Nor are they purely a matter of

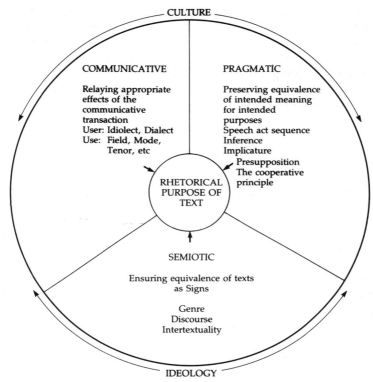

Fig   11.4

transferring nomenclature from more to less prestigious languages. They are a direct reflection of cultural specificity. The challenge to the translator is to perceive terminologies as **vehicles of a culture,** be it that of the latest in laser technology or the multitude of kinship terms among the peoples of an island in the Pacific.

Pragmatic action

Pragmatic aspects of discourse are important in all fields of translating but they are especially apparent in such activities as liaison interpreting. When two people of the same culture and language converse with each other, there is constant use of politeness strategies to ensure cooperative interaction. When an interpreter mediates between interlocutors of different languages, he or she is faced with two sets of problems: on the one hand, politeness strategies are likely to vary from culture to culture. On the other hand, there is always a danger that in the effort to relay propositional meaning, subtle indicators of the way the interaction is going, as well as those of interactive strategies such as hedging and down-toning, may be overlooked and the exchange may become more brusque than intended.

Semiotic interaction

Intertextuality, or the way texts rely on each other, is a semiotic dimension which is powerful in reinforcing social attitudes. An area in which this is apparent is translation for the theatre. What is important in the speech of Shaw's Elisa Dolittle or Pinter's caretaker, for example, is not a particular accent or dialect or reference to some particular cultural feature; rather, it will be the socio-ideological stance reflected in these which is of significance within the play. The ultimate test of translation is: can the consumer of the translated play 'read off' the ideology being signalled? It is in this sense that the study of discoursal values is relevant to the translator.

In treating issues such as these, we hope to have provided a basis for motivated choices on the part of the translator. In charting the relationships which obtain between the context of the communicative activity, its structure and the various cohesive devices at work, we are studying the work of the translator as a particular instance of language in social life.

Glossary

NB The symbol → indicates that the following term is listed in the Glossary

Action The intention to effect a change in the behaviour and/or knowledge state of a receiver of a text, e.g. to rebut an argument.

Adjacency Pairs A sequence in which a second utterance is always seen as a response to the first, e.g. greetings.

Anaphora The use of an item to refer back to another item in the same sentence or text.

Appropriateness The suitability of language use to its context.

Argumentation A text type in which concepts and/or beliefs are evaluated.

Assumed Familiarity What the hearer assumes the speaker assumes, and vice versa

Bottom-up Processing a text on the basis of the textual evidence to hand (cf Top-down).

Cataphoric Refers to the use of a linguistic item to refer forward to subsequent elements in a text.

Channel A particular aspect of → Mode, referring to the vehicle through which communication takes place, e.g. the telephone conversation, the business letter.

Cognitive Environment The set of assumptions, beliefs, knowledge, etc which language users share and refer to.

Coherence The requirement that texts hang together conceptually.

Cohesion The requirement that texts cohere grammatically and lexically.

Communicative Dimension An aspect of context which subsumes all variables pertaining to → Field, Mode and Tenor.

Communicative Dynamism The phenomenon whereby sentences are made up of → Themes followed by → Rhemes and that, in the → Unmarked case, rhemes are the more communicatively important.

Commutability of Signs A basic principle in the development of → Myths, whereby a signifier and a signified give rise to a → Sign which then itself becomes a signifier.

Compensation In translating, the making good of some communicative loss by substituting equivalent effects.

Conceptual Exposition A text type in which the focus is on concepts handled non-evaluatively in terms of either analysis or synthesis.

Connotation Additional meanings which a lexical item acquires beyond its primary, referential meaning.

Context The extra-textual environment which exerts a determining influence on the language used.

Context of Situation All aspects of the situation in which a language event takes place which are relevant to the interpretation of that event.

Contratextuality An aspect of → Intertextual reference which, instead of evoking an image, seems to preclude it, as when political speakers use their opponents' terminology for their own ends.

Conversation Analysis A method of analysis in which investigation of textual evidence takes precedence over contextual factors.

Cooperative Principle The assumption that interlocutors cooperate with each other by observing certain conversational → Maxims.

Co-reference The use of different linguistic items to refer to the same concept.

Co-text The textual environment of a linguistic item (cf Context).

Counter-argument The juxtaposition of a cited thesis and the opposition to it, in order to make a case.

Cultural Codes Conceptual systems which enable → Denotative meanings to take on extra, → Connotative meanings, thus contributing to the development of → Discourse.

Deixis Formal features of language (demonstratives, personal pronouns, tense, etc) which relate the concepts and entities evoked to the time and place of utterance.

Denotation The primary meaning of a lexical item, involving its relationship to the non-linguistic entities which it represents (cf Connotation).

Description An → Expository text type, in which the focus is on the relationship of objects and entities in space.

Dialect (Geographical/Temporal/Social/Standard) Variation in language performance depending on characteristics of the → User.

Discourse Modes of speaking and writing which involve participants in adopting a particular attitude towards areas of socio-cultural activity (e.g. racist discourse, officialese, etc).

Dominant Contextual Focus Another term for → Text type focus.

Dynamic Equivalence Equivalence of effect; the attempt to achieve a similar effect on the TT receiver as the ST is deemed to have on ST receivers (cf Formal equivalence).

Effectiveness Optimum achievement of a communicative goal.

Efficiency Achievement of a communicative goal in the most economic manner possible. Language users normally counter-balance effectiveness and efficiency in order to achieve maximum effect for minimum use of resources.

Ellipsis The omission (for reasons of economy) of linguistic items whose sense is recoverable from context.

Entities (New/Evoked/Inferrable) An entity introduced in a text for the first time is said to be new; if the entity is already present in the context or co-text, it is said to be evoked; if a speaker assumes that a hearer can infer it, then it is said to be inferrable.

Evaluation The determining factor in distinguishing → Argumentation from → Exposition, involving text producers' assessment of alternative belief systems, etc.

Exposition A text type in which concepts, objects or events are presented in a non-evaluative manner.

Felicity Conditions The conditions which have to be fulfilled in order for an utterance to be successful in achieving its intended function.

Field Variation in language according to the use to which it is put in various professional and social settings, e.g. scientific discourse, legal discourse.

Formal Equivalence The attempt to achieve equivalence not only of content but also of form between ST and TT.

Functional Sentence Perspective The assumption that a sentence is to be viewed within a communicative perspective, in which whatever is mentioned first (→ Theme) is normally of less communicative importance than what follows (→ Rheme).

Genre (Generic) Conventional forms of texts associated with particular types of social occasion (e.g. the sonnet, the cooking recipe, etc).

Hearer Meaning The model of the meaning of a speech event which the hearer constructs on the basis of the textual and contextual evidence available.

Hybridisation The multifunctionality of texts, i.e. the fact that texts always serve more than one rhetorical purpose.

Hypertheme The tendency for → Themes of a given type to predominate in certain types of text (e.g. time adverbials in narrative).

Idiolect Features of language variation characteristic of an individual language user.

Illocutionary Having to do with the intentions of the speaker of an utterance.

Implicature An implied meaning derived from an utterance on the basis of certain conversational → Maxims (cf Cooperative Principle).

Inference A meaning inferred from an utterance on the basis of certain conversational → Maxims (cf Cooperative Principle).

Informativity The degree of unexpectedness which an item or utterance displays within a given context.

Initiator That part of a → Sign which serves to identify it (cf Object, Interpretant).

Instruction A text type in which the focus is on the formation of future behaviour, either 'with option' (as in advertising) or 'without option' (as in treaties, contracts, etc).

Intentionality A feature of human language which determines the appropriateness of a linguistic form to the achievement of a communicative goal.

Interaction The successful implementation of intended → Actions, implying on the one hand the perception by receivers of producers' intentions and, on the other hand, the relationship which a given utterance as a sign enters into with other utterances.

Interpretant The effect a → Sign is meant to relay (cf Object, Initiator).

Intertextuality A precondition for the intelligibility of texts, involving the dependence of one text upon another.

Junction The linking of one sentence, clause, etc to another, either explicitly (*but, and, because, etc*) or implicitly (e.g. *He came in. He sat down*).

Lexis The vocabulary of a language; the stock of words available to language users.

Locutionary Having to do with the act of uttering.

Macro-text Processing Another term for → Top-down processing.

Managing Steering discourse towards speakers' goals (cf Monitoring).

Marked See Unmarked.

Maxims Sets of norms which language users adhere to, in order to uphold the → Effectiveness and → Efficiency of communication, e.g. the Maxim of Quantity: 'Be brief'.

Meaning Potential "The paradigmatic range of semantic choice that is present in the system, and to which the members of a culture have access in their language" (Halliday 1978: 109).

Mediation The extent to which text producers and receivers feed their own beliefs into their processing of a given text.

Metalanguage The use of language to comment on language; ranging from a set of terms used for the description of language (as in this Glossary) to the use of language to draw attention to itself (as in plays on words, rhyme, alliteration, etc).

Micro-text Processing Another term for → Bottom-up processing.

Mode The medium selected for language activity; essentially the choice between speech and writing but such distinctions as monologue, dialogue are also seen as variables of mode.

Monitoring Expounding in a non-evaluative fashion (cf Managing).

Motivation/Motivatedness The set of factors which regulate text users' choices, whether conscious or unconscious.

Myth The way in which a given → Sign undergoes a series of transformations until it achieves cultural status in the collective mentality of a community.

Narration An → Expository text type, in which the focus is on situating events in time.

Nominalisation Referring to whole processes by encapsulating them in a single noun, e.g. *He was taken to court for drunken driving. The case dragged on for months.*

Object That part of a → Sign which serves as a vehicle of the sign itself (e.g. the product sample in an advertisement) – cf Initiator, Interpretant.

Paradigmatic The relationship of an item in a text to whatever other items might have stood in its place.

Performative A type of sentence in which an act is performed by its very utterance, e.g. *I declare the meeting open.*

Perlocutionary Having to do with the effect intended in uttering a sentence.

Pragmatic Dimension A dimension of context which regulates → Intentionality.

Pre-text The source of an intertextual reference, ranging from a literary allusion to a body of texts, e.g. the Bible.

Process The procedures involved in the production of texts.

Product Any output of text processing, considered as an object of analysis.

Pro-forms Forms which stand for other text items or constructions.

Recurrence The reiteration of an item or phrase in a text.

Redundancy Saying more than is necessary; often for a particular purpose, e.g. to achieve an implicature.

Register The tendency to pattern language behaviour in relation to a particular type of activity, level of formality, etc.

Reiteration Another term for → Recurrence.

Relevance One of the aspects of the cooperative principle, whereby interlocutors seek to relate their utterances to the current situation.

Restricted Register Any variety of language use which is characterised by a restricted range of formal properties (phonology, lexis and grammar), e.g. shipping forecasts, cooking recipes.

Rheme That part of a sentence which occurs last and which has most communicative importance.

Rhetorical Purpose The overall intention of a text producer, as instantiated by the function of a text, e.g. to narrate, to counter-argue.

Saliency The assumption that some entity is currently to the forefront of interlocutors' consciousness.

Sapir/Whorf Hypthesis The belief that formal features of a language have a determining influence on thought patterns.

Semiotic Dimension A dimension of context which regulates the relationship of texts to each other as → Signs.

Shared Assumptions Another term for → World Knowledge, which recognises the fact that speakers can never *know* what hearers know, and vice-versa.

Sign A unit of signifier + signified, in which the linguistic form (signifier) stands for a concrete object or concept (signified).

Speaker Meaning A model of the meaning which a speaker intends to convey and to which hearers have no direct access.

Speech Acts The action which is intended in the utterance of a sentence. Speech acts may be direct (e.g. *Get out!*) or indirect (e.g. *It's hot in here* = Open a window).

Structure The composition plan of a text, relating → Context to → Texture.

Style Variation in language use, occasioned by conscious choice from the range of phonological, grammatical and lexical resources of language in order to achieve some effect.

Syntagmatic The relationship of an item in a text to those items which occur in its immediate → Co-text.

Systemic Functional Model A model of language description developed by Halliday and others, in which the language system is treated in terms of its potential for fulfilling social functions.

Tenor The relationship between addresser and addressee, as reflected in use of language (e.g. level of formality, relative distance).

Text A set of mutually relevant communicative functions, structured in such a way as to achieve an overall → Rhetorical purpose.

Text Act The dominant → Speech act in a text.

Text linguistics That branch of linguistics which concerns itself with the analysis of spoken and written texts above the level of individual sentences. It involves, for example, the description of the way sentences link together to form → coherent and → cohesive texts.

Text-presented Knowledge The increment of information available from a text (cf World knowledge).

Text-type Focus That aspect of → Context which is seen to be the primary function of a text and which determines the text type.

Textual Indices Signals of the rhetorical intent in a text.

Texture Aspects of text organization, including → Cohesion, → Theme and Rheme, which reflect the compositional plan of a text and its context.

Thematic Progression The tendency for → Themes or → Rhemes to concatenate in particular patterns, relating to → Text Type Focus.

Thematisation The tendency to arrange sentences in such a manner as to draw attention to what is communicatively most important.

Theme That part of a sentence which occurs first and which normally has less communicative importance than the → Rheme.

Through-Argument Citing a thesis and then substantiating it.

Top-down Predicting the meaning of a text on the basis of the information gathered from textual and contextual evidence accruing so far (cf Bottom-up).

Transaction The framework of → Field, Mode, Tenor, etc of discourse, within which communicative intentions are perceived as being mutually relevant.

Transformational grammar A type of grammatical description in which a set of rules is used to derive one linguistic structure from another, more basic structure. The rules should be capable of generating all and only the grammatically well formed sentences of a language.

Unmarked The state of certain lexical or grammatical items or structures which are considered to be more basic or common than other structures, marked for particular effects. The cleft sentence *It was John who did it* is a marked form for *John did it*.

Usage The meaning of a linguistic item in terms of its denotation within the linguistic system.

Use Aspects of language variation relating to what a → User is doing with language (→ Field, Tenor, etc), as opposed to who he/she is.

User Any participant in language activity; the term embraces speakers, writers, hearers and readers.

World knowledge Whatever extra-linguistic or real-world factors are brought into text processing activity.

List of Sources of Text Samples

Arab–British Commerce, Journal of the Arab–British Chamber of Commerce, November 1981.

The Bible: Matthew 20, v.1–16 The Authorised Version 1611.

Revised Standard Version 1954.

New English Bible 1961.

Bronowski J. and B. Mazlish 1960 *The Western Intellectual Tradition*. London.

Bretécher, C. 1978 *Les Frustrés*. C. Bretécher.

Bretécher, C. 1983 *More Frustration*. Methuen.

Chandler, R. 1944 *The Lady in the Lake*. London: Hamish Hamilton.

The Economist 4.01.86 'For the tenth time give us a chance'.

Encyclopaedia Britannica: entry for J-J Rousseau.

Gainsville Sun 20.12.78, quoted in Beaugrande and Dressler 1981.

Gallois, P. M. in *Politique Internationale* 20 (summer 1983): 315.

Goscinny and Uderzo 1972 *Les Lauriers de César* Paris: Les Editions Albert René.

Goscinny and Uderzo 1974 *Asterix and the Laurel Wreath*, translated by A. Bell and D. Hockridge. London: Hodder Dargaud.

The Guardian 18.09.85: B. Le Gendre and E. Plenel 'Third military team involved in sinking'.

1982: Editorial: 'The verdict of Kahan and the context'.

Gulf News, English-language daily published in Bahrain.

Hussain, T. 1932 *An Egyptian Childhood*, translated by E. H. Paxton. London: Routledge.

Iberia, in-flight magazine of Spanish airline, 1987.

IRAQ, English-language monthly, Ministry of Information and Culture, Baghdad 1980.

Lawrence, D. H. 1960 *Lady Chatterley's Lover*. Harmondsworth: Penguin p. 131.

Lawrence, D. H. 1969 *Lady Chatterley* (German translation). Reinbek bei Hamburg: Rowolt Verlag. p. 116.

Le Monde 18.09.85: B. Le Gendre and E. Plenel 'Le *Rainbow Warrior* aurait été coulé par une troisième équipe de militaires francais'.

Majod, A. 1983 *Head-Hunter* in *Modern Malaysian Short Stories*. Kuala Lumpur: Dewan Bahasa dan Pustaka. p. 55.

Molière 1958 *Dom Juan ou le Festin de Pierre*. Oxford: Blackwell p. 13.

Molière 1953 *Five Plays* translated by John Wood Harmondsworth: Penguin p. 209.

Molière 1929 *Molière's Comedies*, Vol 2, introduction by F. C. Green. London: Dent p. 14.

New Statesman 1983: Claudia Wright 'A Back door to war'.

   5.12.86: Christopher Hitchens 'No mistake: this *is* Reagan's foreign policy'.

Orwell, G. 1945 'Politics and the English Language' in *Shooting an Elephant and other Essays*. New York: Harcourt.

Pomonti, J-C 1979 *L'Afrique trahie* Paris: Fayard.

Powell, E. quoted in Sykes (1985).

Pragnell, F. A. 1984 *A Week in the Middle East: An Arabic Language Reader*. London: Lund Humphries.

Proust, M 1914 *Du Côté de chez Swann*. Paris:

Rousseau, J-J. 1969 *Oeuvres complètes IV: Emile ou L'Education*. Paris: Pléiade. pp. 245–6.

Rousseau J-J. 1911 *Emile*, translated by B. Foxley. London: Dent. pp. 5–6.

Rousseau J-J. 1963 *Emile oder Über die Erziehung*, translated by E. Sckommodau. Stuttgart: Philipp Reclam. pp. 107–8.

Sartre, J-P. 1953 *Situations*.

Shakespeare, W. *Macbeth*, Act V, Scene V.

Spark, M. 1958 *You Should Have Seen the Mess!* in Penguin Book of English Short Stories. Harmondsworth: Penguin.

The Sunday Times 13.11.83 John Mortimer 'Week in Focus'.

   15.03.87 'Revealed: The secrets of Israel's nuclear arsenal'.

Tarabishi, G. 1984 *Woman against her Sex*. Beirut: daar Al Adaab.

Tarabishi, G. 1987 *Woman against her Sex*. Translated by B. Hatim and E. Orsini. London: Al Saqi Books.

The Times Editorial: 'The cohesion of OPEC'.

UNESCO Courier July 1984 M. Pereira 'Biografía de la Habana Vieja'. Translated as 'Enchanted Seashell; A Portrait of old Havana'.

UNESCO *Prospects* 1986 P. G. Altbach 'Education and Society: Follow the leader'.

United Nations 9.09.86 Report of the Secretary General.

   9.09.87 Report of the Secretary General.

   14–25.08.78 Conference Report 'World Conference to combat racism and racial discrimination'.

William Carlos Williams 1938 *This is just to say*. In *The Collected Earlier Poems of William Carlos Williams*. New York: New Directions.

World Health Forum 5, 1984: J. S. Bulman 'Dental public health and disease prevention'.

   Editorial: 'The Universities and health for all'.

   Letters to editor.

Bibliography

Aitchison, J. (1976) *The Articulate Mammal. An Introduction to Psycholinguistics*. London: Hutchinson.

Alderson, J. and A. Urquhart (1985) *Reading in a Foreign Language*. London: Longman.

ALPAC (1966) *Language and Machines: Computers in Translation and Linguistics*. A report by the Automatic Language Processing Advisory Committee, Division of Behavioural Sciences, National Academy of Sciences, National Research Council Publication 1416. Washington: NAS/NRC.

Anderson, R. B. (1975) 'Perspectives on the role of the interpreter', in R. W. Brislin (ed.), *Translation Applications and Research*. New York: Gardner Press, pp. 208–28.

Arnold, D. and L. des Tombe (1987) 'Basic theory and methodology in EUROTRA', in Nirenburg (1987), pp. 114–35.

Astington, E. (1983) *Equivalences. Translation Difficulties and Devices, French–English, English–French*. Cambridge University Press.

Austin, J. L. (1982) *How to do Things with Words*. Cambridge, Mass.: Harvard University Press.

Badawi, A. (1968) *La Transmission de la Philosophie Grecque au Monde Arabe*. Paris: Librairie Vrin.

Barthes, R. (1957) *Mythologies*. Paris: Seuil (trans. London: Paladin, 1973).

Barthes, R. (1970) *S/Z* Paris: Seuil (trans. London: Cape, 1975).

Beaugrande, R. de (1978) *Factors in a Theory of Poetic Translating*. Assen: van Gorcum.

Beaugrande, R. de (1980) *Text, Discourse and Process*. London: Longman.

Beaugrande, R. de and Dressler W. (1981) *Introduction to Textlinguistics*. London: Longman.

Bell, R. (1987) 'Translation theory: where are we going?' *Meta* 32, 4:403–415.

Bloomfield, L. (1933) *Language*. New York: Holt.

Bourdieu, P. (1982) *Ce Que Parler Veut Dire*. Paris: Fayard.

Brislin, R. W. (1980) 'Expanding the role of the interpreter to include multiple facets of intellectual communication', *International Journal of Intellectual Relations*, **4**, 137–48.

Brower, R. A. (ed.) (1959) *On Translation*. Harvard: Harvard University Press.

Brown, G. and G. Yule (1983) *Discourse Analysis*. Cambridge: Cambridge University Press.

Brown, P. and S. Levinson (1978) 'Universals in language usage: politeness phenomena', in E. N. Goody (ed.) *Questions and Politeness: Strategies in Social Interaction*. Cambridge: Cambridge University Press, pp. 56–289.

Candlin, C. N. (1976) 'Communicative language teaching and the debt to pragmatics', in C. Rameh (ed.), *Semantics: Theory and Applications*. Georgetown University Round Table on Language and Linguistics, pp. 237–57.

Candlin, C. N. and L. K. Saedi (1983) 'Processes of discourse', *Journal of Applied Language Study*, **1** (2), 103–31.

Catford, J. C. (1965) *A Linguistic Theory of Translation*. Oxford: Oxford University Press.

Chafe, W. L. (1976) 'Givenness, contrastiveness, definiteness, subjects, topics, and point of view', In C. Li (ed.), *Subject and Topic*. New York: Academic Press, pp. 25–55.

Chau, S. (1984) *Aspects of Translation Pedagogy*. Unpublished PhD thesis, University of Edinburgh.

Corder, S. P. (1973) *Introducing Applied Linguistics*. Harmondsworth: Penguin.

Crombie, W. (1985) *Process and Relation in Discourse and Language Learning*. Oxford: Oxford University Press.

Crystal, D. and D. Davy (1969) *Investigating English Style*. London: Longman.

Daneš, F. (1974) 'Functional sentence perspective and the organization of the text', in F. Daneš (ed.), *Papers on Functional Sentence Perspective*. Prague: Academia.

Dressler, W. (ed.) (1977) *Current Trends in Textlinguistics*. Berlin: Walter de Gruyter.

Eco, U. (1973) 'Looking for a logic of culture', in *Times Literary Supplement*, 5 and 12 October 1973.

Fairclough, N. (1985) 'Critical and descriptive goals in discourse analysis', *Journal of Pragmatics*, **9**, 739–63.

Fairclough, N. (1989) *Language and Power*. London: Longman.

Ferrara, A. (1980a) 'An extended theory of speech acts: appropriateness conditions for subordinate acts in sequences', *Journal of Pragmatics*, **4**, 233–52.

Ferrara, A. (1980b) 'Appropriateness conditions for entire sequences of speech acts', *Journal of Pragmatics*, **4**, 321–40.

Ferrara, A. (1985) 'Pragmatics' in T. van Dijk (ed.) *Handbook of Discourse Analysis*, vol. 2 *Dimensions of Discourse*. London: Academic Press.

Firbas, J. (1975) 'On the thematic and the non-thematic section of the sentence', in H. Ringbom (ed.), *Style and Text: Studies Presented to Nils-Erik Enkvist*. Stockholm: Skriptor.

Firth, J. R. (1935) 'The technique of semantics', *Transactions of the Philological Society*, reprinted in Firth (1951), pp. 7–33.

Firth, J. R. (1951) *Papers in Linguistics: 1934–1951*. Oxford: Oxford University Press.

Foucault, M. (1972) *The Archaeology of Knowledge* (trans. M. Sheridan Smith). London: Tavistock.

Fowler, R. (1985) 'Power', in T. van Dijk (ed.), *Handbook of Discourse Analysis*, vol. 4. London: Academic Press.

Fowler, R. (1986) *Linguistic Criticism*. Oxford: Oxford University Press.

Garcia Yebra, V. (1982) *Teoría y práctica de la traducción*, vols. 1 and 2. Madrid: Gredos.

Garcia Yebra, V. (1983) *En Torno a la traducción*. Madrid: Gredos.

Graustein, G. and W. Thiele (1983) 'English monologue as complex entities', in *Linguistische Arbeitsberichte*, 41, Sektion Theoretische und angewandte Sprachwissenschaft, Karl-Marx-Universität, Leipzig.

Green, G. and J. Morgan (1981) 'Pragmatics, grammar and discourse', in P. Cole (ed.), *Radical Pragmatics*. New York: Academic Press.

Greenberg, J. H. (1968) *Anthropological Linguistics: An Introduction*. New York: Random House.

Gregory, M. J. (1967) 'Aspects of Varieties Differentiation', *Journal of Linguistics*, 3, 177–98.

Gregory, M. J. (1980) 'Perspectives on translation from the Firthian tradition', *Meta* 25 (4), 455–66.

Gregory, M. and S. Carroll (1978) *Language and Situation: Language Varieties and their Social Contexts*. London: Routledge & Kegan Paul.

Grice, H. P. (1975) 'Logic and conversation', in Cole P. and Morgan J. L. (eds), *Syntax and Semantics*, vol. 3: *Speech Acts*. New York: Academic Press.

Grice, H. P. (1978) 'Further notes on logic and conversation', in Cole (ed.), *Syntax and Semantics IX: Pragmatics*. New York: Academic Press, pp. 113–27.

Grimes, J. E. (1975) *The Thread of Discourse*. The Hague: Mouton.

Gülich, E. and W. Raible (1975) 'Textsorten-Probleme', in *Linguistische Probleme der Textanalyse*. Jahrbuch des Instituts für Deutsche Sprache in Mannheim. Düsseldorf: Pädagogischer Verlag Schwann.

Gumperz, J. J. (1977) 'Sociocultural knowledge in conversational inference', in M. Saville-Troike (ed.), *28th Annual Round Table Monograph Series on Language and Linguistics*. Washington DC: Georgetown University Press.

Gumperz, J. J. (1982) *Discourse Strategies*. Cambridge: Cambridge University Press.

Halliday, M. A. K. (1967) 'Notes on transitivity and theme in English, Part 1/2', *Journal of Linguistics*, 3, 199–244.

Halliday, M. A. K. (1971) 'Linguistic function and literary style: an inquiry into the language of William Golding's *The Inheritors*', in S. Chatman (ed.), *Literary Style: a Symposium*. New York: Oxford University Press.

Halliday, M. A. K. (1978) *Language as Social Semiotic: The Social Interpretation of Language and Meaning*. London: Edward Arnold.

Halliday, M. A. K., McIntosh, A. and Strevens, P. (1964) *The Linguistic Sciences and Language Teaching*. London: Longman.

Halliday, M. A. K. and R. Hasan (1976) *Cohesion in English*. London: Longman.

Halliday, M. A. K. and R. Hasan (1985) *Language, Context, and Text: Aspects of Language in a Social-Semiotic Perspective*. Victoria: Deakin University Press.

Harris, B. (1981) 'Observations on a Cause Célèbre: Court interpreting at the Lischka Trial', in R. P. Roberts (ed.), *L'Interprétation auprès des tribunaux*. Ottowa: University of Ottowa Press.

Hartmann, R. R. K. (1980) *Contrastive Textology*. Heidelberg: Julius Groos Verlag.

Hasan, R. (1976) 'Socialization and cross-cultural education', *International Journal of Social Linguistics*, **8**

Hasan, R. (1977) 'Text in the Systemic–Functional Model', in W. Dressler (1977), pp. 228–46.

Hasan, R. (1985) 'Texture', in M. A. K. Halliday and R. Hasan, *Language, Context, and Text: Aspects of Language in a Social-Semiotic Perspective*. Victoria: Deakin University Press.

Haslett, B. (1987) *Communication: Strategic Action in Context*. London: Lawrence Erlbaum Associates, Inc.

Hawkes, T. (1979) *Structuralism and Semiotics*. London: Methuen.

Hörmann, H. (1975) *The concept of sense constancy*. Mimeo. University of Bochum.

Horner, W. B. (1975) *Text Act Theory: A Study of Non-fiction Texts*. Unpublished PhD thesis, University of Michigan.

House, J. (1976) *A Model for Translation Quality Assessment*. Tübingen: Gunter Narr Verlag.

Hutchins, W. J. (1986) *Machine Translation, Past, Present and Future*. Chichester: Ellis Horwood.

Hymes, D. (1972) 'On communicative competence', in J. B. Pride and J. Holmes (eds), *Sociolinguistics*. Harmondsworth: Penguin.

Jakobson, R. (1959) 'On linguistic aspects of translation' in Brower (1959), pp. 232–9.

Jakobson, R. (1971) 'Language in relation to other communication systems', *Selected Writings*, vol. II, The Hague: Mouton.

Jakobson, R. (1974) *Main Trends in the Science of Language*. New York: Harper & Row.

Johnstone, B. (1987) 'Arguments with Khomeini: Rhetorical situation and persuasive style in cross-cultural perspective', *Journal of Pragmatics*.

Keenan, E. O. (1976) 'The universality of conversational postulates', *Language in Society*, **5**, 67–80.

Kelly, L. (1979) *The True Interpreter*. Oxford: Basil Blackwell.

Knapp-Potthoff, A. and K. Knapp (1987) 'The man (or woman) in the middle: discoursal aspects of non-professional interpreting' in Knapp, Enninger and Knapp-Potthoff (eds), *Analyzing Intercultural Communication*. Berlin: Mouton de Gruyter.

Kress, G. (1985) *Linguistic Processes in Sociocultural Practice*. Victoria: Deakin University Press.

Kristeva, J. (1969) *Semeiotike. Recherches pour une sémanalyse*. Paris: Seuil (translated as *Desire in Language: a semiotic approach to literature and art*, edited by L. S. Roudiez, translated by A. Jardine, T. A. Gora and L. S. Roudiez. Oxford: Blackwell).

Lefevere, A. (1975) *Translating Poetry: Seven Strategies and a Blueprint.* Assen: Van Gorcum.

Lemke, J. L. (1985) 'Ideology, intertextuality, and the notion of register', in J. D. Benson and W. S. Greaves (eds) *Systemic Perspectives on Discourse,* vol 1. Norwood, N.J.: Ablex Publishing Corporation.

Levinson, S. (1983) *Pragmatics.* Cambridge: Cambridge University Press.

Lotman, J. M. et al (1975) 'Theses on the semiotic study of cultures (as applied to Slavic texts)'. In *The Tell-tale Sign: A Survey of Semiotics.* Lisse: de Ridder Press pp. 57–84.

Lyons, J. (1979) 'Pronouns of address in *Anna Karenina*: the stylistics of bilingualism and the impossibility of translation', in S. Greenbaum, G. Leech and J. Svartvik (eds), *Studies in English Linguistics (for Randolph Quirk).* London: Longman, pp. 235–49.

Lyons, J. (1981) *Language and Linguistics: An Introduction.* Cambridge: Cambridge University Press.

Malinowski, B. (1923) 'The problem of meaning in primitive languages'. Supplement 1 to C. K. Ogden and I. A. Richards, *The Meaning of Meaning.* London: Kegan Paul.

Malinowski, B. (1935) *Coral Gardens and their Magic,* vol. 2. London: Allen & Unwin.

Martin, J. R. (1983) 'Conjunction: the logic of English text', in J. S. Petofi and E. Sozer (eds), *Micro and Macro Connexity of Texts.* Berlin: Helmut Buske.

Martin, J. R. (1985) *Factual Writing: Exploring and Challenging Social Reality.* Victoria: Deakin University Press.

Mauro, T. de (1973) 'The link with linguistics', *Times Literary Supplement,* October.

Melby, A. K. (1982) 'Multi-level translation aids in a distributed system', *Coling 82.* North Holland Linguistic Series, no 47. Amsterdam: North Holland, pp. 215–20.

Melby, A. K. (1987) 'On human–machine translation' in S. Nirenburg (1987), pp. 145–54.

Meschonnic, H. (1973) *Pour la Poétique II.* Paris: Gallimard.

Nabokov, V. (1964) 'Translator's introduction', in A. Pushkin, *Eugene Onegin,* translated from the Russian, with a commentary, by Vladimir Nabokov. New York: Bollingen Foundation.

Namy, C. (1979) 'Du mot au message. Réflexions sur l'interprétation simultanée', *Paralleles,* **2,** 48–60.

Nash, W. (1980) *Designs in Prose.* London: Longman.

Neubert, A. (1985) *Text and Translation.* Ubersetzungswissenschaftliche Beitrage **8.** Leipzig: VEB Verlag Enzyklopadie.

Newmark, P. (1981) *Approaches to Translation.* Oxford: Pergamon.

Newmark, P. (1988) *A Textbook of Translation.* London: Prentice-Hall.

Nida, E. A. (1959) 'Bible translating', in R. Brower (1959), pp. 11–31.

Nida, E. A. (1964) *Toward a Science of Translating with Special Reference to Principles and Procedures Involved in Bible Translating.* Leiden: E. J. Brill.

Nida, E. A. and C. R. Taber (1969) *The Theory and Practice of Translation.* Leiden: E. J. Brill.

Nirenburg, S. (ed.) (1987) *Machine Translation. Theoretical and Methodological Issues*. Cambridge: Cambridge University Press.

O'Donnell, W. R. and L. Todd (1980) *Variety in Contemporary English*. London: Allen & Unwin.

Orwell, G. (1945) 'Politics and the English language', in *Shooting an Elephant and other Essays*. New York: Harcourt.

Payne, J. (1987) 'Revision as a teaching method on translation courses', in H. Keith and I. Mason (eds), *Translation in the Modern Languages Degree*. London: CILT.

Peirce, C. (1931–58) *Collected Papers* (ed. C. Hartshone). Cambridge, Mass.: Harvard University Press.

Perfetti, C. A. and S. R. Goldman (1974) 'Thematization and sentence retrieval', *Journal of Verbal Learning and Verbal Behaviour*, **13**, 70–9.

Picken, C. (ed.) (1983) *The Translator's Handbook*. London: ASLIB.

Picken, C. (ed.) (1985) *Translation and Communication. Translating and the Computer 6*. London: ASLIB.

Porter, B. (1972) *Found Poems*. New York: Something Else Press.

Prince, E. F. (1978) 'A comparison of WH-clefts and it-clefts in discourse', *Language*, **54**, 883–907.

Prince, E. F. (1981) 'Toward a taxonomy of given–new information', in P. Cole (ed.), *Radical Pragmatics*. New York: Academic Press.

Reiss, K. (1971) *Möglichkeiten und Grenzen der Übersetzungskritik*. Munich: Max Heuber.

Reiss, K. (1976) *Texttyp und Übersetzungsmethode. Der Operative Text*. Kronberg: Scriptor.

Sager, J. C. (1983) 'Quality and standards – the evaluation of translations', in Picken (1983), pp. 121–8.

Sampson, G. (1980) *Schools of Linguistics: Competition and Evolution*. London: Hutchinson.

Sapir, E. (1921) *Language*. New York: Harcourt Brace (reprint, Harvest Books, 1949).

Saussure, F. de (1959) *Course in General Linguistics* (translated from the French by Wade Baskin). New York: Philosophical Library.

Schank, R. C. and R. Abelson (1977) *Scripts, Plans, Goals and Understanding*. Hillsdale, N.J.: Lawrence Erlbaum.

Schmidt, S. J. (1977) 'Some problems of communicative text theories', in W. Dressler (1977), pp. 47–60.

Scinto, L. F. M. (1977) 'Textual competence: a prelim⁀. v analysis of orally generated texts, *Linguistics*, **194**, 5–34.

Searle, J. R. (1969) *Speech Acts*. Cambridge: Cambridge Univ ⁀. Press.

Searle, J. R. (1976) 'A classification of illocutionary acts ⁀. ⁀uage in Society*, **5**, 1–23.

Sebeok, T. A. (ed.) (1986) *Encyclopedic Dictionary of Semiotics*, v⁀ ⁀–3. Berlin: Mouton de Gruyter.

Silverman, K. (1983) *The Subject of Semiotics*. Oxford: Oxford University Press.

Simpson, E. (1975) 'Methodology in translation criticism', *Meta*, **20**, 251–62.

Sperber, D. and D. Wilson (1981) 'Irony and the use-mention distinction', in P. Cole (ed.), *Radical Pragmatics*. New York: Academic Press.

Sperber, D. and D. Wilson (1986) *Relevance: Communication and Cognition.* Oxford: Basil Blackwell.

Stalnaker, R. C. (1972) 'Pragmatics', in D. Davidson and G. Harman (eds), *Semantics of Natural Language.* Dordrecht: Reidel.

Steiner, G. (1975) *After Babel: Aspects of Language and Translation.* Oxford: Oxford University Press.

Steiner, T. R. (1975) *English Translation Theory 1650–1800.* Assen: Van Gorcum.

Stratton, C. R. (1971) *Linguistics, Rhetoric and Discourse Structure.* Unpublished PhD thesis, University of Wisconsin.

Stubbs, M. (1983) *Discourse Analysis: The Sociolinguistic Analysis of Natural Language.* Oxford: Basil Blackwell.

Sykes, M. (1985) 'Discrimination in discourse', in T. van Dijk (ed.), *Handbook of Discourse Analysis,* vol. 4, *Discourse Analysis in Society.* New York: Academic Press.

Traugott, E. C. and M. L. Pratt (1980) *Linguistics for Students of Literature.* New York: Harcourt Brace Jovanovitch.

Trimble, L. (1985) *English for Science and Technology.* Cambridge: Cambridge University Press.

Tucker, A. B. (1987) 'Current strategies in machine translation research and development', in S. Nirenburg (1987), pp. 22–41.

Tytler, A. F. (1907) *Essay on the Principles of Translation.* London: Dent.

Van Dijk, T. (1982) 'Towards an empirical pragmatics', *Philosophica,* **27** (1), 127–38.

Werlich, E. (1976) *A Text Grammar of English.* Heidelberg: Quelle & Meyer.

Whorf, B. L. (1958) *Language, Thought and Reality.* Selected writings, edited by J. B. Carroll. Cambridge, Mass.: MIT Press.

Widdowson, H. G. (1979) *Explorations in Applied Linguistics.* Oxford: Oxford University Press.

Wilss, W. (1982) *The Science of Translation. Problems and Methods.* Tübingen: Gunter Narr.

Yngve, V. H. (1964) 'Implications of mechanical translation research' *Proceedings of the American Philosophical Society,* **108,** 275–81.

Index

cultural codes, 70
cultural norms, 125

Danish, 45
De Saussure, 107–8
decode, 192
deep structure, 31–2
deixis, 27, 196
demonstratives, 28
denotation, 57, 71, 99, 112
Description, 155, 158–9, 174, 183,
    199
dialect, 39, 41–54
Dialect, Geographical, 40
Dialect, Social, 42
Dialect, Standard, 42
Dialect, Temporal, 41, 135, 227
discourse, 22, 69, 71–5, 139–43
Dutch, 40
dynamic equivalence, 7

editor, 25
editorial, 152
effectiveness, 93, 100, 144
efficiency, 93, 100, 144
ellipsis, 94–5
encode, 192
Enhancers, 230, 235
equivalence, 8, 56
equivalence probability, 26, 27
EUROTRA, 34
expansion, 198
exposition, 2, 144, 147, 154–5,
    158–9, 187
extended reference, 202
external relations, 207
extra-linguistic, 39

felicity conditions, 62, 64
Field, 48–9, 55–6
Firth, 26, 37–8
focus, 138–9, 145–6, 148, 168
footnote, 18
form, 192
formal correspondence, 26

formal equivalence, 7
frame, 160
frames, 35, 159
Free, 5, 15, 36
freelance, 21
French, 28, 44–5, 49–50, 74, 82,
    89, 94, 96–7, 99, 136, 196,
    200, 203, 211, 232–3, 235
function, 1
Functional Sentence Perspective,
    212
Fuzziness, 51

Gaelic, 26
genre, 2, 13, 22, 69–70, 71, 72–5,
    139–43, 161, 171, 186
German, 40, 45, 196, 211, 231–3, 235
Given-New, 217
global patterns, 191
goals, 35

hearer meaning, 92
honorifics, 65–6
Hopi, 30
host text, 133, 137
Hungarian, 167
hybridization, 146–8, 159, 164, 220
hypertheme, 235

ideology, 11, 71, 125, 127, 141,
    160–61, 223, 224, 238
idiolect, 10, 43–4
Illocutionary act, 60
illocutionary force, 61, 64, 76, 78–9,
    83, 86, 90
illocutionary structure, 77–8, 86
implicature, 63, 97–8, 103
Indonesian, 26
inference, 198–9
inferences, 150
inferencing, 93, 208
inferrable, 22
information core, 106, 118
initiator, 118–19
Instruction With Option, 157